Springer Series on Cultural Computing

More information about this series at http://www.springer.com/series/10481

Jennifer Seevinck

Emergence in Interactive Art

Springer

Jennifer Seevinck
Queensland University of Technology
Brisbane
Australia

ISSN 2195-9056 ISSN 2195-9064 (electronic)
Springer Series on Cultural Computing
ISBN 978-3-319-45199-2 ISBN 978-3-319-45201-2 (eBook)
DOI 10.1007/978-3-319-45201-2

Library of Congress Control Number: 2016962037

Printed on acid-free paper

This Springer imprint is published by Springer Nature
The registered company is Springer International Publishing AG
The registered company address is: Gewerbestrasse 11, 6330 Cham, Switzerland

For Joseph and Adriaan

Foreword

Interactive Art gained wide recognition in the early 1990s, when the Ars Electronica Festival in Linz, Austria, introduced this category into their annual Prix Ars Electronica competition. Even though audience participation can be traced back to the early 1920s and to art forms such as Happenings, Fluxus, Cybernetic Art, Kinetic Art as well as Expanded Cinema, Electronic Art pushed the possibilities of user involvement to a whole new level.

Designers and artists have become excited about the possibility of using the creative input of the audience to complete a work of art. These interactive systems were designed to be quite open, thus enabling new image, sound, and interaction events to emerge. The concept of the Open Work as expressed by Eco, Benjamin, Barthes was put into practice with the help of sensor technologies and computer programs. Subcategories such as Artificial Life Art, Robotic Art and Generative Art then appeared. It was this emergence that fascinated artists, as the interaction triangle artist-artwork-audience led to a whole new level of creative feedback.

Jennifer Seevinck's book about Emergence and Interactive Art gives an in-depth account of the motivation of artists and designers who deal with emergence in their art practice. She provides an excellent framework for constructing and evaluating emergence in interactive art by proposing a taxonomy that classifies different levels of emergent behaviours. She thereby distinguishes between physical and perceptual emergence and introduces the notion of intrinsic and extrinsic emergence. This is especially useful for the expanding field of interactive art, where openness, unpredictability and the use of generative methods are becoming ever more popular.

This book is highly recommended for all scholars who are interested in open and generative systems in electronic art, as it provides an excellent, well-structured overview. It also represents a best practice case of artistic-scientific research, combining theory and practice in an innovative and constructive manner.

Participation and interaction are now the key metaphors of our times. From user-created content, crowd-sourced art and open creative platforms, the trend towards the involvement of the audience in social media is accelerating. Since we are being increasingly tracked, measured and evaluated, artists and designers need to reflect upon the effect of these interactions and provide a critical and creative discourse on these emergent phenomena. Books such as "Emergence and Interactive Art" will help us develop this kind of reflective evaluation.

Linz, Austria
November 2016

Christa Sommerer

Acknowledgements

The completion of this book has been at various times solitary and collaborative. Reflective creative and theoretical investigations occurred in parallel to soliciting the experience and insight of others, such as through the naturalistic evaluations on artworks to generate evidence and the insights presented here. The scope of this book therefore extends beyond the manuscript and into the various places the creative works were installed and the conversations that surrounded the staging and evaluation of those works; and my deepest thanks to the people that assisted in these efforts. Realising a manuscript as a book has similarly been an effort where I have relied on the guidance, good nature and direct assistance of some wonderful people and for this too I am very grateful.

I would however like to acknowledge specific people that have helped me in this journey. From the earliest projects discussed in this text, I benefited from support and conversations around art, augmented reality and emergence with Yani Seevinck, Hector Garcia, Rick McKenzie and Roelof Seevinck. Thanks as well to Ralph Crispino for the formative opportunities rendered through the I-Park artist in residency project, which have facilitated deeper considerations of landscape in the interactive artwork *+−now*. Deborah Turnbull and Matthew McConnell were extremely helpful and I gratefully acknowledge their assistance in facilitating the installation and evaluation of *+−now* at the Beta_Space, Sydney Powerhouse Museum; similarly I appreciate the time and thought of the staff and study participants there. Special thanks are extended to my colleagues and friends at the Creativity and Cognition Studios (CCS) at University of Technology Sydney (UTS) for their participation in early evaluations and for the camaraderie around a shared passion for interactive art and research. My Ph. D studies at CCS UTS led to this book project and my deepest thanks go to supervisors Ernest Edmonds and Linda Candy for their mentoring and friendship.

Subsequent work *Of me With me* project (2012–2015) benefited from the insight of collaborating print artists and staff at ArTel, particularly Elizabeth Saunders, Robert Oakman, Louise Taylor and Dillon Carlsson. Their time, thoughts and creative responses were highly significant to the conceptual evolution of that project. Special thanks as well to Jared Donovan at the Queensland University of Technology (QUT) for his processing code contribution and to Geoff Ward for assistance with installation furnishing and design. Thank you as well to Angelique Coetzee at the Redcliffe City Gallery for supporting the installation and participant evaluation, and to the staff and study participants there. This project was partly funded by Arts Queensland through their Regional Arts Development Fund and also received support from QUT.

For the more recent creative investigations into the *Lightworks* body of work (2015-ongoing), I am grateful to Daniel Flood and Alex Winter at The Edge and the Brisbane Powerhouse Theatre (BPH) for their support through the *Made with Light* artist-in-residence project. Special thanks to Lachlan Currie and Geoff Ward for programming support and installation furnishings, respectively, for *Dichroic Wade*. Thank you as well to Chenoa Pettrup at the State Library of Queensland (SLQ) for supporting the interactive artwork installation and evaluation in 2016, and to SLQ staff and study participants.

In theoretical reflections on artworks and the TEIA, I must also thank the artists discussed in this text. It has been inspiring to study their work through the lens of emergence and their creative contributions set an extraordinary stage to practice in. Thank you to the artists, authors and organisations that kindly granted permission to republish images here. Special thanks to Anthony Hearsey for his photography of much of my work and to Andy Bates for the graphic design of a number of the figures, such as the TEIA image and mapping schemes. Special thanks too to Sam George-Allen and Roelof Seevinck for proof reading.

Finally my deepest thanks are extended to Ernest Edmonds, Linda Candy, Helen Desmond and James Robinson at Springer, Christa Sommerer, Mandy Thomas, Gavin Sade, and Oksana Zelenko at QUT, and my family. Ernest and Linda were with me from the first days of inquiry into emergence and interactive art and without their early support, many thoughtful conversations and ongoing encouragement, this book would not have eventuated. Similarly Helen Desmond has been extremely kind with all my questions. Her expert guidance, along with James' has been invaluable in the final realisation of this book. I would also like to thank Christa Sommerer for writing the foreword. I have long admired her work with Laurent Mignonneau in emergence and open-ended interactive experiences and it is an honour to have her consideration and thoughts here. Many thanks to Mandy Thomas who encouraged me to write this book and thank you to Gavin, Oksana and other colleagues at QUT for support including teaching relief, which was invaluable.

To my wonderful parents Yani and Roelof Seevinck, always ready with creative and rational critiques and never-ending emotional and practical support, my very deepest thanks for supporting me from the start of this journey. We have lost Adriaan and in many ways he is in every page, alongside Joseph who was such a guiding light when days were dark. And finally, at the coalface with me in completing this book is my partner. Thank you dear Geoff and thank you to our three boys Joseph, Matthew and Anthony. Your patience, warmth, curiosity and joy for living are ongoing inspiration for future writing and making.

Contents

Chapter 1
Introduction

Abstract This book is concerned with emergence and interactive art. It looks at what sorts of emergent interactions can occur with digital, interactive art systems, with a particular focus on participant experience. But what is emergence? What is an emergent experience? How can we create one and how will we find it? Emergence is a debated area within and across domains. In this chapter, two approaches to emergence are briefly reviewed: one from design research and the other from the natural sciences. They are reconciled into a broad definition of emergence. The relatively new area of interactive art and its key concern with an active, participating audience are also introduced. These discussions set the stage for analytical emergence tools and creative works presented in Chap. 2 and throughout the text. They also lead to *perceptual emergence* which, with its focus on the subjective experience of emergence, provides the means to understand and create new and surprising participant interactions with art systems.

Emergence and Experiencing Interactive Art

When you think of emergence, you might be thinking about the processes of biological life and how it comes about from the interactions between molecules and atoms. You could also be thinking about how colonies of termites construct large structures of earth without a leader or direction. Or you might be thinking about how we come up with new ideas and how designers perceive new forms while drawing. While these all seem to be different things, they are all instances of emergence. Their diversity reflects the range of disciplines that investigate emergence and hints at the debates between them. In this book I reconcile a number of these differences. Emergence is, accordingly, understood as occurring *when a new form or concept appears that was not directly implied by the context from which it arose. This new 'whole' is more than a simple sum or grouping of its parts*. The literature reviews that have informed this definition and other analytical tools are discussed throughout this book. This is combined with case studies of emergence in digital interactive art systems to explore the topic of emergence in interactive art.

J. Seevinck, *Emergence in Interactive Art*, Springer Series on Cultural Computing,
DOI 10.1007/978-3-319-45201-2_1

Interactive art is a new form of art. It emphasises audience interaction with the work and reconfigures the relationship between artwork, audience and artist. For some artists this entails a consideration of participant experience with the interactive artwork. The field of Human Computer Interaction (HCI) is similarly concerned with a 'user's' experience. But what does it mean to work with experiences that are digitally augmented?

As the world becomes increasingly populated with networks and computing devices, our interaction with it is increasingly augmented by data. The internet layers onto physical space and changes the meaning of that space and our experience of it. But what are the dimensions and nuances of this new hybrid digital-physical space, and our experience of it? This is a pressing question for artists and designers working with interactive media.

Perceptual emergence is valuable here. It is a new concept presented in this text that has been informed by theories of emergence and creative, practical explorations. It is new to interactive art and interaction design, but well suited to exploring participant experiences of creative and complex systems. It can reveal new, surprising interactions with systems to inform an artist's understanding of that system. It can also provide us with a more differentiated understanding of the quality of interaction as a medium to work in. We speak of millions of colours; shouldn't we likewise be thinking about the many 'tones and textures' of interaction? A more differentiated understanding of participant interaction benefits artists, researchers and designers alike. And what better way to explore the potentials of interaction than through the open-ended domain of emergence, with its inherent affinity to the natural world?

Core concepts to this text are emergence, interactive art, computing and interaction. These are introduced next, with a focused introduction of emergence in Chap. 2 and discussions of interactive art, participation and computing in Chap. 3. After the theoretical discussion of emergence in interactive art in the early chapters, case studies of interactive artworks are discussed. This includes a review of artworks from around the world (Chap. 4) and my own work, subsequently evaluated to evidence aspects of emergence (Chaps. 5, 6). These reveal insights into facilitating emergent interactions through design, as well as what these experiences can be like for the participants.

Emergence

Emergence can be understood as occurring when a new form or concept appears that was not directly implied by the context from which it arose. This new 'whole' is more than a simple sum or grouping of its parts. This broad definition implies some key criteria for emergence: it is new, unpredictable, and a Gestalt whole that comes about from interactions between the parts.

The definition and criteria are drawn from literature in physics, biology, computer science and other sciences as well as Gestalt theory and design research. It

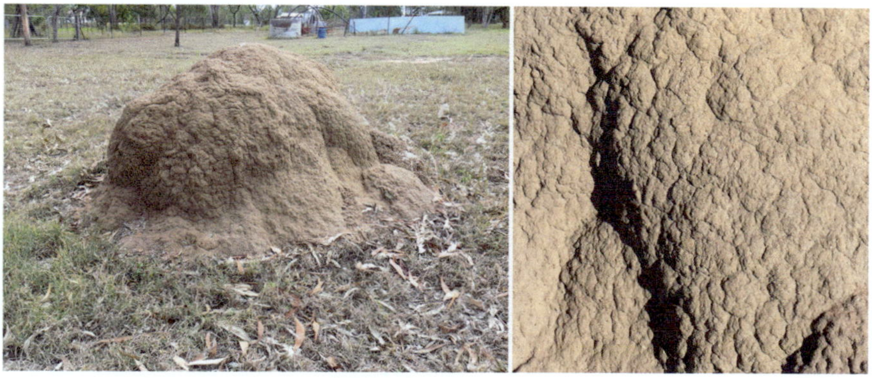

Fig. 1.1 Termite mound in Coominya, Australia. Photography © Yani Seevinck 2016

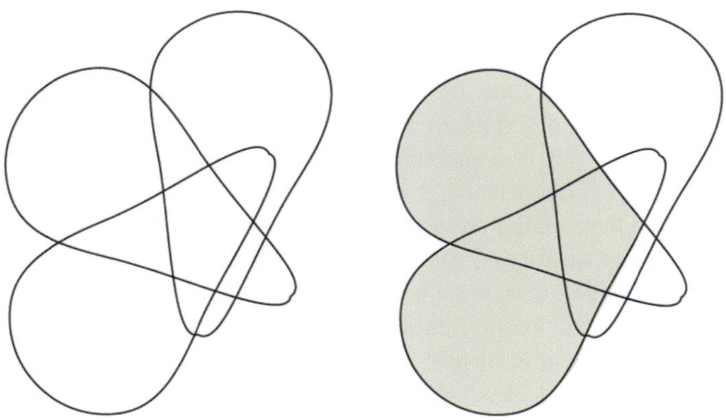

Fig. 1.2 An emergent 'heart' shape emerges from overlapping teardrop shapes

bridges varying understandings of emergence to describe structures and phenomena across these domains. The termite mound is a new structure created through simple interactions of ants and, as such, can be understood as emergent (Fig. 1.1). Similarly, our creative interpretation of new shapes and structures, such as the heart shape that can be perceived from overlapping tear drops in Fig. 1.2 can be understood as an instance of emergence. In both cases we see the core characteristics of emergence—something *new* (the mound structure and the heart) has appeared that is qualitatively different and surprising, or *unpredictable* from what was there before. It is a Gestalt '*whole*' that has come about from interactions between its lower level '*parts*' (the ants and teardrop shapes).

Core differences do, however, remain between these examples and the areas of emergence research. One main distinction is the differing role of an observer. For example, emergence can be understood as occurring as a part of our process of perceiving and creating new meaning while interacting with images, or it may be said to occur independently of an observer. This distinction in approaches informs a classification difference in the Taxonomy of Emergence in Interactive Art (TEIA), and is discussed in Chap. 2.

Another difference in emergence literature and understandings reflects the tension between reductivism and holism. In mathematics for example, a combination of parts yields no more and no less than the sum. Here the idea of something that is 'greater than the sum of the parts' can be contentious. There are however many situations in our natural, physical world that challenge an understanding in terms of parts alone. Are such situations explainable or are they mystical? Or are they perhaps a reflection of our ignorance or subjectivity? And, given these concerns, can we usefully engage with concepts of emergence in the digital interactive arts? I believe so. In this book I propose logical and pragmatic means for applying emergence in interactive art and, in so doing, broadening our understanding of interaction. I bridge different approaches, including the role of the observer, through the TEIA (Chap. 2) and provide the interested reader with a deeper discussion of emergence, including the concerns around explainability, in Chap. 7.

The TEIA is an organising framework for emergence in interactive art. It draws on emergence in the literature by categorising positions in terms of criteria for emergence to position different views of emergence alongside one another and within the one 'map'. It is a practical effort that can facilitate new insights for practitioners and researchers in art, design and computing. It consists of three levels of hierarchy, or differentiation, as follows:

The first, primary distinction differentiates between emergence that relies on an observer and that which can be understood to exist independently of an observer. An example of the latter is the termite mound. This is an emergent structure that does not rely on observation. It was created without need for us to perceive it. The flocking behaviour of birds is another example. They organise themselves and in so doing reduce wind resistance for each individual bird. Termite mounds and flock formations exist independent of whether we are there to observe them or not. Computer simulations of flocking and models of ant behaviours in artificial life research are also relevant here (For example see Langton 1987; Reynolds 1987; Johnson 2001). In the TEIA this type of emergence is called *physical* emergence, named after the physical, world structures it describes.

On the other hand we have perceptual, subjective structures like the heart shape in Fig. 1.2. This is an instance of emergence that comes about through the processes of seeing, making it reliant on an observer. We can understand a melody in the same way. It is an emergent whole that is more than a collection of notes, qualitatively new and different to them and not obvious or predictable from those notes. However, there is a need for someone to hear (perceive) the melody for it to exist. In the TEIA these are called *perceptual* emergence, named after the necessity for someone to perceive them.

Perceptual emergence is particularly useful in interactive art. This is not only because art is similarly a subjective experience for the viewer or audience. It is also useful because interactive art is concerned with an active audience, a participant. Here there is opportunity for the observer to interact with a system and effect emergence. By looking at emergence in a 'participant-observer', we can understand emergent experience.

Interactive Art

Interactive art differs from traditional, static art such as painting because interactive art entails reciprocal response or influence between artwork and audience. In interactive art there is an implication of audience participation rather than passive spectatorship. This more participatory role for the audience is a defining aspect of the art form. It is why terms such as 'audience', 'viewer' and 'spectator' have been replaced by 'participant' in discussions of interactive art, a practice I also follow in this book (Ascott 1966; Edmonds et al. 2004).

The idea of audience-as-participant implies other insights into the nature of interactive art. This is the notion that the work is, in part at least, also realised by that participant and the participant can in many ways be considered a co-creator who helps to realise the work. These provocations lead us to consider questions around the artwork—does authorship rest solely with the artist? Does the work exist without participant interaction? And, ultimately, what is important about the participant's interaction? For example, in Marcel Duchamp's *Rotary Glass Plates* (1920) an optical effect could be perceived by the audience—but only once they switched on the engine and stepped back. John Cage's 4′33″ (1952) included the audience in the sound composition, not only challenging the idea that he was the only creative agent or artist in control of the experience of music but also highlighting the active role we play in listening to decide what is sound and what is silence. These works help us consider the question of interpretive and creative audience experiences.

A few years later Alan Kaprow's *18 Happenings in 6 Parts* (1959) challenged the role of the audience in still another way. This work also involved the audience, though in a more physical and active manner to explicitly choreograph their movement throughout a series of installations. In so doing, the observable form of those works changed dynamically. The audience is treated like human theatre set pieces (Schimmel 1989), perhaps revealing more of a focus on visual form than creative or critical participant experience.

These examples demonstrate some of the historical considerations of interaction in art, but the area is still largely undefined. This is particularly the case when we consider the potential for interaction with digital art systems, as in this text.

Pioneering work in this digital art domain includes the efforts of artist and researcher Ernest Edmonds and his colleagues. Edmonds has been explicitly concerned with interactivity in art for a number of years (Cornock and Edmonds 1973; Edmonds et al. 2004; Edmonds 2011). Their classification of art addresses some of the questions and potential around participation in art raised above. It also points out that while a viewer may respond to all art, traditional and interactive; to qualify as interactive this influence must be reciprocated by the work in some way. I'll come back to this classification system—and other discussions of interactive art, participation and experience—in more detail in Chap. 3. In looking at interactive art research it is also useful to review creative works. In Chap. 4 I discuss six case studies from artists around the world that relate to participation and interaction in art in diverse ways. They also reveal possibilities for participant experience of emergence. Later I present some of my own interactive artworks informed by concepts of emergence, as well as evaluation studies of these which found audiences to experience emergence.

Openness, Interaction and HCI

A history of participation in art locates the new area of interactive art within arts discourse. That same arts discourse has also produced the notion of the 'open work' (Eco 1962), that is, one which is not predetermined but is instead still open to interpretation. It is, in some ways, unfinished, until someone else—audience, performer, participant—comes along and acts to 'complete' it. As for Cage above, the open work invites the participant or performer to "*make the work together with the author*" (Eco 1962). They interact with it to make an interpretation or creative decision. With many conclusions possible this means the work also tends towards being inexhaustible, infinite as well as ambiguous in its form. For example, every rendition of an open work will involve an act of interpretation by the performer, and every performance will be different.

Open-ended design processes also facilitate ambiguity and multiple interpretations (Sengers and Gaver 2006). And openness has also characterised certain game play. For example, video game theorist Jesper Juul compares the possibilities of open-ended gameplay versus progressive game structures where challenges are laid out serially (Juul 2002). In the former there is greater opportunity for 're-play value' precisely because of the multiple outcomes. The open-ended experience implies a range of variations, meanings and possibilities.

As I worked on an interactive art sketch in 2005 I found myself seeing the natural landscape in multiple ways. A lake was a place of leisure for some and quiet reflection for others. Still others would fish for dinner there. In the natural, real world there is an incredible diversity and depth of detail that can support a rich range of interaction experiences and possibilities. Looking into still water can reveal the depths below, but it can also mirror the sky. Every tree, every conversation is different. In many ways, our natural world and our interaction with it is 'open' (Seevinck and Edmonds 2009). While the natural world may be open-ended, typical design for Human Computer Interaction (HCI) does not allow for ambiguous or open-ended interactions. Instead the traditional focus of HCI has been on routine, well defined or low level tasks (Edmonds 1995). As mentioned, some progress into complex interactions such as ambiguous or open-ended interactions has been made (e.g. Gaver et al. 2003; Sengers and Gaver 2006; Gaver and Martin 2000) but these are still few in number. Bødker's articulation of a 'third wave' of HCI (2006) overtly states a need to focus design on people's creative, emotional and non-work interactions, but the design of such systems is still little understood. Emergence in interactive art can provide some insight. As is discussed more in Chap. 3, emergence is implicitly open-ended and as such can facilitate open-ended experiences as well as third wave—and beyond—HCI design approaches.

The concepts of emergence and open-ness have driven this creative work and research. They recur throughout the text—from landscape studies and other practice through theory, evaluation of participant experience and the design insights these revealed. Emergent and open-ended designs are a mechanism whereby we can expand the domain of HCI to more complex and creative, next generation, human–computer interactions.

Approach

This book comes out of both creating artwork and doing research. Specifically, a Practice-Based Research (PBR) has been used. PBR facilitates shareable knowledge outcomes from an agenda prioritising practice (Candy 2006; Candy and Edmonds 2010; Edmonds and Candy 2010). The way in which the research and practice relate, varies for different PBR researchers and practitioners. (See for example Candy 2011; Candy and Ferguson 2014 for collections of artists reporting on their research and practice). My approach involves the creative practice of making digital interactive artworks and sketches, accompanied by a combination of theoretical enquiry and qualitative research into participant experience. The creative efforts span three bodies of work presented in Chap. 5: *Traces* (2005–8), *Iterative Drawing* (2012–15) and *Lightworks* (2015–2016). Various art making techniques as well as methods from Reflective Practice (Schön 1983) and iterative software development have informed their creation, as is also discussed there.

In many ways the artworks set the research agenda; however, ensuing research findings have also influenced and set the direction for practice. For instance, after an artwork is at a certain point of completion where it is functional and mostly resolved, people's interaction with it is evaluated in naturalistic field studies where they are observed and asked about their experience and thoughts (Preece et al. 1994). What I learn from this informs further creative work and growing understanding about what emergent participant experiences can be like and how to create for them. Practical design insights into facilitating emergent interactive experiences through to a theoretical framework for organising emergence, the TEIA, as well as the creative artworks themselves have all eventuated from this PBR approach.

Overview of the Book Structure

Emergence in interactive art entails discussion around emergence, interaction, art and computing. More specifically, it involves characterisations of the debated area of emergence and the new area of interactive art. These form a basis for insights into creating interactive artworks that facilitate emergence and insight into the nature of emergent participant experiences. The different chapters in this book address these aspects, in turn.

Chapter 2 provides more detail on the defining aspects of emergence. A classification of emergence in interactive art, the TEIA is also presented. This organising framework sits across the various domains of emergence literature with a focus on how it can be applied to interactive art. Perceptual emergence is presented as a means to reconcile some of the domain differences as well as facilitate deeper understanding of people's experience of interactive art. This chapter and the TEIA are a baseline for the discussion and identification of emergence in interactive art in Chaps. 4, 5 and 6. Additional discussion of emergence theory is provided for the interested reader in Chap. 7.

Chapter 3 focuses on interaction, art and computing. It provides an overview of these areas for the novice. It also positions interactive art relative to emergence—through a discussion of openness in art, participation, computing designs and computer games. Openness is a characteristic of both emergence and of the natural world and this chapter integrates prior discussions of emergence, art, interaction and computing to provide some theoretical insight into *emergent open interactions.*

Chapter 4 reviews six artworks from across the world. These digital, interactive artworks by Christa Sommerer and Laurent Mignonneau, Ken Rinaldo, Simon Penny and Jamieson Schulte, Romy Achituv and Christina Utterback, Rafael Lozano-Hemmer, and David Rokeby are characterised through a lens of emergence. That is, the TEIA and qualities of emergence are used to review each work to understand its potential for emergence. The discussion draws on image, video and textual descriptions of the works in various art and online sources. It starts to illustrate, through graphic examples, the potential for emergence in interactive art. It also reveals some of the different ways we can think about emergent participant behaviours and experiences with art systems.

Chapter 5 concerns three of my interactive art works: *+−now* (2008), Seevinck (2014, 2016). All were found to facilitate emergence in some way. The works and their methods for making are described in this chapter, including the PBR methods for practice used (e.g. Schön 1983). The works vary in the interaction modes, gestures and materials they use as well as computing technology. The conceptual strategy behind each work is also distinctive. In my approach to PBR, concept in the art works to integrate research with practice. All three works are similar in that all three facilitate emergence—however, the second artwork, *Of me With me*, draws on different types of emergence. It was created using methods of physical emergence while the outcome facilitates participant experience of emergence (perceptual emergence).

Chapter 6 presents evaluation research into people's experience with each of the three works in Chap. 5. The processes of conducting these studies are described, along with details about how the data was analysed to identify and classify instances of emergence. This includes drawing on the TEIA to use emergence criteria codes and a mapping scheme. These tools and the documented processes provide the reader with insight to identify and classify instances of emergence in interaction with other artworks. A brief review of the methods for evaluation and analysis used, accompany this discussion (e.g. Glaser and Strauss 1967; Preece et al. 1994; Richards 2006; Braun and Clarke 2008).

Chapter 7 provides a more in depth discussion on emergence for the interested reader. Some of the 'hairier' questions around emergence in the physical sciences are explored here. These include our ability to explain emergence and the questions surrounding emergence in the finite and deterministic domain of the computer (e.g. Cariani 1991; McCormack and Dorin 2001). More of the design research efforts in emergence is also provided including the role of collaboration and efforts into modelling different types of emergent shapes using computer processes (e.g. Edmonds and Soufi 1992; Edmonds et al. 1994; Gero 1996).

Finally, Chap. 8 provides design insights for other artists, designers and researchers into creating for, and identifying, emergence in interactive art. It draws on the preceding theoretical discussions, creative works and case studies as well as evaluation research findings to provide insights to look at the potential for interactive art and interaction that emergence can provide.

Conclusion

Since the area of interactive art is still quite young a great deal remains to be investigated. Emergence has an inherent ability to support a complex understanding of interaction, one that includes creative, open-ended perception and interaction. Perceptual emergence, in particular, allows us to focus on such participant experiences of interactive art systems. Given its focus on the subjective interpretation of emergence, it is very useful for understanding people's experiences with these systems. This book enhances our understanding of emergence in interactive art. This intersection, with its emphasis on participant experience, has not been investigated before. It holds much potential for interactive art and the creation of interactions, generally.

Perceptual emergence is concerned with the interpretation of forms, patterns and structures. It is, in effect, about a person's 'creative sense-making', something that is also becoming increasingly relevant to our everyday lives. As more and more data surrounds us, we need more ways of making sense of this data and increased capacity for creative visual thinking. We also need a more differentiated understanding of digitally mediated interactions. That is, interaction in the real physical world is highly differentiated and nuanced, affording many interpretations and subtleties. Shouldn't we be looking at interaction with the digital realm in a similar way? The aesthetics and dimensions of interaction are, I would argue, as critical to creative expression in interactive art as the myriad of hues and tones are to the painter.

Emergence, with its affinity for the natural world, can enhance our understanding of complex and creative interactions and experiences. And emergence research is vast, crossing domains from the natural, physical sciences through to design research and Gestalt theory. Researchers have developed theories, models and techniques that can be applied in different areas, innovating across them. The following chapter describes how one might navigate all this research—through a map of emergence criteria and qualities. This is the Taxonomy of Emergence in Interactive Art (TEIA). As shown later in the book, the TEIA also facilitates understanding interactive artworks and participant experiences of them.

References

Ascott R (1966) Behaviourist art and the cybernetic vision. Cybernetica 9:247–264

Bødker S (2006) When second wave HCI meets third wave challenges. ACM Press, New York, USA, pp 1–8

Braun V, Clarke V (2008) Using thematic analysis in psychology—qualitative research in psychology—Volume 3, Issue 2. Qual Res Psychol 3:77–101. doi:10.1191/1478088706qp063oa

Cage J (1952) 4′33″, music composition

Candy L (2006) Practice based research: a guide. Creativity and Cognition Studios, University of Technology, Sydney, Australia

Candy L (2011) Research and creative practice. In: Candy L, Edmonds EA (eds) Interacting: art, research and the creative practitioner. Libri Publishing Ltd., Farrington, Oxon, pp 33–59

Candy L, Edmonds EA (2010) The role of the artefact and frameworks for practice-based research. In: Biggs M, Larsson H (eds) The Routledge companion to research in the arts. Routledge, New York, USA, pp 120–136

Candy L, Ferguson S (eds) (2014) Interactive experience in the digital age evaluating new art practice. Springer International Publishing

Cariani P (1991) Emergence and artificial life. In: Langton CG, Taylor C, Farmer JD, Rasmussen S (eds). Addison-Wesley, pp 775–797

Cornock S, Edmonds EA (1973) The creative process where the artist is amplified or superseded by the computer. Leonardo, The MIT Press 6:11–16

Duchamp M (1920) Rotary Glass Plates (Precision Optics), motorized artwork

Eco U (1962) The poetics of the open work. In: Bishop C (ed) Participation. Whitechapel, The MIT Press, London, England, pp 20–40

Edmonds EA (1995) Creativity: interacting with computers (panel discussion). In: Edmonds EA, Katz I, Mack R, et al. (eds) CHI '95 conference on human factors in computing systems. SIGCHI: ACM Special Interest Group on Computer-Human Interaction. ACM Press, Denver, USA, pp 185–186

Edmonds EA (2011) Interactive art. In: Candy L, Edmonds EA (eds) Interacting: art, research and the creative practitioner. Libri Publishing Ltd., Faringdon, UK

Edmonds EA, Candy L (2010) Relating theory, practice and evaluation in practitioner research. Leonardo, The MIT Press 43:470–476

Edmonds EA, Candy L, Jones R, Soufi B (1994) Support for collaborative design: agents and emergence. Commun ACM 37:41–47

Edmonds EA, Soufi B (1992) The computational modelling of emergent shape in design. In: Gero JS, Sudweeks (eds) Computational models of creative design. University of Sydney, Sydney, Australia, pp 173–190

Edmonds EA, Turner G, Candy L (2004) Approaches to interactive art systems. ACM Press, Singapore, pp 113–117

Gaver W, Martin H (2000) Alternatives exploring information appliances through conceptual design proposals. In: Proceedings of CHI 2000. pp 209–216

Gaver W, Beaver J, Benford S (2003) Ambiguity as a resource for design. In: Proceedings of CHI 2003. ACM Press, Ft Lauderdale, Florida, USA, pp 233–240
Gero JS (1996) Creativity, emergence and evolution in design. Knowl Based Syst 9:435–448
Glaser BG, Strauss AL (1967) The discovery of grounded theory strategies for qualitative research. Aldine Publishing Company, New York, USA
Johnson S (2001) Emergence: the connected lives of ants, brains, cities, and software. First Scribner, New York, USA
Juul J (2002) The open and the closed: games of emergence and games of progression. In: Mäyrä F (ed) Computer game and digital cultures conference proceedings. Tampere University Press, Tampere, Finland, pp 323–329
Kaprow A (1959) 18 Happenings in 6 Parts, artwork
Langton CG (1987) Artificial Life. In: Langton CG, Taylor C, Farmer JD, Rasmussen S (eds) Proceedings of the workshop on artificial life I. Addison-Wesley, Los Alamos, USA, pp 1–47
McCormack J, Dorin A (2001) Art, emergence, and the computational sublime. Proceedings of the second international conference on generative systems in the electronic arts. Centre for Electronic Media Art (CEMA), Victoria, Australia, pp 67–81
Preece J, Rogers Y, Sharp H et al (1994) Human computer interaction. Addison-Wesley, USA
Reynolds CW (1987) Flocks, herds, and schools: a distributed behavioral model. In: Stone MC (ed) Proceedings of the 14th annual conference on computer graphics and interactive techniques (Siggraph 87). ACM Press, pp 25–34
Richards L (2006) Handling qualitative data a practical guide. Sage Publications, London, England
Schimmel P (1989) Leap into the void: performance and the object. In: Schimmel P (ed) Out of actions: between performance and the object. The Museum of Contemporary Art, Thames and Hudson, Los Angeles, USA, pp 1949–1979
Schön DA (1983) The reflective practitioner how professionals think in action, 1995th edn. Temple Smith, London, England
Seevinck J (2014) Of me With me, interactive artwork
Seevinck J (2016) Dichroic Wade, interactive artwork
Seevinck J, Edmonds E (2009) Open in art, nature and emergence. ACM Press, Melbourne Australia, pp 365–368. doi:10.1145/1738826.1738898
Sengers P, Gaver B (2006) Staying open to interpretation: engaging in multiple meanings in design and evaluation. In: Designing Interactive Systems DIS'06. ACM Press, pp 99–108

Chapter 2
Emergence

Abstract This chapter establishes a broad understanding of emergence and provides a tool for classifying it, the Taxonomy of Emergence in Interactive Art (TEIA). This framework sits across the debated concept of emergence. It draws on the variety of understandings of emergence in the physical and life sciences through to design research communities, to reveal differences and similarities between them. The classifications fit an overarching, broad understanding of emergence as occurring *when a new form or concept appears that was not directly implied by the context from which it arose; and where this emergent whole' is more than a simple sum of the parts*. Emergence also has some core qualities and characteristics. As implied by the definition, something *new* is created that is a *whole* with *parts,* which exists across *levels* and has the potential for *feedback* between those levels, namely from the whole to the parts. *Unpredictability, creativity* and *open-endedness* and the subjective interpretation of emergence are other key concerns that have come out of emergence literature. A new concept that I introduce here is *referencing*. While new to the domain of emergence it is significant to the visual arts. It facilitates a more differentiated understanding of emergence in the context of interactive art by distinguishing those instances of emergence that are associated with something else in the world (as in figurative and representational work in the visual arts) from the more direct and material concerns of Concrete art. The various qualities of emergence and organizing TEIA discussed here go on to inform the analytical and creative activities in later chapters. A more in-depth discussion of emergence follows in Chap. 7, for the interested reader.

Two Approaches to Emergence

The concept of emergence has challenged philosophers through to biologists and scientists since the time of Aristotle. Questions about the origins of life and qualities of being alive have directed enquiry for many (Weber and Esfeld 2008; Aristotle in Pickard-Cambridge 2015). Questions of life, particularly through computer models of artificial life (AL), have also informed contemporary arts practice (for example

J. Seevinck, *Emergence in Interactive Art*, Springer Series on Cultural Computing,
DOI 10.1007/978-3-319-45201-2_2

Sommerer and Mignonneau 1998; Rinaldo 1999 as discussed later in the book). Computer scientists and artists have modelled theories of emergence in the natural, physical world through computer based simulations through iteratively applying simple rules to collections of simple entities. Organic structures of trees through to ant colonies have been re-created digitally in this way, facilitating understanding into their structure and the natural world as well as aesthetic outcomes (e.g. Prusinkiewicz and Lindenmayer 1990; Resnick 1994). These research and creative efforts in emergence understand it as something that occurs in the natural, physical world.

In another context, however, emergence is understood as a subjective concept one that explains how we can come up with new design solutions, such as how an observer can interpret a new shape like the triangle in Fig. 2.1 (e.g. Mitchell 1990; Edmonds and Soufi 1992).

While these understandings may at first seem to be about different things, they share some key characteristics. In each case *a new form or concept has appeared, that was not directly implied by the context from which it arose.* And in each case, *this emergent 'whole' is more than a simple sum of the parts.* Whether it is a flock of birds or an emergent triangular shape, it is qualitatively new and different to its constituting parts—birds or the simple Pac-man shapes in Fig. 2.1.

The two understandings each draw upon different bodies of research in emergence. Design research including Gestalt theory and visual thinking takes a personal, subjective approach to focus on emergent structures that seem to appear, such as the emergent shape and the new understandings that it can facilitate. Here the emergence is something that is occurring in the eye of an observer, or as relevant to that body of research, being a designer or artist.

On the other hand, research in the physical and natural sciences is focused on emergence as it occurs in that natural, physical world. This is not as something that occurs perceptually, rather here the concern is with structures originating from living and non-living physically based processes in the real world. The

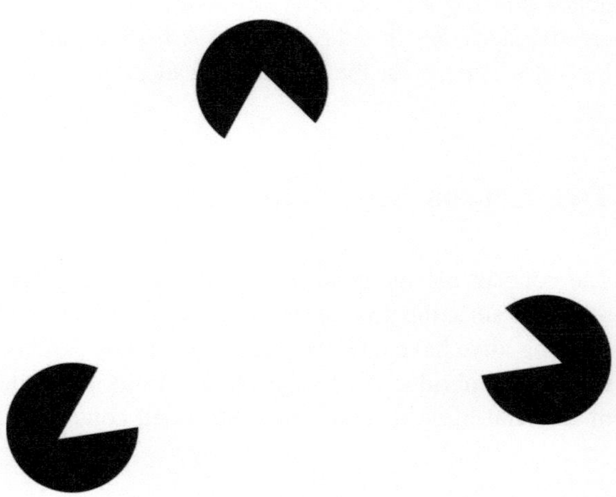

Fig. 2.1 The Kanizsa triangle illusion is not perceived as a result of an image on the retina, rather it is induced by the three Pac-Man shapes

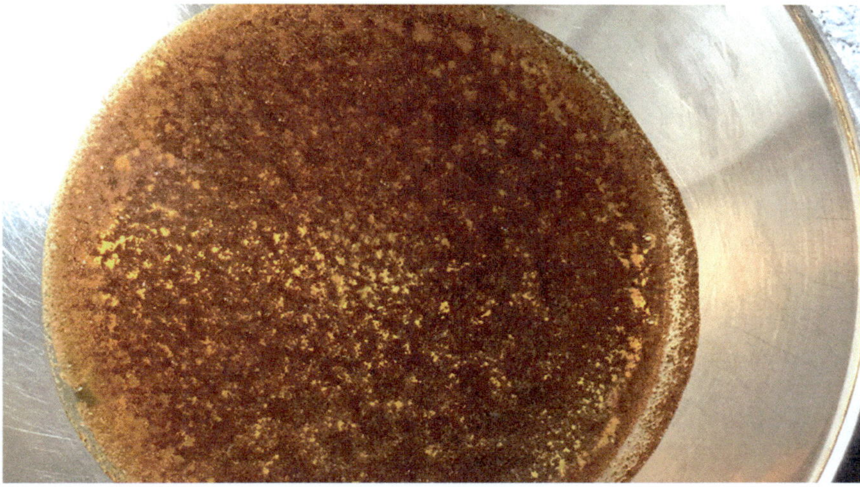

Fig. 2.2 As chilli powder is heated in oil, hexagonal structures (Bénard cells) become evident. Photo © Yani Seevinck 2016

characteristic V-Shape of snow geese flying in formation is an emergent structure or behaviour that becomes physically manifest and can be differentiated from a disordered group of birds. The organisation of ant colonies or formation of termite mounds can be characterised the same way (Flake 1998). Non-living systems also exhibit this 'self-organisation'. Scientist Stephen Wolfram describes such systems as those that "*...start disordered and featureless but then spontaneously organize themselves to produce definite structures*" (Wolfram 2002). For example, when heating oil and chilli in a pan, one can see self-organisation of the chilli powder. It will rearrange from its disorganised configuration to settle into beehive patterns, or Bénard cells (Emmeche 1994) as shown in Fig. 2.2. Such natural structures challenge our assumption of the world as moving towards randomness, intriguing researchers and artists alike.

Theories of evolution and adaptation can help us understand new organisms and life forms. Complex systems research also provides insight, as is discussed in more depth in Chap. 7. A fine grained view of physical materials and context can also provide insight into how natural form comes about. D'Arcy Thompson articulated the concept of *Morphology* in 1917) to explain the shape of an antelope horn in terms of the horn's increasing weight over time and uneven rate of growth parallel to the axis; factors which direct the growth of the animals' horns to mirror logarithmic spirals (Thompson 1992). Thompson proposed these explanations as alternatives or complementary to natural selection. As Phillip Ball describes it more recently, "*as an explanation for natural form, natural selection is not entirely satisfying. Not because it is wrong, but because it says nothing about mechanism*"(1999). The morphologists approach can also render a more economical answer than evolutionary theory.

There are a number of approaches to understand emergence, within and across disciplines. They do however share the above broad definition. They also share some key or core qualities, which is discussed next. Some of the controversy between qualities of emergence is also discussed here while more depth is offered to the interested reader in Chap. 7. The primary aim of the current chapter is establishing a basic understanding of emergence in the context of interactive art, and presenting an organizing framework for applying it, the TEIA. This Taxonomy for Emergence in Interactive Art is a pragmatic effort to aid understanding and navigation of emergence across the literature. It can also facilitate the application of models and understandings of emergence from one domain into to the next.

Qualities of Emergence

Emergence has some key qualities. To begin with, there is a whole with constituting parts. This also implies the idea of different *levels* between that *whole* and its *parts*. Similarly the idea of something qualitatively *new* appearing implies a notion of surprise or *unpredictability*. As the following discussion shows, each quality can be unpacked to reveal some depth in understanding emergence. These qualities become useful to characterise interactive artworks, as is shown throughout the book.

The Whole and Parts

The term 'emergent' was coined by philosopher George Henry Lewes in 1875 to describe a phenomenon that is neither a mixture nor a sum of constituting parts but rather heterogeneously new and irreducible to those parts (1875). Max Wertheimer's articulation of Gestalt psychology in 1924 sounds very similar: "*There are wholes, the behaviour of which is not determined by that of their individual elements, but where the part-processes are themselves determined by the intrinsic nature of the whole*" (Wertheimer 1938).

50 Years later computer scientist John Holland describes emergence in very similar terms to those of Wertheimer: "*for emergence, the whole is indeed more than the sum of its parts*" (1998). Other researchers within the natural sciences have also described emergence in this way (e.g. Emmeche et al. 1997; Flake 1998).

The notion of a whole that cannot be understood reductively and in terms of parts alone has been familiar for some time and it has featured across different disciplines. However, while there is agreement on this concept, there is also debate. Not being able to explain something in terms of its constituting parts alone has, in the past, challenged the concept of emergence by leaving it open to mystical explanations. A holistic view of emergence is, however, increasingly gaining traction in physics (Laughlin and Pines 2000; Bar-Yam 2002; Chap. 7).

Explaining and Predicting Emergence

The tension between reductivism and holism accounts for much of the debates between theories of emergence. A reductionist position seeks to understand things in terms of their parts alone (Oxford Dictionaries 2010). However, when a concept cannot be simplified to theories or properties of the parts (Lewes 1875) this can become problematic. One argument to reconcile reductivist explanations with unexplainable outcomes asserts that our understanding of the parts is simply inadequate… and more knowledge here could sustain an explanation of the so-called emergent phenomenon as a sum of those parts. This argument is part of a broader idea of emergence as "*relative to some transient state of scientific knowledge*" (Weber and Esfeld 2008). It does, however, have its own problems, as is detailed in Chap. 7.

For example, deterministic chaos systems are, by definition explainable because we can trace every causal step to arrive at the outcome. They are also predictable—at least in the short term. For example, we can look outside to see if it will rain this afternoon, but predicting the weather for next week is less reliable.

Considering the design research view of emergence yields a more nuanced understanding again. Here the focus is on something become explicit that was previously implicit, or the appearance of something that is "*not present in its source*" (Mitchell 1993; Edmonds et al. 1994). Emergent shapes, like the triangle in Fig. 2.1 are more than a simple sum of their parts—the pacman shapes. They are qualitatively different and new relative to their parts. This research therefore understands emergence as possibly, but not necessarily, being wholly unpredictable. Rather the question of unpredictability is more usefully understood as unpredictable from the vantage point of the parts. Put another way and as is discussed next, it is concerned with the appearance of something heterogeneously different and new to what was there before.

The Appearance of Something New

The creation of something new is another core quality of emergence. For Danish philosophers Claus Emmeche, Simo Køppe and Frederik Stjernfelt, emergence involves the "*…creation of new properties*" (Emmeche et al. 1997). Similarly for design researchers "*…an emergent form displays characteristics not present in its source*" (Edmonds et al. 1994). A whole that is more than the sum of its parts is necessarily new relative to those parts. Specifically, the newness is qualitatively different to what was there before. It is *heterogeneously* new (Lewes 1875; Mill 1889) or, as physicist John Crutchfield describes, it is different to the system's pre-existing character (Crutchfield 1994).

These first three aspects—the system as a *whole* with *parts,* exhibiting relative *newness*—provide a starting point for understanding emergence. A nice example here is von Ehrenfehls 1890 experiment on the perception of a musical melody. He found that it could not be distinguished from exposure to the separate notes. We intuitively understand this too—a melody is a whole that is qualitatively different, new and more than a simple sum of its parts, the notes (1890 von Ehrenfels experiment described in Wertheimer 1938).

Creativity Through Emergence

The occurrence of something qualitatively new can also mean that something creative has occurred. As Edmonds argues, "*emergence is fundamental to creative thought because the creative thought introduces something new*" (1995). For example, when you look at Fig. 2.1 you can interpret a new shape, the triangle. As architectural designer and theorist William Mitchell describes, designers can respond to their drawings to come up with new understandings: "*Designers ... frequently recognize emergent subshapes, and subsequently structure their understanding of the design and their reasoning about it in terms of emergent entities and relationship*" (1990). These new shapes are interpreted through the designer's reflection on their drawing. It is an activity that is integral to the creative drawing process.

Creativity is an integral concern in emergent shapes research. The design research community has pursued Computer-Aided Design (CAD) tools to facilitate the designer in their creative and less routine design tasks. The efforts aim to facilitate computer recognition of emergent sub-shapes, something which is not straightforward given that CAD systems explicitly specify shapes, while an emergent shape like the triangle in Fig. 2.1 is, instead implied (Mitchell 1993; Gero 1996). Various computational models that address these questions to support creative design processes have been proposed (e.g. Mitchell 1990; Soufi and Edmonds 1995; Poon and Maher 1996; Gero 1996).

One such system differentiates between four types of emergent shapes—these range from those that are embedded within the original drawing, such as the heart appearing from overlapping teardrop shapes in Fig. 1.2, through to emergent shapes that function through perceptual qualities responding to occlusion or spatial extension. A fourth kind is an illusory emergent shape such as the Kanizsa triangle pictured in Fig. 2.1 where interpolation or subjective contours contribute to perception of this triangle (Soufi and Edmonds 1995).[1]

Emergence can also lead to creative behaviours in interactive art, such as the ability of a participant to interactively *compose* music through navigating the audio-visual virtual world *Feeping Creatures* (Berry 1998). In this artificial life environment, creativity occurs as you move through the virtual world to compose new soundscapes with the evolving virtual creatures in the art system. That is, both new acoustic

[1]Further discussion of emergent shapes can be found in Chap. 7.

compositions are created and, at the same time, virtual creatures are also 'created', while the biological life simulation unfolds. Other examples of creative, emergent interactions and experiences are discussed in Chaps. 4, 5 and 6. Emergence is integral to creativity but both are also intertwined with ambiguity and openness. As stated by Umberto Eco: when someone is completing the open work (as participants of interactive art systems arguably do) they are, in many ways, acting creatively (Eco 1962).

Perceiving Emergence

Computer artists and scientists have pursued the digital modelling of life processes to emerge new forms and virtual creatures. Such simulations can, however, be contentious. Neuroscientist and researcher Peter Cariani argues that most computer simulations cannot really generate emergence. This is because within the domain of the computer nothing truly new can emerge: given the same starting conditions, the result will always be the same. Put another way, emergence within the closed domain of the computer will be predictable because the system is 'informationally closed'. Cariani believes the only true emergence to occur in this situation is that which occurs within the observer's mind: those new understandings or concepts that might form in an observer watching the simulation. Emergence here, says Cariani, is through "*...creating new ways of seeing the world [and] ...changing the way we think and interact with the world*" (Cariani 1991); and the emergence that occurs in simulations is '*computational emergence*'.

Of course the simulation of emergent processes, including artificial life, remains useful for understanding natural phenomena, creating art, supporting design practices and so on. However, Cariani's concept of computational emergence also reminds us that finite, deterministic computer simulations differ from the natural world in terms of openness. Openness is a recurring theme throughout this book due to its relationship to both emergence and art (and is discussed in more depth in Chap. 3).

Through articulating the concept of computational emergence, Cariani also describes emergence in subjective, personal and experiential terms.This parallels the approach to emergence taken in visual thinking and design research. It demonstrates another similarity in how emergence is understood between disciplines. In the design research approach, however, there is a focus on the actual creative experience of perception; such as the shapes, patterns or order that can be *perceived* by an observer. In the context of interactive art this observer can be a participant with that interactive artwork. We can then say that where such a 'participant-observer' is interacting with the system, they would be experiencing emergence in interactive art.

The perception and experience of emergence are key concerns here. Their consideration has informed two primary classes of emergence: *perceptual* and *physical*. The first type of emergence is focused on the subjective, interpretive action of *perceiving* emergence, and the creativity this involves. It draws on research from the design research and Gestalt domains, including emergent shapes research. The second type of emergence is concerned with the real, natural world and living and non-living physically-based processes, and does not rely on an observer. For example, a group of birds will flock regardless of whether or not we are there to observe them. This latter class of *physical* emergence is informed by research in the complex sciences, biology and physics as well as the tools used in those domains, including simulations of these processes such as artificial life research.

Emergence Across Levels

Another useful aspect to the concept of emergence is the different types of relations between the level of the whole and the level of its constituting parts. Contemporary Gestalt psychologist Rudolf Arnheim points out that there is feedback between the emergent whole and the parts: "*In a gestalt, each unit [part] is affected and modified by its relations to other units of the system [whole]. Each relation [whole], in turn, is affected by the agent generating it [parts]*" (Arnheim 1996). While the whole gains its meaning from some combination of the parts that is more than a simple summing, the parts are also affected.

As noted earlier, the distinction between a whole and constituting parts logically implies a difference in scale, or levels. An emergent new aspect is occurring on one level of organisation that is not predictable from a lower level. Philosopher Emmeche and his colleagues recently described four such levels in our world: physical-chemical, biological, psychological and sociological. Each level has its own sub-levels, and emergence occurs any time a level is transcended—for example, as we move from physical-chemical building blocks to biological life, or as we move from disordered groups of atoms to crystalline structures. In each case, there is something 'heterogeneously new' occurring at one level up (Emmeche et al. 1997). Furthermore, this emergent phenomenon cannot be explained or anticipated in terms of its originating level or parts.

From this characterisation of emergence as something that occurs across levels we can see there is a capacity for mutual dependence and feedback between the levels of the parts and the whole. For example, an emergent crystal structure is not only heterogeneously new to constituting molecules, that structure will also affect the solubility of the molecules; that is their state, at a local, lower level. There is feedback from the higher level of the whole back down to the level of the parts.

Physicist James Crutchfield describes this as intrinsic emergence.[2] He characterises newness as occurring at two scales or levels (Crutchfield 1994). Firstly, new behaviour such as pattern formation occurs at a global scale where the system as a

[2]Interestingly, the early Gestalt conception of a whole as both coming about from the interaction of parts and informing how those parts relate to one another mentioned above also expresses this idea of feedback (Wertheimer 1938). Once again we can see similar understandings of emergence across disciplines.

whole exhibits this emergent property. Secondly, it can also occur at a local scale, when the local interactions between the parts themselves change. New patterns of structure can be said to emerge at a local level and this "*newness with respect to other structures in the underlying system*" is described as intrinsic emergence (Crutchfield 1994). The change in interactions between the parts at a local scale creates a feedback loop between global and local levels, where they inform one another. For example, when birds fly in a flock they both affect and are affected by the changing formation of the flock. Each bird flies differently when in formation than it would on its own. When in formation, a change in one bird's flight affects its neighbours (for example, to avoid collision), who in turn affect their immediate neighbours. Thus the behaviour of the individuals affects the flock. Conversely, flying in a flock benefits the birds through reduced wind resistance, which in turn creates new local bird behaviour because it improves their performance. In an emergent system, the whole and its parts can relate to one another through feedback loops. This notion of feedback informs the second layer of the taxonomy. That is, emergence can be further differentiated as firstly *intrinsic*, where the emergent whole affects the system across levels at both the level of the whole and of the parts… On the other hand, in *extrinsic* emergence there is no feedback from the whole back to the parts. The parts remain unchanged by the emergent whole and as such, emergence is said to occur at the level of the whole only.

To recap, the definition of emergence provided at the start of this chapter identified some core qualities that have now been discussed: *new*, *unpredictable*, a *whole* that is made up of *parts* and the *levels* that these sit across. Creativity is another quality that has also been discussed. The remainder of this chapter builds on this understanding of the qualities of emergence to describe an organising framework for emergence in interactive art.

The Taxonomy of Emergence in Interactive Art (TEIA)

The TEIA organises the debates and qualities of emergence discussed above into one framework to position emergence in the context of interactive art. In many ways it is a pragmatic effort: the characteristics that differentiate classes of emergence seek to serve the creative arts and particularly interactive art. A practitioner seeking to instantiate the characteristics of emergence can look towards the models and approaches collected here, to identify possible approaches or mechanisms. That is, an approach for creating emergence in one domain can be used to affect it for another. While the TEIA is largely informed by theory, empirical evidence from participant interactions with artworks as well as the creation of artworks themselves have also influenced its development. The TEIA is summarised in Fig. 2.3.

The above discussion of emergence research has already identified some of the different ways in which emergence is understood in the natural and computer sciences through to Gestalt theory and design research. These inform the first two levels of the TEIA. First is the role of the observer and second is the concept of

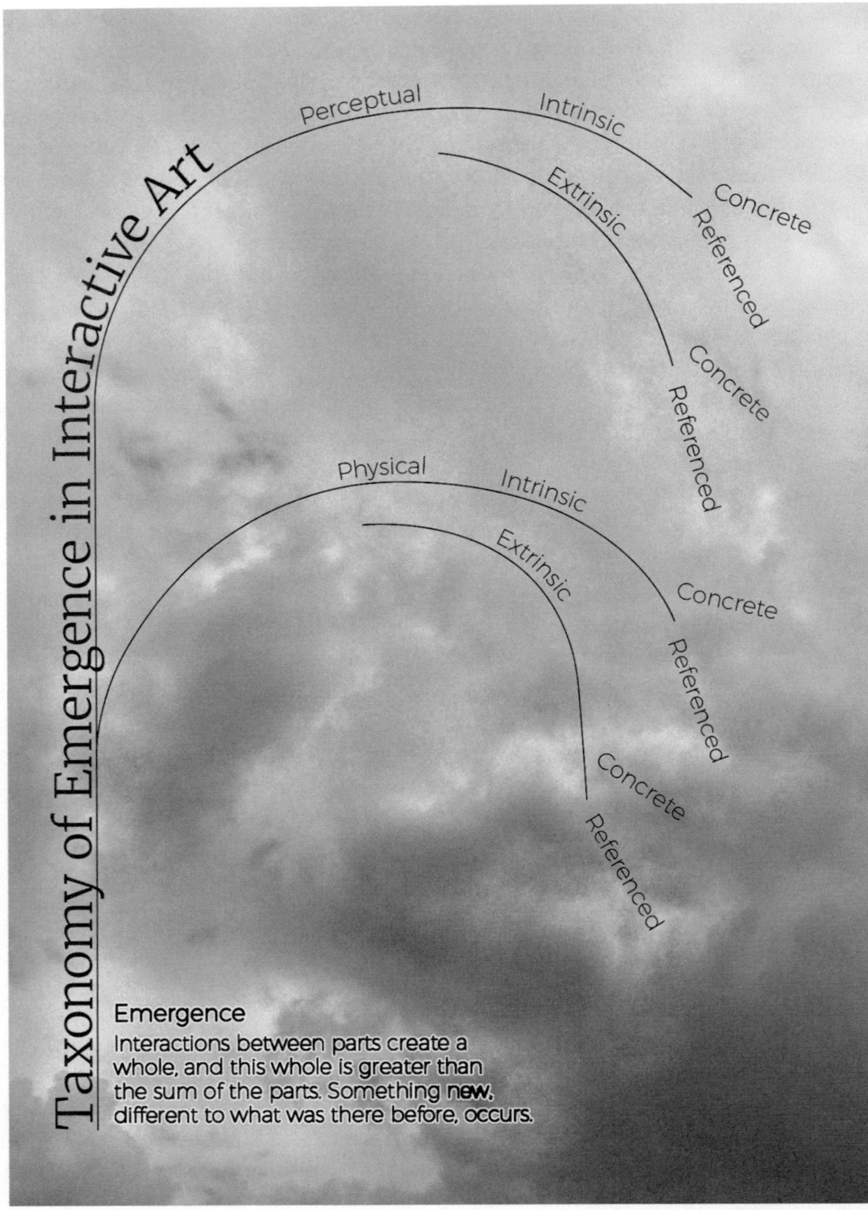

Fig. 2.3 The TEIA comprises three differentiating factors, resulting in eight classes of emergence in interactive art.

feedback across the levels. The third and final layer of differentiation in the TEIA concerns how the quality of novelty, or newness can characterise the emergent instance within an art context. In this section I discuss each of these layers in detail.

First Level: The Observer

To start with, it is useful to differentiate emergence that is experienced by us from that which occurs in the natural world. The first level of the taxonomy therefore distinguishes between situations where the emergent 'whole' relies on the perception of an observer to exist (*perceptual* emergence) and situations where the emergent 'whole' is considered independently of an observer (*physical* emergence). These two primary types of emergence, *perceptual* and *physical* emergence, are non-exclusive and may be spatial or temporal. To recap, the first includes research into the perception of shapes in the field of design and composition in the arts. The second includes structures in natural systems and the efforts to model or simulate these.

It's useful to note that the perceptual type of emergence often occurs at the same time as physical emergence has occurred. For example, when we perceive patterns or order in the natural world, such as the emergent hexagonal shapes that form in the hot oil as in the Bénard cells pictured in Fig. 2.2, there is not only the physical emergence that is occurring through the self-organisation of these complex systems, there is also the perceptual emergence occurring within us as we perceive these shapes and develop this new understanding.

Since the context of this book is digital, interactive art, *perceptual* emergence is a critical concern. It is also more novel—mostly the research into emergence and interactive art is in the simulated rendering of natural processes rather than being concerned with a participant's emergent perception and experience.

Second Level: Feedback

The second level of classification differentiates between instances where the emergent whole 'feeds back' into the parts and alters them, and those instances where there is no feedback from the whole to the parts. Where there is feedback, the emergent quality is *intrinsic* to the structure, and where there is no feedback it is *extrinsic* to it (e.g. Wertheimer 1938; Crutchfield 1994; Arnheim 1996).

These two first layers of the taxonomy can be illustrated with an example. Consider the typical V-shape formation of snow geese. We can think of this as an emergent structure or behaviour that is physically manifest in the world independent of our perception. In this sense it is an instance of *physical* emergence. Furthermore, the flock formation benefits the individual birds by providing reduced wind resistance to the individuals. In this sense, the emergent whole structure is 'feeding back' into the level of the parts and it can be understood as a *physically intrinsic* instance of emergence. On the other hand, where a person is watching these birds and remarks on their characteristic V shape, they are also experiencing a form of emergence, specifically *perceptual* emergence. However, unless that person acts on their new, emergent understanding to influence the birds, the emergence is solely at the level of the 'whole': the emergent V shape we perceive. In this case it is, at the same time as demonstrating *physically intrinsic* emergence, also an instance of *perceptually extrinsic* emergence.

Third Level: Referencing

The final third distinction in the TEIA has not yet been discussed. This concerns the quality of emergent newness by drawing on concepts of the figurative, abstract and concrete in art. Specifically, it draws on a distinction in aesthetics that differentiates artwork that refers to something, such as a figure or landscape, from the type of abstract artwork that eschews all reference to the outside world. This latter class is the 'Art Concrete' movement. It was proposed by artist Theo van Doesburg in 1930 (Baljeu 1974). Here the plastic, essential or 'concrete' elements of the art work (for example colour and form) are employed for their own sake. This is rather than them being in the service of a representation (Gooding 2001; Chilvers 2009).

Other art movements, such as Constructivism and De Stijl, hold similar ideas about the plastic, or concrete, elements that make up an artwork. Constructive artist Naum Gabo describes the content and form of an artwork as being "*one and the same thing. It does not separate Content from Form ...they have to live and act as a unit, proceed in the same direction and produce the same effect*" (Gabo 1937). Art historian Herschel Chipp writes of a similar focus on form in De Stijl: "*in terms of painting the plastic means were reduced to the constitutive elements of line, space and colour, arranged in the most elemental compositions*" (Chipp 1968). A Mark Rothko painting, for example, is concerned with the material aspects of the medium such as the brush stroke or interaction between adjacent colours. This is different to the reference the painting may make to that outside itself, to the outside world—such as a portrait of the *Mona Lisa*, or the abstracted, colourful city lights in Mondrian's *Boogie Nights*. Identifying instances of concrete emergence in interactive art can, potentially, facilitate better understanding of the material aspects of interaction.

The taxonomy therefore differentiates between emergence as relating to representation, and art in these two ways. That is, emergence that references something else in the world such as through modelling or interpreting something familiar can be considered *Referenced* emergence. Conversely, emergence that does not reference anything and is completely local to its plastic or 'concrete' elements can be called *Concrete* emergence.

In addition to aesthetic theory, this last level of the taxonomy has also been informed by observations of people interacting with artworks. As is discussed later in Chap. 6, this includes instances in which people have interpreted images and then manipulated these images during their interaction with a work. In one case during interaction with the art system +−*now* (Seevinck 2008), a participant perceived a stick figure in the computer imagery. He subsequently interacted with the figure to 'make it walk'. This is an example of *Referenced Intrinsic Perceptual* emergence, as shown in Fig. 2.3). The image is a perceived object which relies on the participant to interpret it in order to exist as the 'walking man' composition. The 'walking man' interpretation also works to sustain the composition because the participant creates gestures in the sand to 'keep the stickman walking'. Each of these gestures is a stroke in the sand for the legs, sharing the meaning of the stick figure walking. The emergent *whole* therefore informs the *parts*, *feeding back* into them. As such it is *intrinsic* to the whole. Finally, the interpretation *references* a 'stickman walking'.

Through these three levels of differentiation we can think about emergence in interactive art in terms of eight types. Each of these classes is now briefly reviewed.

Concrete Extrinsic Perceptual Emergence This first class of emergence relies on being perceived to exist, and is where the emergent whole does not change or affect the parts that make it up. Here the emergent whole also does not refer to anything. For example, a melody is qualitatively different and new, whole to its constituting musical notes (the parts), and it does not change the notes. In this case it would also lack references to other sounds such as a babbling brook or canons firing or familiar sound motifs to evoke other aural compositions. The shifting rhythms one can perceive in a Steve Reich composition is an example of concrete extrinsic perceptual emergence.

Referenced Extrinsic Perceptual Emergence This is a type of emergence that relies on being perceived to exist, where the emergent whole does not change or affect the parts that make it up, and where the emergent whole refers to something else in the world. The emergent heart shape pictured in Fig. 1.2 is one example. This came about from the transformation of the teardrop shapes. Furthermore, the emergent shape, such as the heart (whole) does not change the constituting shapes (parts); while the interpretation of this heart is in reference to our pre-existing understanding of this symbol. Another example is the emergent composition of a face, perceived during interaction with +−*now* (Seevinck 2008), discussed in Chap. 6. Here the interpretation of the face compositions (whole) does not affect the constituting shapes and gestures (parts). It also refers to faces in the real world.

Concrete Intrinsic Perceptual Emergence This is a type of emergence that relies on being perceived to exist, where the emergent whole changes or in some way affects the parts that make it up, and where the emergent whole does not refer to anything. It can include new strategies or behaviours—for example, *bluffing* in the game of poker (Salen and Zimmerman 2004) and the 'following lights' behaviour during interaction with +−*now* (Chap. 6). Here the *bluffing* behaviour (whole) affects the way in which cards (parts) are treated (e.g. with suspicion).

Referenced Intrinsic Perceptual Emergence This is a type of emergence that is independent of an observer's perception, where the emergent whole changes or in some way affects the parts that make it up, and where the emergent whole refers to something else in the world. For example, during the collaborative design of the *Lotus* bicycle the creative team would recognise aspects of the drawings in different ways, as is consistent with their own area of expertise (Edmonds et al. 1994). When shared among the group, these varied interpretations resulted in surprisingly new design intentions. The emergent intentions would 'feed back' to change the meaning of the drawings and their emergent shapes. Thus the emergent design (whole) feeds back to change the condition of the shapes recognised in those drawings (parts). Another example is the interpretation and animation of a 'stick-man' during one participant's interaction with *+−now*. As described earlier, the animation behaviour (whole) affects the way in which the sand, coloured and white image are interacted with (e.g. rhythmically, to make a 'man' 'walk'). Furthermore, this interpretation is referenced in that the behaviour is referring to animation and a man walking in the real world. Interestingly, this also points to *analogy* as being, by definition, referenced.

Concrete Extrinsic Physical Emergence This is a type of emergence that exists independently of being perceived, where the emergent whole does not change or affect the parts that make it up, and where the emergent whole does not refer to anything. A coastline's shape is one example. We can understand that this edge between land and sea does not refer to anything, and that its self-similar structure does not feed back in to affect the rocks that it is made up of (parts).

Referenced Extrinsic Physical Emergence Once again, as a form of physical emergence, this class is considered to exist independently of being perceived. It is also a case of where the emergent whole does not change or affect the parts that make it up. Finally, as an instance of referenced emergence, in this case it will refer to something else in the world. For example, this might be a fractal rendering simulating a coastline. Here the fractal algorithm (whole) does not affect the constants within this algorithm (parts). It also refers to a coastline.

Concrete Intrinsic Physical Emergence As another case of physical emergence this class also describes instances of emergent processes in the natural world which can be understood to exist independently of being perceived. Here however there is feedback and the emergent whole changes or in some way affects the parts that makes it up. Also here the emergent whole does not refer to anything outside of what it is. Examples include an insoluble crystal or a skein of geese flying in formation. Here the insoluble crystal (whole) affects the molecules (parts) by changing their solubility. Similarly, a flock (whole) affects the individual birds (parts) by reducing their wind resistance and flying effort.

Referenced Intrinsic Physical Emergence This last class of emergence is also physical. Here the emergent whole changes or in some way affects the parts that make it up. The emergent whole also refers to something else in the world. An example of this type of emergence is the *Boids* computational model that simulates the flocking behaviour of birds (Reynolds 1987). Within this simulation the 'flock' (whole) affects the individual behaviour of the 'birds' (parts), demonstrating feedback from that whole to the parts. As a simulation of real-world bird flocking behaviour it is also necessarily a form of referenced emergence.

Conclusion

The Taxonomy of Emergence in Interactive Art (TEIA) organises the literature and various positions on emergence into one view. It facilitates understanding and comparisons between different types of emergence. In the first instance it differentiates between emergence that is reliant on an observer to exist, from that which relates to the physical and biological processes of the natural world to exist independently of being perceived. The second and third layers of distinction concern feedback between the whole and the parts and whether or not the instance of emergence refers to anything.

The TEIA can also function as a map, locating mechanisms to facilitate emergence in interactive art alongside aspects of audience experience of it. In so doing, it can facilitate a more differentiated understanding of emergence. Furthermore, the explicit focus on the concrete, material and local aspects of an emergent system means that the TEIA provides the opportunity to look at aspects of emergence that are local to an artwork and not, for example, metaphorical or based on analogy. This also serves to orient the taxonomy in the context of interactive art.

As mentioned, the TEIA can *map* across the different enquiries into emergence, providing a route that might facilitate one kind of emergence by effecting another kind. For example, a physically emergent simulation can facilitate perceptual emergence. The practitioner interested in different ways of facilitating perceptual emergence can look at the models and understandings in physics and computer science as well as biology and artificial life communities (i.e. physical emergence). Conversely, the researcher who is interested in how people understand and interpret their simulation of natural systems could look towards the ways the design research community understands and models (perceptual) emergence. My interactive artwork *Of me With me* (Seevinck 2014) demonstrates such a cross-mapping. Here an understanding of self-similar structures (physical emergence) has informed a creative participant experience. That is, the work employs a generative, fractal algorithm to take incoming gestures of a participant drawing and 'echo' these for transformed and iterated imagery. The overall participant experience is one of drawing interactively 'with their own mark'. It is a work that seeks to enable agency and ownership as well as compositional unity through visual pattern and rhythm. As discussed in Chap. 6 *Of me With me* was found to facilitate emergent participant experiences (perceptual emergence). The art system employs an understanding and model of emergence from one side of the TEIA tree to facilitate instances of emergence as shown on the other side.

Understanding the potential of interactive artworks to facilitate emergent participant experiences is another useful application of the TEIA. I demonstrate this application through evaluation of participant experience of my own works (Chap. 6), as well as through the characterisation of six key interactive artworks from around the world (Chap. 4). The TEIA and the qualities of emergence that have been discussed here will also inform the data analyses and critiques to identify various aspects and potentials for emergence.

References

Arnheim R (1996) Form as creation. In: Arnheim R (ed) The split and the structure twenty eight essays. University of California Press, Berkeley, pp 151–155

Baljeu J (1974) Theo van Doesburg, First American Edition. Macmillan Publishing Co. Inc, New York

Ball P (1999) The Self-Made Tapestry: Pattern Formation in Nature. Oxford University Press, Oxford

Bar-Yam Y (2002) General features of complex systems. Encyclopedia of life support systems EOLSS. UNESCO Publishers, Oxford

Berry R (1998) Feeping Creatures, interactive artwork

Cariani P (1991) Emergence and artificial life. In: Langton CG, Taylor C, Farmer JD, Rasmussen S (eds). Addison-Wesley, pp 775–797

Chilvers I (2009) Concrete art. Oxford University Press, Oxford

Chipp HB (1968) Neo plasticism and constructivism in abstract and non-objective art. In: Chipp HB (ed) Theories of modern art a sourcebook for artists and critics. U.C. Press, USA, pp 309–366

Crutchfield JP (1994) Is anything ever new? Considering emergence. In: Cowan G, Pines D, Melzner D (eds) Complexity: metaphors, models, and reality. Addison-Wesley, Reading, pp 479–497

Eco U (1962) The poetics of the open work. In: Bishop C (ed) Participation. The MIT Press, London, pp 20–40

Edmonds EA (1995) Creativity: interacting with computers (panel discussion). In: Edmonds EA, Katz I, Mack R et al (eds) CHI '95 conference on human factors in computing systems. SIGCHI: ACM Special Interest Group on Computer-Human Interaction. ACM Press, Denver, pp 185–186

Edmonds EA, Soufi B (1992) The computational modelling of emergent shape in design. In: Gero JS, Sudweeks (eds) Computational models of creative design. University of Sydney, Sydney, pp 173–190

Edmonds EA, Candy L, Jones R, Soufi B (1994) Support for collaborative design: agents and emergence. Commun ACM 37:41–47

Emmeche C (1994) What is Life? In: The Garden in the Machine The Emerging Science of Artificial Life. Princeton University Press, pp 23–46

Emmeche C, Køppe S, Stjernfelt F (1997) Explaining emergence towards an ontology of levels. J Gen Philos Sci 28:83–119

Flake GW (1998) The computational beauty of nature computer explorations of fractals, chaos, complex systems, and adaptation. A Bradford Book, Cambridge

Gabo N (1937) The constructive idea in art. In: Circle: international survey of constructivist art, 1st edn. London

Gero JS (1996) Creativity, emergence and evolution in design. Knowl Based Syst 9:435–448

Gooding M (2001) Abstraction: an introduction. In: Gooding M (ed) Abstract Art. Tate Publishing, Cambridge University Press, Cambridge, pp 6–11

Holland JH (1998) Emergence from chaos to order. Addison-Wesley, Redwood city

Laughlin RB, Pines D (2000) The theory of everything. Proc Nat Acad Sci (PNAS) 97:28–31. doi:10.1073/pnas.97.1.28

Lewes GH (1875) Resultants and emergents. Problems of life and mind. James R. Osgood and Company, Boston, pp 368–375

Mill JS (1889) On the composition of causes. In: a system of logic ratiocinative and inductive being a connected view of the principles of evidence and the methods of scientific investigation, Peoples. Longmans, Green, & Co., London, pp 242–247

Mitchell WJ (1990) A new agenda for computer aided design. In: McCullough M, Mitchell WJ, Purcell P (eds) The electronic design studio architectural knowledge and media in the computer era. The MIT Press, Cambridge, pp 27–43

Mitchell WJ (1993) A computational view of design creativity. In: Gero JS, Maher ML (eds) Modeling creativity and knowledge-based creative design. Laurence Erlbaum Associates Inc., Hillsdale, pp 25–42

Dictionaries Oxford (2010) Reductionism. Oxford University Press, Oxford

Pickard-Cambridge WA (tran) (2015) Topics/Aristotle. eBooks@Adelaide, Adelaide

Poon J, Maher ML (1996) Emergent behaviour in co-evolutionary design. Artificial intelligence in design. Springer, The Netherlands, pp 703–722

Prusinkiewicz P, Lindenmayer A (1990) The algorithmic beauty of plants, electronic version published Springer, New York, in 1990 and reprinted in 1996. Springer

Resnick M (1994) Turtles, termites, and traffic jams explorations in massively parallel microworlds. The MIT Press, Cambridge

Reynolds CW (1987) Flocks, herds, and schools: a distributed behavioral model. In: Stone MC (ed) Proceedings of the 14th annual conference on computer graphics and interactive techniques (Siggraph 87). ACM Press, pp 25–34

Rinaldo KE (1999) The Flock. Leonardo, The MIT Press, pp 405–407

Salen K, Zimmerman E (2004) Rules of play game design fundamentals. The MIT Press, Cambridge

Seevinck J (2008) +-now, interactive artwork

Seevinck J (2014) Of me With me, interactive artwork

Sommerer C, Mignonneau L (eds) (1998) Art as a living system. In: Art @ science. Springer, Vienna

Soufi B, Edmonds EA (1995) A framework for the description and representation of emergent shapes. In: Teh M, Tan R (eds) Proceedings of computer-aided architectural design (CAAD) futures. Singapore, pp 411–422

Thompson DW (1992) On growth and form: the complete revised edition. Dover Publications, Momence

Weber M, Esfeld M (2008) Holism in the sciences. Encyclopedia of Life Support Systems (EOLSS), vol 1. UNESCO, Paris, pp 91–109

Wertheimer M (1938) Gestalt theory. In: Ellis WD (ed) Source book of gestalt psychology. Harcourt, Brace and Co., New York, pp 1–11

Wolfram S (2002) A New Kind of Science. Wolfram Media, Inc., Champaign, IL USA

Chapter 3
Interaction in Art and Computing

Abstract The questions surrounding emergence in interactive art necessitate insight from different domains. While the previous chapter established an understanding of emergence, here the focus is on interaction. A selection of contemporary arts practices and computing approaches are reviewed as these can point to new ways of thinking about the relationships between audience, art system and artist. Participation, experience and open interactions form the core of the chapter's discussions, leading to insight into open and emergent digital interactions.

Interactive art is still a relatively new area. Here it can be understood as a system which requires an active audience in order to function and respond to their presence or actions. As interactive arts pioneer Ernest Edmonds describes art as being interactive "*when audience participation is an integral part of the work*" (Edmonds 2011a). Similarly, Digital Art Museum (DAM) founder and gallerist Wolf Lieser describes interactive art as involving external signals—for example, from the body of participant, or from the outside world more generally—to display them in a perceivable form (Lieser 2010). In both cases interactive art involves some sort of active audience participation with the work. An interesting facet of this discussion is the consideration that if the artwork necessitates an active audience to respond to, then it can also be argued that the interactive artwork is only fully realised once someone is participating with it.

Participation and Influence

In 1973 British artists Edmonds and Stroud Cornock were working with computation and audience involvement and, a part of these considerations, they identified four classes of art (Cornock and Edmonds 1973). The first class they identified corresponds to traditional forms of art such as painting, and is termed *static*. Their second class is *dynamic-passive* art. As its name suggests, this changes over time, but does not facilitate active audience involvement. Kinetic art like a Calder mobile

J. Seevinck, *Emergence in Interactive Art*, Springer Series on Cultural Computing,
DOI 10.1007/978-3-319-45201-2_3

is an example of this type of art. It is an artwork which moves but which is not responsive to the audience.

The other two classes are concerned with audience involvement. The third, *dynamic-interactive* type of art describes work that reacts to a viewer and where they can change its performance. It changes over time like the preceding *dynamic-passive* category, but is also responsive because there is a feedback loop between audience and work such that the audience affects the work directly. Much of the interactive art that we see today would fall in this category.

The last class identified in 1973 is *dynamic-interactive (varying)* work. As its name suggests, this form also changes over time and with audience interaction. However, it has the added aspect of internally modulating the feedback loop. In *Heron* (Edmonds 2002) Edmonds implemented such a feedback loop using a generative software agent. Specifically, the work's vertical line imagery would become thinner as one approached responding to immediate audience presence in a way that seems like 'retreating'. Audience movements throughout the day also accumulate to modify the behaviour of the imagery the next day, through a programmed modification of the threshold of sensitivity to the audience. Edmonds describes the behaviour of this modifying agent metaphorically, referencing the behaviour of the bird: "*One could say that Heron can become tired of people jumping and waving in front of it all day long*" (Edmonds et al. 2004).

The dynamic-interactive and dynamic-interactive (varying) classes focus on artworks that change with participant interaction. Edmonds has continued to explore other ways of thinking about interactive art, including temporal and distributed aspects of audience engagement as well as longer term interaction. *Heron*'s capacity to vary its behaviour from day to day is an example of this sort of distended, longer term interaction.

Longer term interaction has become a concern for Edmonds. He differentiates it from the immediate, direct, 'action-response' feedback model that we often see in computer games. Rather, longer-term engagement is more 'influencing' in its character. It may only create an effect, that is, *influence* the performance some time later, and there may not even be an immediately perceivable reaction. In more recent writing he draws on his creative work to describes this as another type of art, that is as *dynamic-interactive (influencing)* art (2011b).

The communicating technology of the internet has also informed understanding of interactive art. *Cities Tango* (Edmonds 2009) constitutes 'nodes' of the artwork at different geographic locations. These communicate with one another and the work is, correspondingly, described as a dynamic-interactive (communicating) artwork. They are affected by people's interaction with them locally but also by each other. In this sense the interaction can also be understood as distributed across the works and geography.

Lieser similarly identifies interactivity in artworks as ranging from 'direct interaction' through to some sort of 'time-delayed action'. He observes that while works can range from "'*simple*' *interactivity, where the visitor only pushes a button, up to complex procedures between the installation and the recipient,*" it is usually only the latter that retain audience interest (Lieser 2010).

Delayed and influencing interactions can start to move us towards more complex understandings of interaction. They resemble the way in which memory works, and the way in which influence can travel across large system with interconnected elements. In many ways, they evoke similar character to our relationships with other people or animals who remember how we treated them yesterday; or with our world, in which tomorrow's climate is influenced by our behaviour today.

This is not something we typically see in interactive applications. Instead there is a prevalence of the action-response type model of interaction. Similarly, immediate interaction feedback tends to be more common. Explorations of interactions and complex models that challenge the status quo are needed. These can affect the way in which we relate to information and environment. They can help identify the potential for creative expression within interactivity as a medium. Furthermore, it may be that explorations of formal aspects of the interactive medium such as these become increasingly expressive, complex and experimental, in a bid to differentiate themselves from the every growing landscape of interactive applications and devices in our everyday lives.

Rules and Computers

Interestingly, the earlier definitions and descriptions of an interactive artwork seem only to require a feedback loop between the work and the audience, and some sort of change in the work itself. They do not state the necessity for a computer. While much interactive art today does typically use computer hardware and software systems, or a microcontroller chip such as the Arduino (Ivrea Interaction Design Institute 2005) this was not always the case. In fact, interactive art predates the digital computer. It is the involvement of the audience, rather than technology, which has brought us here.

A number of art movements—such as Dada, Fluxus and the Situationists—have influenced this evolution. Marcel Duchamp's *Rotary Glass Plates* (Duchamp 1920) is understood as one of the earliest interactive artworks (Paul 2015). This machine required the viewer to turn the handles then stand back and view the optical effects. Better known as an interactive artwork is Myron Krueger's *Videoplace*. Originally this work also did not use a computer, but was instead reliant on analogue video technology for rendering the audience for interaction. Only in 1985 were computer vision issues resolved, allowing the work to incorporate a computer (Krueger 1974; Krueger et al. 1985).

Edmonds also believes a work may be both interactive art and *not* use a computer. While today we use computers to execute a set of conditional rules, this effort does not, strictly speaking, need to be completed by a machine. It could, albeit slowly and possibly arduously, also be accomplished by a person: it is for example feasible for an artist to 'update' an artwork based on the active audience input, perhaps on a daily basis (Edmonds et al. 2004).

The execution of a set of conditional rules is at the core of much software and hardware technology, but rules have also been used as a part of the process of artmaking. In Dadaist poetry, Fluxus events and conceptual art works, precise instructions are followed to make the work. In 1922 Moholy Nagy ordered an enamel sign by instructing the fabricator over the telephone. Similarly in 1966 Robert Morris sent fabrication instructions to a gallery in Chicago to build his work anew for display there, given this was cheaper than transporting from New York. For art historian and critic Jack Burnham these efforts exemplify a shift "*from an object oriented to a systems oriented culture. Here change emanates, not from things, but from the way things are done*" (Burnham 1968).

The shift in emphasis from product to processes in art making is significant for interactive art. This is because it embraces the conceptual effort behind the rule-making, explicitly acknowledging this as something creative. Here the artist works to procedurally set the boundaries for the art system, which may contain the audience and other people, materials, or ideas, through to aspects of the environment surrounding them.

Integral to this systems view is the relations between all these aspects. As artist Hans Haacke describes it:

> A "sculpture" that physically reacts to its environment is no longer to be regarded as an object. The range of outside factors affecting it, as well as its own radius of action, reach beyond the space it materially occupies. It thus merges with the environment in a relationship that is better understood as a "system" of interdependent processes… (Burnham 1968)

A systems art approach emphasises the intangible interactive relations we can have with an artwork. It also reminds us that we can think beyond our immediate interaction with an artwork or device to consider the world more broadly—be it the environment beyond this local interaction between me and my device, or the influence and consequence of today's actions on my future.

Audience as Participant

Allan Kaprow's *Happenings* were similarly procedural artworks. They were orchestrated events with a clear sequence of activities. However, they also emphasised a participatory aesthetic: each *Happening* consisted of an environment through which the audience was manipulated to a degree that was "*virtually unprecedented in 20th century art*" (Schimmel 1989). Situationists such as Kaprow and DeBord advocated active audience participation for the political purpose of redefining passive 'watching' to instead prioritise 'active living'. In his 1957 essay DeBord outlines participatory events that require physical involvement, and rejects a passive role for the audience (1957).

Other efforts towards audience involvement challenge the authorship of the work. For example, John Cage's 1952 performance *4'33"* (Cage 1952) was a turning point for the composer, who subsequently went on to 'surrender' authorship and 'open' the form of the work up to other interpretations and meanings. In this controversial performance, the audience heard four minutes and 33 s of 'silence'. That is, the performer took no action; rather it was the environment—such as the audience—that contributed to the soundscape. This is an example of an open-ended work and, as discussed later in the chapter, the open artwork tends to have greater capacity for creative engagement.

Cage and the Situationists were among the first to initiate active audience participation. In 1963, artist Nam Jun Paik explored critical audience engagement with live television broadcasts in his *Participation TV 1* (Paik 1963). This was the first instance of viewer interaction with the previously passive medium and heralded the start of Video Art (Arns 2004; Daniels 2008). It was around then that artist and theorist Roy Ascott first distinguished the term *participant* to describe the audience of the interactive artwork (Ascott 1966).

The use of the term *participant* is significant. It acknowledges the legacy of contemporary arts practice, including the potential for open-ended interaction. Participation also resonates with the idea of perceptual emergence—that is, that emergence is something that someone can interpret and experience. Inherent in the notion of participation and perceptual emergence, then, is the assertion that meaning is actively constructed through our interaction with the world. In this book the term *participant* is therefore used to describe the active audience of the interactive artwork.

Human-Computer Interaction

We can also gain insight into the experience of interactive systems by looking at human computer interaction (HCI). This field of research is broadly concerned with "*studying humans and computers in communication*" (Hewett et al. 1992). Its focus has shifted from technology implementations, efficiency and usability to more complex concerns, such as more involved or open-ended interactions between the human and computer, and these latter concerns can relate directly to emergence in interactive art.

Early on in HCI the primary concern was with human factors, namely solving ergonomics-type issues and understanding how people could feasibly interact with computers for work. As HCI researcher Liam Bannon explained, addressing those questions was a matter of identifying specifications. The human being in the equation was treated as just one more set of 'specifications' (Bannon 1992). Human performance would be evaluated in controlled laboratory tests to determine things like the human eye's persistence of vision to inform a minimum refresh rate for a screen. The user's involvement with the design process did not, however, tend to go beyond this passive role of being a 'factor for design integration' or 'test subject'. As research in HCI developed, the end users of the computer became more important. They became more actively involved in the design process—after all, who better to articulate the users' needs than the user themselves? This 'second wave' of HCI would aim to start with the user and solicit their needs in consultation with them, then learn if they are actually able to use the system in the context of use. The emphasis shifted to treating the human as an *actor rather than a factor*, that is, as an active member of the design process.

While the research and development of the first and second wave remain relevant and necessary, in the third wave of computing we see HCI environments that go beyond questions around work, efficiency and usability. Here we're starting to see the sorts of questions art and culture can bring to computer-mediated interactions and consideration of the broader context, not just the device itself (Bødker 2006). As HCI broadens its understanding of interaction design for the human condition we increasingly see philosophical, psychological and social concerns directing enquiry.

Interactive Construction of Meaning In his articulation of embodied computing, computer scientist Paul Dourish argues our ability to make meaning is through being present and participating in the world. Meaning does not reside in the technology; rather it comes about through interaction with the technology, and this is how technology can become re-purposed (Dourish 2001). How we understand the world around us, and the things within it, is through interaction.

This resonates with the theory of affordances put forward by psychologist James J. Gibson. Affordance theory describes the integrated relationship between an actor (such as an animal or person) and environment with its objects, in terms of the actions that those objects can support for that actor (Gibson 1977, 1979). These qualities are, however, subjectively perceived and constructed; they are not fixed in that object—rather, they can differ for different animals. For example, a berry that is food for an insect can be poison for a horse. Gibson argues that when we perceive qualities of objects in our environment, what we actually perceive is the affordances of those objects (Gibson 1979), that is, we see them in terms of how they relate to ourselves.

In the 1990s Tangible Computing (TC) sought to leverage the rich affordances that we have with everyday objects to facilitate a similarly rich experience of human computer interaction. TC researchers argued that the emphasis on graphical user interfaces (GUI) have ignored the rich languages, cultures and design of instruments, physical objects and architecture, that have been informed by haptic interaction with real physical objects and evolved throughout our history (e.g. Fitzmaurice et al. 1995; Ishii and Ullmer 1997; Ishii et al. 2012). These criticisms arguably still apply today given the prevalence of GUIs in everyday computing interactions, such as the ever-present smartphone and tablet.

Ambient Media and Hybrid Places TC researchers Ishii and Ullmer also criticised the focus on designing for tasks that require direct, foreground attention. There are other equally significant ways in which we understand and experience the world. For example, I will know that it is getting late in the day without needing to look out the window, because I inadvertently notice changes in ambient light levels and temperature. Research into ambient media is an aspect of the TC philosophy they proposed and one which would explore design for this sort of background information processing.

Architects Dunne and Raby's *Benches* project demonstrates the idea of an ambient augmentation to every day life. Here an area on one park bench is heated up when that same position is occupied on another park bench, located elsewhere (Dunne and Raby 1996). The *D-Tower* in Doetinchem, The Netherlands is another example. This visualises data about the emotional state of town residents by changing the building's colour at night (NOX et al. 2004).

The layering of digital devices and data into our physical surroundings is growing. We increasingly see smart home and office designs to monitor and moderate temperature, lighting and so on. Data and computation are integrated into our physical surroundings, effecting 'hybrid spaces' (de Souza e Silva 2006). Interaction and experience of these places is also now different, affected by the connectivity to others and the network. Contextual reminders, location-based 'push' notifications and social media and gaming all interrupt and redirect movement. Ubiquitous data and devices change the way we think and act. As MIT media scholar Sherry Turkle's studies have revealed, our behaviour is now affected to the extent that simply the presence of a mobile device will impact a conversation: the tone remains light as there is an expectation of being interrupted (Turkle 2015). Connection to the outside world through social media and email is affecting the depth to which we engage with one another. This connectivity is also changing the meaning of places. The experience of a memorial or temple is similarly less reflective given the expectation of interruption from a mobile device. The data network that overlays a place affects our experience of it and, by extension, its meaning. When my children became enthralled by the internationally popular augmented reality and geo-caching game, *Pokémon Go* (Hwang 2016), a large local tree and landmark for us changed. We started to refer to it as 'the Pokestop', referring to the fact that we could stock up on virtual 'poke balls' at this geocache location. Here the physical location and place was superseded by the gameplay and its virtual associations.

Interface for Experience As data networks and devices increasingly influence our everyday experience it becomes important to think about the quality of these digital interactions and interfaces. Early on in interface and interaction design the emphasis was on ubiquity and seamless integration with the everyday setting (Weiser 1991, 1994). This translated into a design approach that prioritises invisibility of design. It reflects a focus on the task and content over the interface or tool: *I don't want to think about the word processor, I just want to write.*

The emphasis on interface 'transparency' is valuable in many contexts. There are however, other approaches to creating with interactivity. For example, ART+COM are an artistic studio and company who work with interactivity as a medium for expression and not just as a tool (Lieser 2010 on ART+COM). Similar, more complex, expressive approaches may better reflect the rich understanding we already have of interaction with the physical, real world; affording considerations of experience.

It's worth discussing the status quo on interface design, particularly from the perspective of art and creativity. That is, rather than considering the interface as something that should be transparent and the interaction as solely about receiving information, we can focus on the experience that the interface and interaction can facilitate. Digital media researchers and artists Jay Bolter and Diane Gromala argue that designers have a choice in the role that the interface plays, and that it need not be relegated to 'transparency' or so-called 'natural' interaction. In fact, they caution against situations where the user believes they are interacting directly with the information instead of realising that there is a mediating, transformative agent—the interface—influencing understanding. At some point in the process of designing an interface, the designer will need to interpret and represent aspects of system functionality and operation, and things are naturally left out of this process. We run risks of error when we think that we actually see through an interface as a 'window' to reality, instead of realising that this view is itself a representation:

> The instrument is an interface and is never completely transparent.... In fact the glass may be a mirror, reflecting what the user is inclined to believe rather than a transparent window (Bolter and Gromala 2003).

We are actively constructing our process of seeing and sense-making, and maintaining some awareness of this is often useful, if not necessary for digital media.

Bolter and Gromala advocate a second strategy for interface design, which can be used alongside as an alternative to the strategy for transparency. This prioritises audience reflectivity, or active awareness of what they are looking at and seeing. It positions the interface as a mirror rather than a window, as something we 'look at' rather than just 'look through'. Instead of looking "*...through the experience to a world beyond, ... rather ...we look right at the surface*" (2003). Here the experience of engaging with the medium is deliberately crafted and goes beyond the communication of information. The interactive art work *Text Rain* (Achituv and Utterback 1999, discussed in Chap. 4) demonstrates this. Here a participant can see themselves as represented through a live video image. By moving their body and image of it, they are able to capture and direct falling letters and phrases from a poem. It is a compelling, reflective experience—one where the interface (their body) is something they look directly at, not through.

This work demonstrates how the interface can both facilitate information delivery (the goal of the transparent interface) and provide a compelling experience. Emotional design for products and experiences (e.g. Norman 2002) is another example of how one can approach that combination of experience and information delivery. As Bolter and Gromala assert, functionality and beauty need not be considered separate qualities and good interaction design and art can do both.

Researching Experience

The creation of an interactive artwork is a complex process, particularly given the intangible nature of experience. Artists, designers, technologists, curators and researchers are exploring and realising various possible interaction modes and experiences. In some cases the work is a collaborative team effort while in others an artist may function as technologist and researcher to create more independently. Detailed discussions of artists reporting on their research and practice can be found in the edited collections of Candy and Edmonds (2011) and Candy and Ferguson (2014).

Since a participant is necessary for the interactive artwork to be fully realised, engaging them with the work is a key consideration for artists working in interactivity. One approach is to involve the participant during part of the creative process by facilitating audience observation and interviewing, in an appropriate (e.g. aesthetic, cultural) public setting. The Beta_Space was an experimental public exhibition space that facilitated this type of research enquiry (Muller et al. 2006).[1] From early 2000 for almost ten years, this 'living laboratory' provided artists and researchers the opportunity to place near-complete work in a public context and observe or interview the visiting public that engaged with it. *+−now* (Seevinck 2008) was installed in the Beta_Space over a 2 month period in 2008 for the evaluation of audience experiences, as is discussed in Chaps. 5 and 6.

Research at the Beta_Space included studies on creative engagement. In 2006, Beta_Space researchers Edmonds, Muller and Connell came up with a threefold interaction model for looking at participant behaviours and interactive work (2006). These concepts are *attract*, *sustain* and *relate*. That is, the work may be attracting, or drawing participants in. This requires it to be appropriately distinct from its context. Next is the question of how to sustain participant engagement rather than having them lose interest and move on. The participant may also have 'related' to the work, in that they want to experience it again and again. Frenetic activity or bright colours are possible means towards attracting audiences to the work, as observed by Edmonds, Muller and Connell (2006). In Edmonds' work *Absolute_4.5* a participant's approach would impact the piece to suddenly 'settle down', initially puzzling them and sustaining their interest. The concepts of *attract*, *sustain* and *relate* are similar to some ideas developed by Nathan Shedroff for experience design (Shedroff 2001). Here, however, the stages are situated in the context of interactive art and research, and exemplified as such.

Over the years, researcher Zafer Bilda and colleagues from Beta_Space would propose a more detailed Creative Engagement Model (CEM) (Bilda et al. 2008; Bilda 2011), drawing on a longitudinal study of audience experience at the Beta_Space from 2004–7. 10 Case study artworks were researched , investigating creative engagement with those works. Among their findings was a definition of interactive experience as "*...a transformative dialogue between the audience and the interactive (art) system*" (Bilda et al. 2008).

Here the notion of transformation is key—that is, where a participant has an intention to interact. Purpose and system outcome inform this. In the first case there is a particular purpose to performing an action, such as for fun, for pleasure or curiosity. Second, there is an outcome that is expected, such as generation of a

[1]Muller pursued a similar project to document audience experience of David Rokeby's *Giver of Names* at the Daniel Langlois Foundation for Art Science and Technology, together with other researchers. The data produced there has informed discussion of Rokeby's work in Chap. 4 (Jones and Muller 2008; Muller 2008).

specific response. If a participant's purpose and outcome were not aligned they were often found to become frustrated and sometimes to give up. This is because their expectations and what they understood the artwork to be doing and mean, were not met. However there were also some participants at this stage that became curious about the system instead of frustrated, and would explore it some more. It is at this point that Bilda and his colleagues argue creative engagement has occurred:

> The participant might find herself re-thinking about her intentions or the outcomes she expects. Therefore, her intentional behaviour can become 'thoughtful'. If s/he shifts her intention to 'enjoying the moment', rather than focusing on the intended outcome, she will have to make sense of her experience in a different way to what it was before. Therefore, there is a shift in her intention and expectation. We define this process as the 'transformative dialogue' between the self and the object/system (Bilda et al. 2008).

They also found that satisfying audience expectations correlated to feeling in control, but that this could turn into boredom. Participants who engaged with systems that afford more uncertainty and are less predictable were less likely to satisfy their expectations, and there was a greater danger of this leading to frustration. At this point there was, however, also the greatest opportunity for creative engagement.

Open and Emergent Interactions

Participation is arguably necessary for interactive art work to be realised, and perhaps it is even necessary for the work to exist in the first place. This necessity can be explained by the characteristic of open-ness. Umberto Eco describes the 'open-ended' artworks as necessitating a participant or performer for its 'completion' (Eco 1962). For example, a musical composition by Stockhausen is considered unfinished until a performer acts creatively to effect an 'oriented insertion' and thus complete it. Its conclusion is not as predictable as a Bach fugue whose score is far more determinant, or prescriptive, of its performance.

Eco goes on to describe these 'works in movement' as open works that are indeterminate and potentially inexhaustible given the large field of possible solutions they can afford: the Stockhausen piece is inexhaustible in comparison to Bach. Here "*...each performance explains the work but does not exhaust it*".

This also demonstrates a creative interaction by the performer. That is, when the performer makes their deliberate 'oriented insertion' into the work they are contributing to its form. In this sense they may be seen to be working creatively together with the composer: "*the 'open' works... are characterized by the invitation to make the work together with the author*" (Eco 1962). The performer or participant has the capacity to 'complete' this work through a creative insertion. However, the completion is merely one of many that have been facilitated by the artists' creative scoping of parameters, and the outcome remains in the realm of possibilities defined by the artist. For Eco, it remains that artists' work.

We can think of interactive art as open-ended simply by virtue of requiring audience participation. However, participation with work can vary qualitatively, and accordingly the quality of the openness can vary. Interactive artwork such as Peter Weibel's *Observation of the Observation: Uncertainty* (Weibel 1973) is a more 'closed' type of interactive art system. Here closed circuit use of cameras and monitors preclude the spectator/participant from ever seeing their front, no matter how much they twist and turn. The mediation of the image conditions the spectator's behaviour. These installations were highly predictable and defined artworks and in this respect they were relatively closed (Arns 2004; Daniels 2008).

On the other hand, the use of the computer and increasing access to the internet has provided more opportunities for openness and interactive feedback from audiences. For example, in Sommerer and Mignonneau's *Verbarium* (1999) the viewer plays an active role in shaping the work. They send emails that are converted into three-dimensional forms. Another example of an open-ended work is Ken Feingold's *The Surprising Spiral* (1991). This computer-controlled interactive artwork consists of a sculptural interface for a large, hypertext-linked database of travel images. The images are organised into a non-linear montage, affording the eternal, recurrent, interaction structure alluded to by the work's title. Feingold describes the work as embodying an ambiguous interaction, something which the audience at that time found frustrating because they couldn't control the system to get what they wanted. He was disappointed by the desire for control and considers it simplistic, lacking a capacity for the abstraction, metaphor and ambiguity employed when viewing traditional art forms like painting. He goes on to critique work that prioritises such control and predictability as

> … Vending-machine menu –driven forms of interaction… [Such as] 'If the viewer does this then computer does that'… [Will result in work that] is too fixed, and as a result lacks mystery, complexity or paradox, which I consider to be essential qualities of a good work of art (Feingold 1991).

The creation of ambiguous, open interaction designs has also been pursued in digital, interactive design research. Through a focus on play, design and interaction researcher Bill Gaver and his collaborators have created open-ended appliances as well as conceptual designs for interactive works (Gaver et al. 2003). Their *Dawn Chorus* is an intelligent bird feeder that would "*teach local songbirds the owner's favourite songs*" (Gaver and Martin 2000). Where such a bird feeder was installed in a garden, the range of potential outcomes is large and unpredictable, depending on its collaborators. These collaborators—birds and residents—will also of course be providing 'creative insertions', or songs, to the system.

Evaluation approaches for understanding the types of interpretation and ambiguity that open-ended design and research can facilitate have also been proposed (Sengers and Gaver 2006). This includes a taxonomy differentiating interpretation in time, quality, and the occurrence of many different interpretations simultaneously. Here interpretation is the process of assigning meaning. Sengers and Gaver argue that by designing objects of ambiguous use more than one meaning can be interpreted, and this, in turn, facilitates open-ended interaction.

Emergence is another method by which multiple interpretations, or openness, can be afforded in an interactive design. This is particularly relevant when dealing with the deterministic and bounded domain of the computer. Early work by artificial life artists Christa Sommerer and Laurent Mignonneau facilitate an open-ended experience in that context. In their 1997 interactive art system *Life Spacies,* the artwork's participants influence the evolution and emergence of visual forms (Sommerer and Mignonneau 1997) through textual input. The artists' use artificial life algorithms as a basis for their custom text-to-form editor. This then takes email messages from the participants to create visual forms, or 'virtual creatures'. The 'birthed' creatures are then also able to clone or reproduce. The artists describe the work as an

> …evolutionary communication and interaction environment that allows remotely located visitors to interact with one another in a shared virtual environment (Sommerer and Mignonneau 1998).

The work is explicitly open: audience participation to create the creatures is necessary. It is different to closed structures of interaction such as choosing options from a finite list, navigating a predetermined set of paths or "*a pre-defined multiple choice interaction*" (Sommerer and Mignonneau 1998). The open-ended interaction here can result in the generation of physically emergent forms, through the evolving virtual creatures. Perceptual emergence could also occur where, for example, participants demonstrate an opportunity for novel, surprising participant interactions.

Video game researcher Jesper Juul provides another perspective of open and emergent interaction. He classifies computer games as progressive or emergent in structure. Progressive structures correlate to closed systems and the emergent structures to open systems. Progressive games are a newer form of game that corresponds to the adventure genre. The player progresses through the game by meeting a series of challenges, with options and solutions explicitly defined:

> In progression games, the player has to perform a predefined set of actions in order to complete the game (Juul 2002).

Emergent games are the older game form and include most card and board games and all strategy games. Here "*a number of simple rules combine to form interesting variation*" (Juul 2002). Emergence implies the ability for strategies to surface and for the game-space to extend beyond the rules. For example, the card game of Poker is an emergent game where the game play extends beyond the rules by including the emergent behaviour of bluffing (Salen and Zimmerman 2004).

The computer game with a low replay value is typically progressive and closed because it is often exhausted during play, with nothing left to engage the player. These will tend to have more explicitly controlled and predefined structures, with limited interaction potential. Conversely a computer game with an emergent game structure is typically more open-ended because it facilitates many options at each playful encounter. It will have opportunities for improvisation during the game play, in ways which may not be anticipated by the author. The open and emergent structures may have more opportunities for interaction, making them more likely to have higher 'replay' value.

The 'replay' value of game provides some insight into people's experience of it, namely the interest the gamer has in returning to the game and playing it again. It corresponds to Edmonds, Muller and Connell's 'relating' descriptor of participant experience (Edmonds et al. 2006).

Emergence naturally supports openness in that it supports ambiguity and the act of interpretation while interpretation implies multiple possibilities—a quality of open systems. Emergence and openness also share qualities of creativity (by completing, or closing the open work and creating something new) and unpredictability (of the final solution or emergent form). By contrast, 'closed' interactions are predetermined, repeatable, with a finite set of possibilities.

It can be argued that any interactive application will tend to be more open than works in media that do not rely on a participant for completion, such as a medieval painting, since to some extent the participant makes the work along with the author. However a range of openness across interactive designs can also be found, as we saw in Weibel's closed circuit video artwork from the 1970s. Similarly, some interactive works such as those based on hypermedia can be finite given their limited dataset as well as exhaustible, with a smaller field of possibilities. On the other hand, where participants have the opportunity to move through actions or images more freely, perhaps finding their own path in unexpected and non-scripted ways, there comes a greater field of possible forms, behaviours etc. and new strategies or behaviours not explicitly defined in the interaction are more likely to arise.

Conclusion

Contemporary arts practices and computing each provide insights into creating interactions. The role of the participant as an iiactive agent is a key aspect for the arts. It is also a distinguishing characteristic of interactive art. In fact, it may be argued that interactive art is reliant on participation for its realisation.

The quality of participant interaction is a core concern. The CEM model demonstrates that at times, a lack of control can be accompanied by frustration but it can also be accompanied by a creative and engaging experience. At the same time as opportunities for interaction increase, open-ness will also increase. As Ken Feingold found, audience experience of systems that do not afford complete control can cause them frustration; and this tends to happen with the more open-ended systems. These tend to facilitate more interaction possibilities, more ambiguity, unpredictability. They are overall less defined. Furthermore, when successful, the open-ended interaction has multiple creative outcomes. As Juul would say, they have higher replay value, facilitating continued engagement with the work. And, as Eco has described, this interaction can be creative.

Mechanisms for creating open-ended systems include the theories and models of emergence. Emergence lends rules and structures to guide interaction/gameplay while still facilitating surprising strategies, such as the perceptually emergent behaviour of bluffing in Poker. Participant input can 'feed into' an emergent system as well, working as a way to open it beyond its deterministic domain through the inclusion of the human being in that system. In Life Spacies audience input at the start was required and it is only after this point that the system could respond to generate the virtual creatures forms and facilitate their interaction (Sommerer and Mignonneau 1997).

The creation of open and emergent artworks, or indeed, any complex interactions, facilitates an awareness of audience experience. TheBeta_Space approach to evaluate audience participation with work, during the process of making these artworks, has been briefly reviewed. Itreflects the approach used in this text as well, where interactive artworks presented in Chap. 5 were evaluated in field studies to understandparticipant experience, described in Chap. 6. Research and prototyping of systems along with audience interviews and observation canfacilitate the successful creation of interactive systems, particularly when difficult concepts such as emergence, openness and their inherentqualities of unpredictability and lack of control are concerned. As was found from the CEM model, in some cases participant frustration at lack ofcontrol could give way to more exploration and thought and, in turn, to a creative engagement with the system.

References

Achituv R, Utterback C (1999) Text Rain, interactive artwork

Arns I (2004) Reception, participation, interaction—from receptive to active participation. http://www.medienkunstnetz.de/themes/overview_of_media_art/communication/. Accessed 18 Jan 2015

Ascott R (1966) Behaviourist art and the cybernetic vision. Cybernetica 9:247–264

Bannon L (1992) From human factors to human actors the role of psychology and human-computer interaction studies in systems design. In: Greenbaum J, Kyng M (eds) Design at work: cooperative design of computer systems. L. Erlbaum Associates Inc., Hillsdale, NJ, USA, pp 25–44

Bilda Z (2011) Designing for audience engagement. In: Interacting: art, research and the creative practitioner. Libri Publishing Ltd., Faringdon, UK, pp 163–181

Bilda Z, Edmonds E, Candy L (2008) Designing for creative engagement. Des Stud 29:525–540. doi:10.1016/j.destud.2008.07.009

Bødker S (2006) When second wave HCI meets third wave challenges. ACM Press, New York, USA, pp 1–8

Bolter JD, Gromala D (2003) Windows and mirrors: interaction design, digital art, and the myth of transparency. The MIT Press, Cambridge, USA

Burnham J (1968) Systems Esthetics. artforum.com 7:30–35

Cage J (1952) 4′33″, music composition

Candy L, Edmonds EA (2011) Interacting: art, research and the creative practitioner. Libri Publishing Ltd., Faringdon, UK

Candy L, Ferguson S (eds) (2014) Interactive experience in the digital age evaluating new art practice. Springer International Publishing

Cornock S, Edmonds EA (1973) The creative process where the artist is amplified or superseded by the computer. Leonardo, The MIT Press 6:11–16

Daniels D (2008) Strategies of interactivity. In: Sommerer C, Jain LC, Mignonneau L (eds) The art and science of interface and interaction design. Springer, pp 27–62
Debord G (1957) Towards a Situationist international. In: McDonough T (ed). The MIT Press, Cambridge, USA, pp 44–50
de Souza e Silva A (2006) From cyber to hybrid mobile technologies as interfaces of hybrid spaces. Space and Culture 9:261–278. doi:10.1177/1206331206289022
Dourish P (2001) Seeking a foundation for context-aware computing. Human-Computer Interaction 16:229–241. doi:10.1207/S15327051HCI16234_07
Duchamp M (1920) Rotary Glass Plates (Precision Optics), motorized artwork
Dunne A, Raby F (1996) Fields and Thresholds. In: Pearce M, Spiller N (eds) Architects in cyberspace. Academy Press, pp 64–71
Eco U (1962) The poetics of the open work. In: Bishop C (ed) Participation. The MIT Press, London, England, Whitechapel, pp 20–40
Edmonds EA (2002) Heron, interactive artwork
Edmonds EA (2009) Cities Tango, interactive artwork
Edmonds EA (2011a) Interactive art. In: Candy L, Edmonds EA (eds) Interacting: art, research and the creative practitioner. Libri Publishing Ltd., Faringdon, UK
Edmonds EA (2011b) Art, interaction and engagement. In: Candy L, Edmonds E (eds) Interacting: art, research and the creative practitioner. Libri Publishing Ltd., Faringdon, UK,
Edmonds EA, Muller L, Connell M (2006) On creative engagement. Visual Communications 5:307–322
Edmonds EA, Turner G, Candy L (2004) Approaches to interactive art systems. ACM Press, Singapore, pp 113–117
Feingold K (1991) The Surprising Spiral, interactive artwork
Fitzmaurice GW, Ishii H, Buxton W (1995) Bricks: laying the foundations for graspable user interfaces. ACM Press, pp 442–449
Gaver W, Martin H (2000) Alternatives exploring information appliances through conceptual design proposals. In: Proceedings of CHI 2000. pp 209–216
Gaver W, Beaver J, Benford S (2003) Ambiguity as a resource for design. Proceedings of CHI 2003. ACM Press, Ft Lauderdale, Florida, USA, pp 233–240
Gibson JJ (1977) The theory of affordances. In: Shaw R, Bransford J (eds) Perceiving, acting, and knowing. Lawrence Erlbaum Associates, Hillsdale, NJ, USA, pp 127–143
Gibson JJ (1979) The ecological approach to visual perception. Houghton Mifflin, London, England
Hewett T, Baeker, Card S, et al (1992) ACM SIGCHI curricula for human-computer interaction. ACM SIGCHI
Hwang D (2016) Pokémon GO! Niantic, USA, http://www.pokemongo.com
Ishii H, Ullmer B (1997) Tangible bits: towards seamless interfaces between people, bits and atoms. Proc. SIGCHI Human Factors. ACM Press, Atlanta, Georgia, United States, pp 234–241
Ishii H, Lakatos vid, Bonanni L, Labrune J-B (2012) Radical atoms: beyond tangible bits, toward transformable materials. Interactions 19:38–51. doi:10.1145/2065327.2065337
Ivrea Interaction Design Institute (2005) Arduino Microcontroller Board
Jones C, Muller L (2008) David Rokeby, The Giver of Names (1991) documentary collection. The Daniel Langlois Foundation collection: DOCAM (Documentation and Conservation of the Media Arts), Montreal, Canada. http://www.fondation-langlois.org/html/e/page.php?NumPage=2121
Juul J (2002) The open and the closed: games of emergence and games of progression. In: Mäyrä F (ed) Computer game and digital cultures conference proceedings. Tampere University Press, Tampere, Finland, pp 323–329
Krueger M (1974) Videoplace, interactive artwork
Krueger M, Gionfriddo T, Hinrichsen K (1985) VIDEOPLACE—an artificial reality. ACM Press, pp 35–40
Lieser W (2010) The World of Digital Art. Har/DVD edition. H.F. Ullmann Publishing Gmbh, Köln, Germany

Muller L (2008) Towards an oral history of new media art. In: Daniel Langlois Foundation for art, science and technology. http://www.fondation-langlois.org/html/e/page.php?NumPage=2096. Accessed 13 Jul 2016
Muller L, Edmonds E, Connell M (2006) Living laboratories for interactive art. CoDesign 2: 195–207. doi:10.1080/15710880601008109
Norman DA (2002) The design of everyday things. Basic Books, New York, USA
NOX, Serafijn QS, Spuybroek L (2004) D-Tower, media architecture in Doetinchem, The Netherlands
Paik NJ (1963) Participation TV 1, interactive artwork
Paul C (2015) Digital Art, Third, edition edn. Thames & Hudson, New York, USA
Salen K, Zimmerman E (2004) Rules of play game design fundamentals. The MIT Press, Cambridge, USA
Schimmel P (1989) Leap into the void: performance and the object. In: Schimmel P (ed) Out of actions: between performance and the object. The Museum of Contemporary Art, Thames and Hudson, Los Angeles, USA, pp 1949–1979
Seevinck J (2008) +-now, interactive artwork
Sengers P, Gaver B (2006) Staying open to interpretation: engaging in multiple meanings in design and evaluation. In: Designing interactive systems DIS'06. ACM Press, pp 99–108
Shedroff N (2001) Experience design 1. New Riders Publishing, Oakland, USA
Sommerer C, Mignonneau L (1997) Life Spacies, interactive artwork
Sommerer C, Mignonneau L (1999) VERBARIUM, interactive artwork
Sommerer C, Mignonneau L (eds) (1998) Art as a living system. In: Art @ science. Springer, Austria
Turkle S (2015) Reclaiming conversation: the power of talk in a digital age. Penguin Press, New York, USA
Weibel P (1973) Observation of the Observation: Uncertainty, artwork
Weiser M (1991) The computer for the 21st century. Scientific American 94–100
Weiser M (1994) The world is not a desktop. Interactions 7–8

Chapter 4
Characterising Artworks for Emergence

Abstract Emergence can occur in artworks, in their participants, and in varying ways. Pioneering artists in artificial life have simulated emergent landscapes, generating computational emergence for participants to interact with. Emergence in interactive art may also be happening in the system's participants—with or without the artist's intention. Such instances may have been anticipated or designed for by the artists, or the artist may not have mentioned the concept of emergence at all. This chapter fleshes out some of these varied instances of emergence in the interactive arts by reviewing six works by artists across the world: Christa Sommerer and Laurent Mignonneau, Ken Rinaldo, Simon Penny and Jamieson Schulte, Romy Achituv and Camille Utterback, Rafael Lozano-Hemmer, and David Rokeby. These digital, interactive artworks are characterised by using a 'lens' of emergence, and by drawing on the TEIA. The discussion broadens our understanding of the forms emergence in interaction can take as well as providing additional ways of appreciating these works.

Approach

The digital, interactive art systems discussed here are *A-Volve* (Sommerer and Mignonneau 1994), *Sympathetic Sentience* (Penny and Schulte 1995), *Autopoiesis* (Rinaldo 2000), *Body Movies* (Lozano-Hemmer 2001), *Text Rain* (Achituv and Utterback 1999) and the ongoing project *The Giver of Names* (Rokeby 1990a). Some of the artists articulate a concern with emergence while others do not. My aim here is to identify aspects of the work and/or participant interactions that can plausibly be considered emergent. This characterisation of the works is deduced from public documentation. Documentation sources include peer reviewed publications, artist statements, websites, videos and media art databases. The evidence and approach means the analysis is not definitive; rather it is a plausible characterisation that can indicate a potential for the work to support emergence. Determining whether or not emergence *did* actually occur typically necessitates more information, particularly when looking for instances of perceptual emergence.

J. Seevinck, *Emergence in Interactive Art*, Springer Series on Cultural Computing,
DOI 10.1007/978-3-319-45201-2_4

In that case it is best to rely on verbal accounts from participants about interesting aspects of their experience, as in the approach I demonstrate in Chap. 6. Since such specially collected data is not available in the artwork documentation sourced here, the discussion is limited to theorizing how emergence may have occurred and its potential for facilitating emergence in the future. The approach I take is therefore more of a theoretical critique, drawing on the theories of emergence and most particularly, the definition and qualities detailed in Chap. 2. The TEIA, also presented in Chap. 2, provides the framework for differentiating the different types of emergence in these works.

I must add that the characterisations suggested here are neither exclusive nor exhaustive. The inherent ambiguity of art with its great variance in audience understanding and experience precludes singular interpretation. Similarly these works exhibit a range of aesthetic and cultural concerns beyond characteristics of emergence. This discussion aims to *add* to those readings, providing another interpretation of them. It also aims to develop our understanding of emergence.

Characterising with the TEIA

Emergence occurs when a new form or concept appears that was not directly implied by the context from which it arose. This new 'whole' is more than a simple sum or grouping of its parts. This definition of emergence from Chap. 2 implies the core qualities of parts to a whole that is greater than the sum of those parts, and which constitutes something heterogenously new and to some degree, unexpected or unpredictable. Further discussion there also identifies the core characteristics of the idea of feedback from the whole back to change the parts, and the idea that the parts and the whole are at different scales or levels. Finally, the TEIA also differentiates between referenced and concrete emergence. In summary, then, there are eight different types of emergence, resulting from three generations of differentiation. Briefly, these three generations are:

1. Firstly, the heterogeneously new, emergent whole can be distinguished in terms of the necessity of an observer for its existence, i.e. as either *perceptual* or *physical* emergence.
2. Next, we differentiate perceptual and physical emergence in terms of the relationship between the whole and its constituting parts: if there is feedback from the whole back to change the parts it is considered *intrinsic* emergence. If there is no feedback and the emergent whole does not impact on the nature of the constituting parts, it is considered *extrinsic* emergence. Therefore we may have either perceptual intrinsic emergence, perceptual extrinsic emergence, physical intrinsic emergence or physical extrinsic emergence.
3. Third and finally, the TEIA positions the classification of emergence in the context of art by differentiating between emergent outcomes that refer to something else in the world (e.g. 'looks like a star'), or are concrete—that is, focussed on the direct,

material or local aspects of the work as in Concrete Art. Therefore we may have perceptual intrinsic concrete emergence, perceptual intrinsic referenced emergence, perceptual extrinsic concrete emergence and so on.

Each of the following six digital artworks is described in terms of the TEIA and the characteristics of emergence. Some aspects are, however, difficult to assert given the available data. In instances of perceptual emergence it is typically necessary to know what the participant perceived and was thinking at the time. This is particularly the case if you want to know if they are reminded of something, i.e. to differentiate between referenced and concrete types of emergence. In situations where the data cannot be persuasive on this, discussion will therefore omit that aspect of the taxonomy.

The approach to identifying these types of emergence in the following artworks also draws, to some extent, on the insights from analysing and identifying emergence through prior evaluations of participant interactions, a process that is detailed in Chap. 6. For instance, the *Object* code is an analytical element used early on in analysis for emergence and it is conceptually useful here as well. In our discussion here, one of the first steps in reviewing these art systems is to identify the different elements that might make up an experience of the work. In doing so we can check that any interesting events relate to the experience of the work and not just a part of it. For example, if a hypothetical interactive artwork constitutes inflated balloons and projected emergent imagery on a screen, these could all be the parts that contribute to an experience of the work as a whole. If someone interacts with that work to bounce the balloons and not pay attention to imagery this may generate, then arguably they are not interacting with the work but really only 'playing with the balloons'. Any novel and surprising behaviours that they may come up with in interacting with those balloons will not properly represent the potential that the work has for emergence and may instead be more a case of demonstrating characteristics of the balloons, not the artwork as intended by the artist.

The six interactive artworks discussed here have been created over the last two decades. The discussion begins with those artworks explicitly concerned with emergence.

A-Volve, Christa Sommerer and Laurent Mignonneau

Christa Sommerer and Laurent Mignonneau are some of the first artists that come to mind when thinking about emergence in interactive art. Their body of interactive artworks has been concerned with life and artificial life and they have created a number of research publications as well as art outcomes in this domain (e.g. Sommerer and Mignonneau 1998, 2002; Stocker 2009). Their work *A-Volve* (1994) is one of the earliest interactive artworks that also worked with artificial life algorithms. It is a multimodal interactive experience that facilitates audience involvement to effect the emergence of new artificial life forms.

The work also exemplifies their concurrent exploration of natural interfaces with a complex system based on artificial life (AL) algorithms. In the artists' words it is

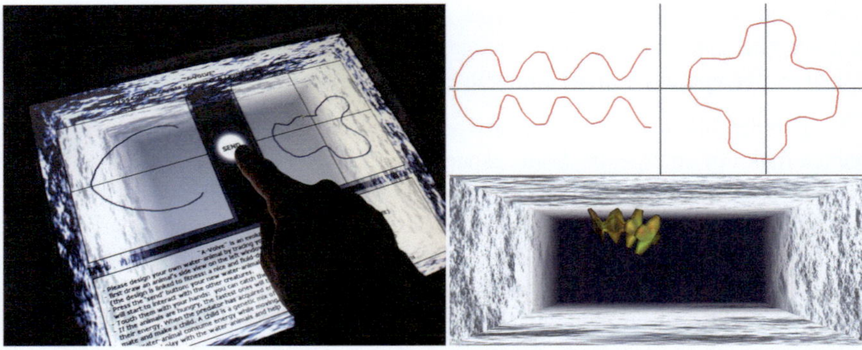

Fig. 4.1 Photograph and screenshot of interaction with the artwork *A-Volve* by Christa Sommerer and Laurent Mignonneau (1993–4) at the ICC-NTT Tokyo, Japan 2006. © Sommerer and Mignonneau (1994)

"*...a pool of artificial living creatures that are open to outside influences, reacting and interacting with their natural and artificial environments* [... and...] *The virtual creatures are created by the visitors of the installation but they can also evolve by themselves* (Stocker et al. 2009).

When interacting with this work, participants draw an initial shape and profile on a touch screen (Fig. 4.1). In this way they "'*give birth' to virtual three-dimensional creatures that are automatically alive and swim in the real water of the pool*" (Sommerer and Mignonneau 1998). Creatures will vary in terms of fitness, lifespan and energy to determine how they function relative to other creatures and within the evolutionary rules of this simulation: some are prey, some are predators and depending on how long a creature can survive, it will reproduce and affect future additional shapes (Dietz 2002).

The audience can also influence the creatures–by, for example, catching them, or protecting them from predator creatures (Fig. 4.2). This is in addition to creating

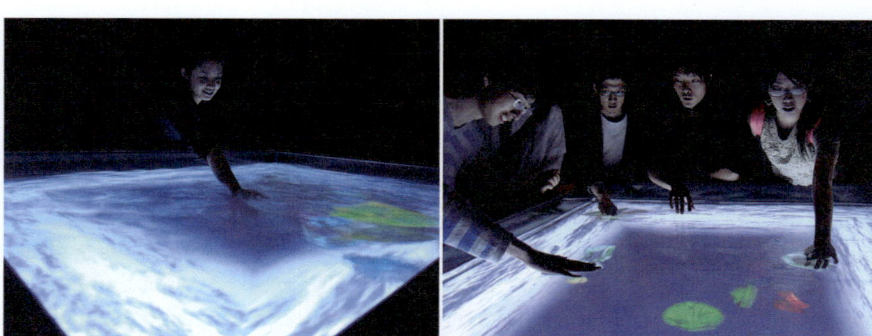

Fig. 4.2 Photographs of interaction with the artwork *A-Volve* by Christa Sommerer and Laurent Mignonneau (1993–4) at the ICC-NTT Tokyo, Japan 2006. © Sommerer and Mignonneau (1994)

them in the first place. Within the simulation the creatures evolve towards greater and greater fitness. This can occur both with and without audience input; however, the system is heavily responsive to the latter. In fact, through opening up to audience input two interesting things happen.

Firstly, the work becomes more open-ended, with a greater range of possible outcomes or 'completions' and greater capacity for creative participation (Eco 1962; see also Chap. 3). Varying audience intentions, behaviours and visitor frequency all provide additional input to the visual form. Secondly, there is potential for feedback between the participant and the system. The system is a form of computational emergence with an active, interacting, 'participant-as-observer', as is discussed in Chaps. 2 and 7. This participant, in providing input to the system, is opening it up informationally and extending the system beyond the bounds of the computer to include their own understandings and subjectivity. This can, as discussed next, facilitate *intrinsic perceptual* emergence as the participant develops new understandings from watching the system, and acts on those emergent meanings to change the work such as by changing the conditions for virtual creatures.

It is useful to note that the creation of open-ended interactions has been integral to these artists' approach for a number of years. They have articulated this point of difference as early as 1998, when hypercard and other branching multimedia structures dominated our understanding of interactivity. They have described how AL interactive art facilitates this through enabling "*continuously evolving levels of experience*". Here interaction would involve the discovery of unexpected new paths for the participant rather than "*choosing between a variety of different choices and paths*" (Sommerer and Mignonneau 1998).

Potential for Emergence in A-Volve

A-Volve is concerned with evolving life processes and includes the participant in that process in a creative way. If we understand the interactive artwork as a simulated life process that a participant can interact with then we can think of the constituting elements as all those aspects contributing to this. In this case it is useful to do this in two ways—for both (a) the simulated life processes in the computer that are a form of *physical* emergence, and for (b) a participant's subjective experience of this; that is, the *perceptual* emergence. The two approaches emphasise what's happening in the system and what the experience might be like for the participant, respectively.

Evolving Creatures and Physical Emergence Firstly we can think of the elements that make up *A-Volve* as each creature and its various, dynamic local and global parameter values. The way in which the creatures relate to one another is informed by both the artists' imposed constraints, such as the dimensions of the pool and their relative scale, and the artificial life rules which direct evolution to continually greater fitness. Other aspects that influence their relation are not predetermined. These include participant interactions—to both add new creatures (through drawing) and to stop or protect some creatures. This is also, given the nature of human interaction, unpredictable.

The overall interplay between the creatures will affect the mating and evolution of new creatures. It results in a "*constantly different look and dynamic*" to the installation (Stocker et al. 2009). Hence we have new and unpredictable *A-Volve* creatures, generated from the evolutionary rules and chance input of participants in directing this evolution. In its simulation of evolutionary theory and biological understandings of life, this can be described as an example of *referenced physical* emergence. Since integral to this is the feedback of a creature to inform evolution of future creatures and the virtual AL landscape, it is also *intrinsic*.

Participant Behaviour and Perceptual Emergence Secondly, the elements can also be understood to include aspects of the participants' interaction. That is, in addition to the creatures and their properties/states/behaviours as above, we can also include participant actions of *drawing* (which will generate a new creature) and certain participant *interacting behaviours* (e.g. putting their hands in the water, touching the creatures to stop or protect). With this view of the interactive artwork and installation system, we can observe how participant behaviours change and the potential for new behaviours to emerge. For example, a participant may perceive their newly 'birthed' creature to have a certain aesthetic quality such as a rhythmic asymmetric movement, which they might interpret and name a 'lame duck'. This would be an instance of *extrinsic perceptual emergence*. If, subsequently, the participant were to act on this understanding, to for example, interact to promote the reproduction of that creature with its unique movement, this could, potentially, be an instance of *intrinsic perceptual* emergence. Here, as with the above scenario, there is an opportunity for the work to become intrinsically dynamic, where the parts are changed by the changing whole.

The range of these possible behaviours demonstrates a capacity for emergent participant behaviours during interaction with the art system. That is, there is capacity for the work to support perceptually emergent behaviours. Determining whether or not they are, in fact, emergent is a question of collecting evidence and conducting an evaluation.

Interaction Across Levels

A-Volve is a complex system that encompasses not only the pool of creatures, but participating visitors as well. The forms that can eventuate are the product of both AL algorithms and creative participant input. Audience interaction is at the level of the parts, as they draw the profiles to describe the initial virtual creatures form, but the audience is also able interact at the level of the whole, i.e. with a god's eye view of the system, to influence the environment. This integration of the participant interaction with the emergent simulation affords them a range of experiences that emphasise the creative process.

This emphasis on the creative process is integral to the artists' conceptual approach. In *A-Volve* they seek to position the audience at the heart of the interaction, or 'art as process'. They liken the artificial life processes to the human, creative process itself, pursuing a way of visual creation that is similar to composer Cage's use of chance for creative outcomes. That is, while the work relies on simulation of life processes, they see this in terms of the notion of '*creation through evolution*' rather than as mimicry of nature. The work *A-Volve* facilitates participant interaction with evolving artificial life and virtual creatures, The work also manifests the artists concern with process, specifically '*Art as Living Process*'.

Sympathetic Sentience, Simon Penny and Jamieson Schulte

Artist Simon Penny has engaged with concepts surrounding interaction and artificial life in his robotics, cybernetics and interactive art works since the late 1980s. In 1993 he created *Sympathetic Sentience* with then-collaborator Jamieson Schulte, with a second version following soon after (Penny and Schulte 1995).

The work consists of 12 independent units that communicate with one another as well as emitting audible 'chirps'. In so doing these individual units combine together to generate "*complex patterns of rhythmic sound out of, and only because of, the process of communication*" (Penny 2015). The units are located around a room and the experience is that of 12-channel sound. Each unit communicates with the next through an infrared beam and transmission of data, that is each is capable of receiving, processing and transmitting data to its neighbour in a circular chain structure that Penny likens to the child's game of 'telephone' (Penny 2015). A random 'chirp' can start the system off, and the system continues to flow on from this original input, slowly building up complexity as a neighbour transmits the chirp. Units may also add silence or another chirp to the message, which is communicated along in turn. In the artist's words: "*This generated a constantly changing but ordered rhythm and melody, and one could hear that melody repeated across the room, delayed and slightly changed by other units in the loop*" (Penny 2015). There is "*recognisable, but not predictable, patterning*" (Penny and Schulte 1995 Artist Statement).

A person moving in the space can interrupt the beam and eventually "silence" the work until they leave, at which point the rhythm will start up again. Penny describes this interaction as 'suppressive', clarifying that the audience could also unknowingly break the communication chain and impose a gap in the 'melodic passage' that had built up. He adds that engendering human agency was less important to him than the performance of this art system.

Each of the units has the same capacity for chirping, processing and communicating. Each emits a chirp at semi-random intervals, which their neighbour would then process and add to its own current state.

The Potential for Emergence in Sympathetic Sentience

While the title of this work references a concern with life and intelligence (a form of emergence in the natural sciences understanding of the term), artist Penny has also recently written about his aims in creating this work—namely creating emergent complex behaviour through the use of minimal physical elements. He defined this emergence as "*a manifestation of behavior more complex than that explicitly coded in the system.*" (Penny 2015)

Melodic Passage and Concrete Emergence The audible chirps, and the silences between them, could be considered the parts of an emergent whole—the rhythmic pattern or melody that the artist describes. When an audience member observes this acoustic composition as a meaningful whole, that is, when they hear it as a melody, there is the opportunity for this to be an instance of perceptual emergence. When they act on their perception of this aural composition, or chirp rhythm, to move through the space again, the whole can be said to be feeding back to change the condition of the parts and the situation may be an instance of *Intrinsic Perceptual* emergence. Finally, when the musical patterning is not perceived as nostalgic or reminiscent of some other tune, it may be considered *concrete*.

The work also, however, facilitates physical emergence. An emergent chirp melody is not only an ordered composition perceived by the audience; it is also an ordered arrangement generated through a complex interaction between these very simple parts. The cyclical arrangement of the units is a feedback cycle—the emergent whole (chirp rhythm) is simultaneously generated by the system and fed through it. As such the work has the capacity for both *intrinsic physical* and *intrinsic perceptual* emergence.

Autopoiesis, Ken Rinaldo

Ken Rinaldo is an American artist working across natural and technological systems, with work that seeks to integrate these and speak "*to the co-evolution between living and evolving technological cultures*" (Rinaldo 2015a). *Autopoiesis* (2000) is an interactive art installation consisting of robotic 'arms'. The individual sculptures are articulated and change shape in response to the changing states of neighbours and changing environmental conditions, as shown in Fig. 4.3. Each creates audible tones depending on its state, also creating soundscapes. They interact with each other and the visitor (participant) as informed by on-board sensing and artificial life algorithms. The artwork is open in the sense that its sensors respond to the physical installation environment, such as the position of people visiting the installation. The work was commissioned for the Helsinki museum Kiasma Museum of Contemporary Art in 2000. Broadly speaking, *Autopoiesis* is a self-organising group of musical and robotic sculptures, with behaviours akin to those from the natural world.

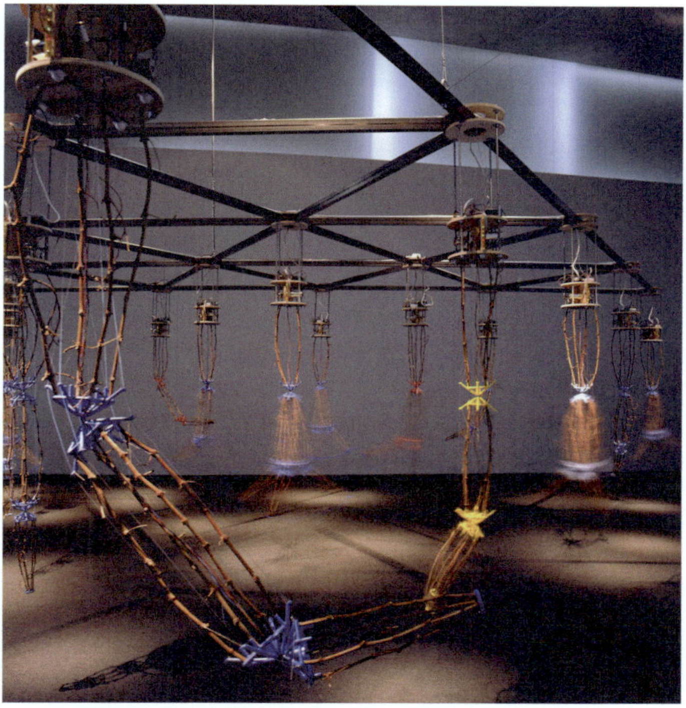

Fig. 4.3 *Autopoiesis* by Ken Rinaldo (2000) installed at the Kiasma Museum of Contemporary Art Helsinki, Finland 2000. © Ken Rinaldo (2000)

The Potential for Emergence in Autopoiesis

The concept of *Autopoiesis* is itself a form of physical emergence. It concerns the self-making aspect of certain living systems. Rinaldo also explicitly describes the work in terms of emergence: "*The interactivity engages the viewer-participant who in turn affects the system's evolution and emergence. This creates a system evolution as well as an overall group sculptural aesthetic*" (Rinaldo 2015b, audio at 1min 10s). This concern with emergence is not, however, limited to the work operating as an evolving, emergent system (i.e. physical emergence). Rinaldo also declares a concern with the aesthetic composition that may be generated. We can also understand this compositional outcome that he is working towards as a form of perceptual emergence.

Dancing, Repulsion, Attraction and Physical Emergence Firstly, in terms of physical emergence, there is the potential for ordered group behaviour to emerge from the moving individual sculptural 'arms'. Each arm's movement is informed both by sensors that detect people in the space, and presence information communicated from other sculptural arms. An overall state control system and artificial life algorithm inform how the arms respond to this incoming data, particularly in terms of group behaviours. Arm behaviours include so-called 'attraction' and 'repulsion'—where the arms can both 'reach out' to a visitor and 'recoil' away from them. Group behaviours mean that they are able to move collectively.

When the arms (art work parts) combine to inform ordered collective behaviours we arguably see physical emergence analogous to the ordered formation of a bird flock. Moreover since this emergent flock can 'feed back' to change the behaviour of an individual arm, the system can be considered *intrinsic physical* emergence.

Perception, Behaviour and Perceptual Emergence While these are the characteristics of the system, the participant experience of this also opens up opportunities for perceptual emergence. For example, when a visitor moving through the flock of sculptures perceives ordered collective behaviour, they are arguably perceiving emergence analogous to how they might similarly perceive a flock of geese as travelling in a V-shape.

If they simply observe it without changing their behaviour then this may be an instance of extrinsic perceptual emergence. On the other hand, if the viewer-participant were to act on this new-found understanding of the system, for example by moving closer to engage with it further, perhaps *dance with* it, they would enter the art system, and a feedback loop with the group of sculptures as a whole could ensue. That is, the person changes their behaviour, and so does the flock, which leads to them being changed in turn, and so on. This is not implausible and such an event would be understood as an instance of intrinsic *perceptual* emergence. Finally, depending on a participant's characterisation of their experience, this could be either referenced or concrete. For example, were they to explain the experience as similar to '*moving through a flock of gulls*' this would be an instance of referenced experience, given that it references the notion of interacting with a flock, something that exists and is known to them.

Body Movies Relational Architecture No. 6, Rafael Lozano-Hemmer

Lozano-Hemmer is a Mexican-born artist who has been exhibiting interactive artworks since the early 1990s. *Body Movies* (2001) is part of his *Relational Architecture* series. It was first shown in Rotterdam, The Netherlands in 2001. The work was partly inspired by *The Shadow Dance*, an etching from 1675 by Dutch painter Samuel van Hoogstraten, with its emphasis on the performative aspect of the viewer. The work has since been installed in other locations around the world, from Germany through to China. The artist uses photographs that are portraits of people from different European cities. These are projected up to 25 metres high on a building façade, but subsequently washed out by extremely powerful spotlights. When people in the plaza pass by these spotlights, they obscure the wash and potentially reveal the portraits. "*In this way, strangers, who were pre-recorded at other locations, popped up as "shadow projections" and were suddenly standing in the person's shadow*" (Lieser 2010).

The Potential for Emergence in Body Movies

The overall impression and experience offered in this work involves this layering of photographic images and live interactive shadows. If we understand this as the extents of experiencing *Body Movies*, the constituting elements could be identified as the *white wash, sound feedback, people's shadows,* and *the photographs* with their varying aspects (i.e. all the system input and output elements). The way in which these parts are integrated in an event is then the subject of an emergence characterisation. Of course, the way in which these parts can relate to each other has been determined by the artist. Therefore this also includes the *context,* e.g. the scale of the Plaza, instructional information that is available, and of course the *rules* the artist has set up—such as only revealing a portrait when a shadow is cast, or of playing a sound if a portrait is revealed. All these parts and their inter-relations go on to inform a diverse range of experiences facilitated by the work as a whole. While some of these are emergent, others are arguably not so.

Online video documentation of the installed work shows people moving through the plaza, changing their scale and manipulating their shadows both individually and while interacting with others. They move their shadows across the projections to reveal the images, as is explained in the accompanying didactic material posted on the building. Since the 'revealing' behaviour is directed from these instructions it is not, however new and emergent. Similarly, the shadow play that people engage with as they interact with others across the plaza is likely also not emergent. Rather, this behaviour can be considered a property of the shadow and not of the work as a whole.

Portrait Collages and Perceptual Emergence Other more playful and seemingly surprising experiences that engage with the work as a whole do, however, appear. These include efforts to transform the portrait with the shadow to create a new image, or meaning, as shown in still images from installations of the work: In Fig. 4.4 when artwork participants hold hands, the shadows they cast are also holding hands. Since these overlay on photographs, those two photos now also become linked and their meaning changes. Similarly shadows change the meaning of the photos in Fig. 4.5, where the authority of the police is mocked through superimposed shadow fingers from participants there, while in Fig. 4.6 a highly expressive (fearful?) portrait of a woman is manipulated through the shadowy addition of multiple arms. In each of these images the participant behaviour could be considered an emergent *whole*—a heterogeneously new occurrence that is not immediately deducible from its parts (separate photos, shadows etc.). These new compositions, or collages, can reasonably be considered to be an instance of perceptual emergence.

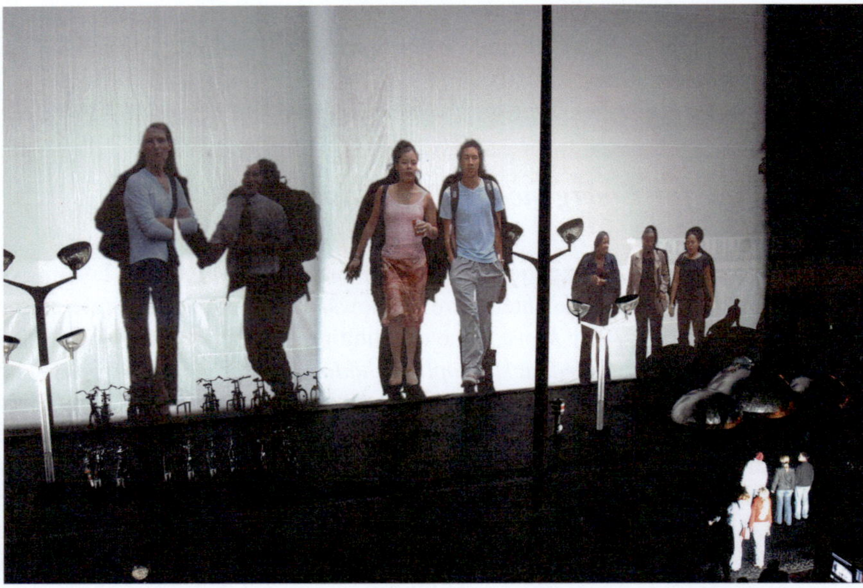

Fig. 4.4 Photograph of interaction with *Body Movies, Relational Architecture 6* by Rafael Lozano-Hemmer (2001) at the Duisburg Akzente Festival, Duisburg, Germany 2003. Image © Antimodular Research 2003

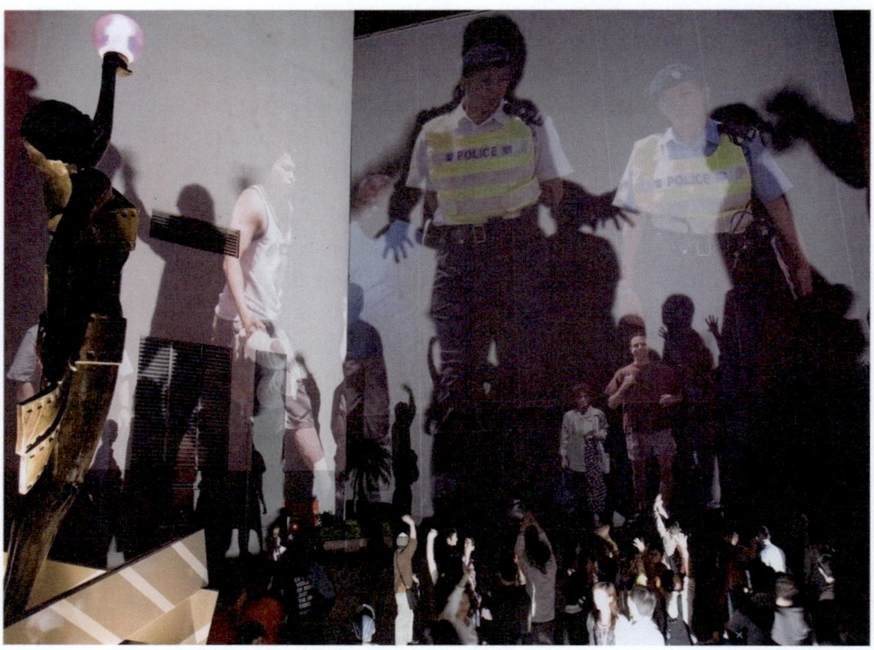

Fig. 4.5 Photograph of interaction with *Body Movies, Relational Architecture 6* by Rafael Lozano-Hemmer (2001) installed at the Museum of Art, Hong Kong, China 2006. Image © Antimodular Research 2006

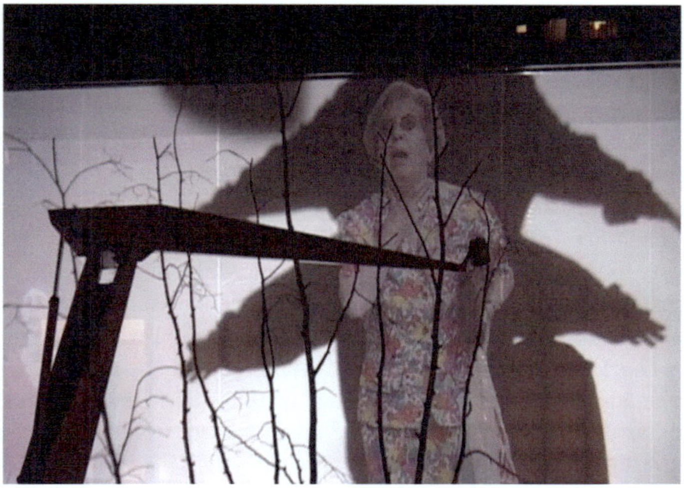

Fig. 4.6 Interaction with *Body Movies, Relational Architecture 6* by Rafael Lozano-Hemmer (2001) at the Cultural Capital of Europe Festival, V2 Grounding, Rotterdam, The Netherlands 2001. Still image from video documentation at 6 min 38 s, www.lozano-hemmer.com/body_movies.php. © Rafael Lozano-Hemmer (2001)

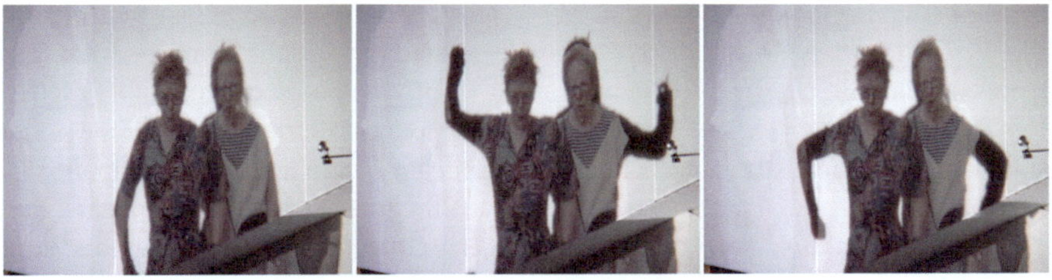

Fig. 4.7 Interaction with *Body Movies, Relational Architecture 6* by Rafael Lozano-Hemmer (2001) at the Cultural Capital of Europe Festival, V2 Grounding, Rotterdam, The Netherlands 2001. Still images from video documentation beginning at 5 min 6 s, www.lozano-hemmer.com/body_movies.php, showing two participants pumping arms repeatedly in an animation of the portrait photographs. © Rafael Lozano-Hemmer (2001)

Pumping Arms and Perceptual Emergence The short series of video stills in Fig. 4.7 depict another scenario again. Here a sequence of shadow arm movements by two participants can be observed. Each participant's shadow has closed hands and bent arms that align roughly with the posture of the women in the photographs. The left participant swings their arms up and down four times during a six-second period, while the right participant does this once. The behaviour ends when someone else starts to interact with them.

Based on the repeated movement by the left participant, and the alignment of the shadows with the portraits, it would appear that the participant gestures are deliberate and focused on those portraits. The meaning of this 'arm pumping' behaviour to the participants is not apparent—it could be anything from mockery to an attempt at animating the person. However, it does appear deliberate and with meaning for those participants. Furthermore, as it is 'feeding back' into the image, such that the shadows (parts) are changing, dynamic, we can argue that it is an instance of intrinsic perceptual emergence. That is, the participant's perception of their newly created collage (the whole with arms bending and fists pumping) is in some way informing their sustained interaction with the work, and they are altering their movement and images created (parts). In this way the whole is feeding back into the parts to change them, and the participant works to sustain the interaction.

Incidences of *Intrinsic, perceptual* emergence seem reasonable within this work as there are a number of places in the video documentation where seemingly novel behaviours appear. To know for sure, one would have to ask those people, that is, conduct evaluations. Other more fine-grained qualities of the event such as whether it was familiar or analogous to something else for them (referenced) cannot however be feasibly proposed. Here most particularly it is necessary to know what people were thinking at that time; that is, evaluation is required. It is therefore not possible to propose characteristics at this level of the TEIA.

Text Rain, Romy Achituv and Camille Utterback

Text Rain (1999) is an interactive artwork created by Israeli Romy Achituv and American Camille Utterback. The work consists of video projection of falling letters from the poem '*Talk, you*' by Zimroth (1993). The letters fall from the top of the screen and come to rest on visual objects in their path such as the image of a participant. The letters can be raised again, pushed up, and when the image obstacle disappears, they resume falling. In this manner the participant can collect letters to form words along parts of their body, the embodying interface to the work. Letters from the poem descend in order such that it becomes possible to see them collect and read phrases from the poem. *Synonym for limbs* is a phrase from the poem that demonstrates this slow, embodied assembly of letters along a participant's arm (Fig. 4.8).

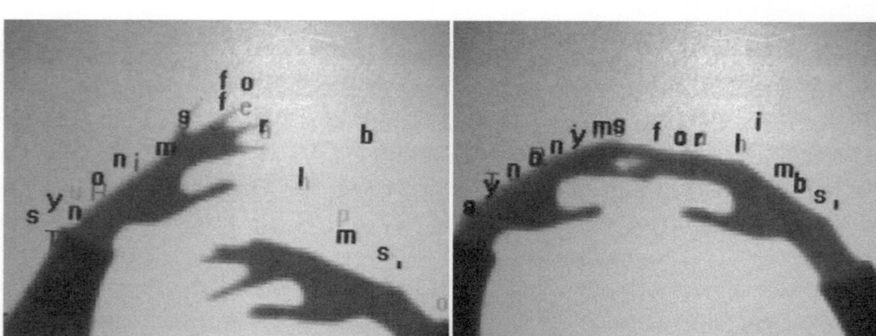

Fig. 4.8 *Text Rain* (1999) by Romy Achituv and Camille Utterback. Interactive installation, screen detail. Photo courtesy of the artists

The Potential for Emergence in Text Rain

If, as informed by the above description, we understand *people's movement, the text letters of words and phrases*—essentially all the system input and output elements —as the parts, then we can consider their combination in terms of emergence in this work. Relations between the parts also influence interaction and any emergent experiences of the work. System constraints—namely, the simulated gravity (text will fall unless encountering an obstacle of a person), and the meaning of the poem are key aspects that inform how the text, body limbs etc can relate to one another. In considering all these elements together with the concepts and qualities of emergence and the TEIA, three interesting interactions and behaviours were identified in the available data. The first of these, *playing with rain*, is not an instance of emergence, though it is worth discussing.

Non-emergence Some of the relevant data to review when considering this work for emergence comes from social media postings by the general public. In publicly uploaded videos at the popular share site YouTube, for example, one can see people manipulating the letters with their bodies in a playful way, but not in a way that acknowledges the meaning of the text or that it is, in fact, text that is 'raining' (as in the title of the work). One example is a post by YouTuber *DangthePhong*. Here someone, presumably Dang himself, calls repeatedly to others in the video to join him in pushing the letters up, chanting *"raise the roof"* and gesturing an upward motion that pushes the letters up, over and over again (dangthephong 2010). This call and behaviour are most likely are most likely a reference to a song of the same name, by Hip Hop artists Public Enemy. It is an interesting behaviour but since it does not engage with falling text as 'letters' that can form words, it is arguably not emergent of this artwork. Rather the interaction is an artefact of an aspect of the work—the falling and interactive visual elements.

Collage and Perceptual Emergence Another interesting behaviour that *does* involve the semantic content of the words is shown in Fig. 4.8, reproduced from Utterback's website (Utterback 2016). Here two hands come together to catch the phrase 'synonym for limbs' from Zimroth's poem: a phrase from the text is combined with a physical illustration of that phrase.

It is likely here that the participant is moving their hands to gather letters and a phrase. The second image suggests a meaningful text and gesture relationship, one that denotes limbs both in terms of the text and in terms of the image, as well as in how they relate to one another—where the text has come to rest on the hands/limbs. This composition has some novelty in terms of its visual form and meaning, though this is also debatable since the phrase is from Zimroth's poem and we could say that the phrase has been predetermined and is not new. Rather we might argue that the emergence comes about in how meaning is interpreted *between* image and text, that it is between the participants' limbs and the text. This collage, or illustration, is a relatively new composition made up of both text and image, and its meaning sits across both elements or parts.

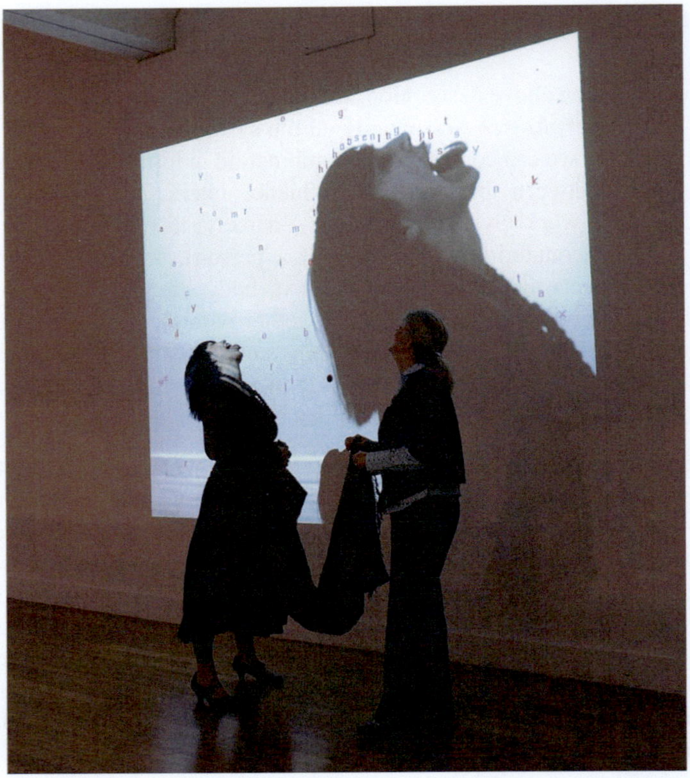

Fig. 4.9 *Text Rain* (1999) by Romy Achituv and Camille Utterback. Interactive installation, installation view. Photo courtesy of the artists

As a new composition, *Synonymn for Limbs* involves the participant in the meaning making. The collage is the emergent outcome, perceived by the participant. This new image is similar to the 'portrait collages' observed during participant interaction with the *Body Movies* work, above. Here too it is an instance of *perceptual* emergence.

Pussy Collage and Perceptual Emergence Another example draws upon a text meaning that is, in fact, new and not predetermined as a result of the poem. This is where, as shown in Fig. 4.9 the arrangement of letters facilitates interpreting the word 'pussy' (Utterback 2016). This word is not in the poem. The accompanying participant posture where those letters fall across the participant's tongue, results in sexual innuendo. Given the novelty and unpredictability of this word appearing as well as the associated participant behaviour, this composition is a particularly interesting instance of new, surprising emergent meaning constructed through interrelating parts: gesture, silhouette, letters and words.

Referenced, Intrinsic or Extrinsic Emergence Both of the above examples are referencing the semantic content of the words. Both would therefore be considered *referenced* emergence.

It can also be argued that both are instances of intrinsic emergence, i.e. feedback was involved. Particularly in the '*pussy collage*', the woman is holding an unusual pose to suspend the letters. We could also say that in *Synonym for Limbs* the arms—limbs—are moved into position to gather the anchoring phrase. The emergent understanding of a text-image collage is affecting the parts, preventing them from falling to prioritise the overall whole composition of text and image.

The Giver of Names, David Rokeby

The interactive artwork *The Giver of Names* by interactive artist David Rokeby is an ongoing project since 1990 (1990a). Installation includes a computer screen, plinth, camera and an array of objects on the floor of a darkened room. The participant is able to select and place objects on the plinth. These are scanned and processed using image analysis algorithms, and aspects of this process are shown on the projected screen behind. Image analysis detects boundaries to the shapes, colour, and texture information to search a database of words and generate a range of related terms shown on another screen. A selection of terms for the objects chosen is then arranged into a grammatically correct sentence, subsequently spoken aloud as audio output from the system, for the participant to hear. In this way the phrase, or 'name' is generated. This image analysis process is illustrated by Rokeby online (Rokeby 1990b).

During an installation of the artwork at the Montreal Museum of Fine Arts, gallery visitors were invited to participate in a new media archiving project with participant evaluations, exploring an oral history of experiencing art (Jones and Muller 2008; Muller 2008). This project involved post-event protocols and interviews with the participants and the project data is hosted online as a part of the Daniel Langlois Foundation's documentary collection. Access to these recordings has meant that this case study differs somewhat from the previous five because here some insight into the thinking processes of the participants is available, even though the discussion was more general and not researching emergence per se. The additional information means it is possible to gain some insight into participants' experiences, such as whether the artwork reminded them of other things—an aspect that relates to the referenced/concrete distinction in the TEIA.

The Potential for Emergence in the Giver of Names

Rokeby describes this work as "*quite simply, a computer system that gives objects names*" (Rokeby 1990a). Shapes or features are detected to inform the phrases, and this results in a meaningful relationship between the phrases or names that the system gives, and the audience's still life arrangement. For example the objects that led to the phrase "*By the timely day, the holy castle of the vermillion floc is unceasingly split by the breathtaking pistol under which the enlightenment does harm*" include a gun and some other bright blue and yellow objects that visually resemble a castle (see 'Two examples of the analysis and naming of objects' in the artists' portfolio online (Rokeby 1990b)). A participant's interactive experience is informed by the objects they can place on the table, their varying profiles and colours, as well as their subsequent representations on screen and in words. Rokeby's software as well as the participant's own behaviours to, for example, select and position objects, determine how the elements interrelate. It is a system that demonstrates many possible combinations and interrelations. The participant's experience of this rich environment has, as is shown next, potential for perceptual emergence.

The Telephone, an Instance of Perceptual Emergence During evaluations by Muller and Jones at the Montreal Museum of Fine Arts, gallery visitor Betty-Jo was observed and interviewed about her experience of Rokeby's artwork. She was recorded both on video and as a verbal description and discussion, and some emergent behaviours seem to have occurred.

One instance is when she and a friend placed a collection of different objects on the plinth in a specific arrangement, as shown in Fig. 4.10.[1] Betty-Jo says of her friend: "*she noticed that it looked like a telephone what she had arranged... and then when reading it The Giver of Names gives it, says the word 'telephone', which is neat*" (Muller 2007). Here an emergent shape—the telephone—has been interpreted based on their arrangement of different objects. This can be understood as an instance of *Referenced Extrinsic* perceptual emergence. Interestingly, the art system similarly identified the overall shape as a telephone.

'See what it would write about me' and Perceptual Emergence Another instance of perceptual emergence can also be identified a little later on in the same interaction session with Betty-Jo and her friend. Here Betty-Jo removed objects that she had been interacting with before placing her elbows and part of herself on the plinth, as in Fig. 4.11. She states that she had seen someone else do this, and that she "*wanted to see what it would write about me*". Her friend similarly posed in front of the camera. The friends subsequently move to the other screen to read the artwork's response to their bodies.

It is feasible that this final behaviour is also emergent—that is, where the audience interacts with the work in a way that is not explicitly intended by the artist or easily deduced from the work itself. And, while their behaviours may have been prompted by someone else, there is still the question of how they arose for that earlier participant. That situation could conceivably have arisen out of the same sort of playful interaction that Betty-Jo is observed to have engaged in. That is, it could

[1]Still images from the video-cued recall sessions with participants of the work *The Giver of Names* by David Rokeby. Interview video production by the Daniel Langlois Foundation for Art, Science, and Technology; interviewer: Lizzie Muller; camera: Raphaëlle Aubin. Courtesy of Lizzie Muller and the Daniel Langlois Foundation.

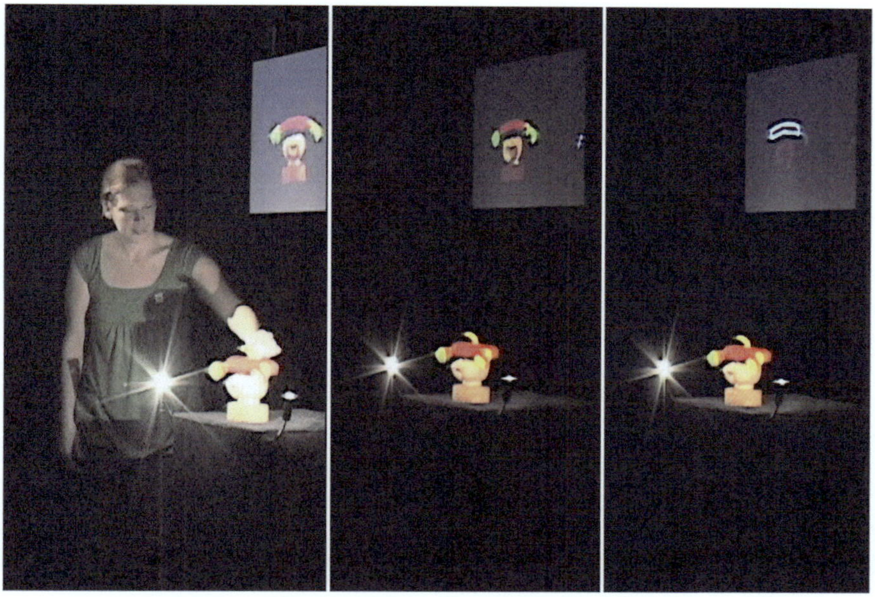

Fig. 4.10 Interaction with *The Giver of Names* by David Rokeby (1991–) installed at the Montreal Museum of Fine Arts, Canada 2007. Still image from video documentation at 6 min 26 s shows the participant with an emergent telephone shape. Image courtesy of Lizzie Muller and the Daniel Langlois Foundation. (Reproduced from Jones and Muller 2008)

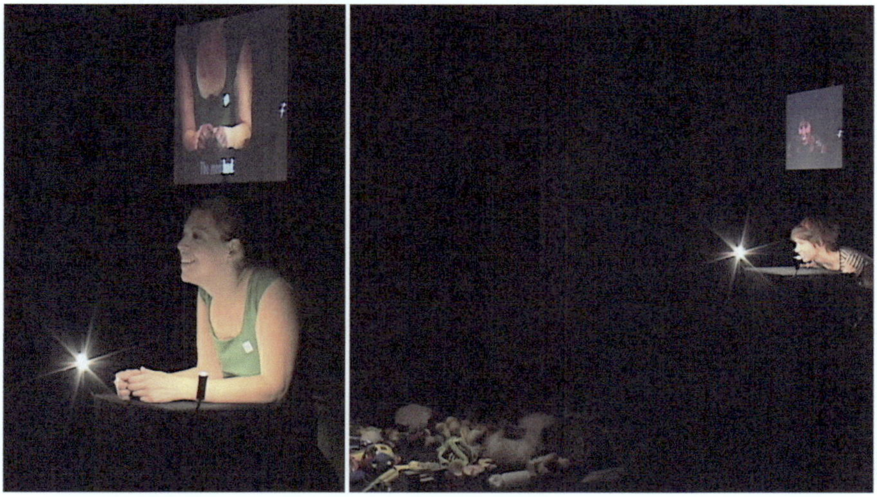

Fig. 4.11 Interaction with *The Giver of Names* by David Rokeby (1991–) installed at the Montreal Museum of Fine Arts, Canada 2007. Still image from video documentation at 8 min 22 s shows participants 'putting themselves into the system'. Image courtesy of Lizzie Muller and the Daniel Langlois Foundation. (Reproduced from Jones and Muller 2008)

set up a feedback loop between the parts and the whole, pointing towards the potential for *intrinsic* perceptual emergence.

For example, Betty-Jo interacts with the work to select and position objects (the parts) on the plinth and observes the compositions of image and text rendered (the combined product, or whole, of those parts). As she interprets compositions, such as the *telephone*, and sees the system do the same in terms of naming it, this understanding then feeds back to the level of the parts to change her subsequent selection of objects. But now she tries a different 'part'—herself. That is, her understanding of the compositional whole 'feeds back' to change the parts that make up that whole, as she selects another, new and unexpected part—her body.

Where the participant is interacting to combine different objects, this is arguably not an instance of emergence. Rokeby's intention, and correspondingly, the installation design itself, suggest and direct this behaviour. That is, a selection of toys is presented in front of the illuminated pedestal. As an intuitive interface it is effective, and it facilitates a range of behaviours from 'figuring out how it works' through to 'trying out combinations' and observing what might be generated. The behaviours of selecting and positioning objects on the pedestal is communicated through the installation set up. In itself it would not be a new behaviour then and therefore not an emergent behaviour either.

While this action of combining elements may not be emergent, the meaning that can be generated through the combinations may effect perceptual emergence. And when the software is doing this, as in properly naming the *telephone*, it resembles the design research efforts that explore the computation of emergent shapes to support creative design with the computer (as discussed in Chaps. 2 and 7).

In talking about the work, Rokeby describes his intention to create an interface that is "*really wide open*" with "*as little as I could imagine pre-constrained so that the experience for each person would be absolutely unique and very fundamentally determined by their contribution*" (Rokeby in Rokeby et al. 2007). The work demonstrates this open-ness through the diverse range of possible outcomes that have been facilitated—each person's choice or positioning or combination of objects is quite unlikely to be repeated by another. Rokeby further describes his role in this, however. It involved ensuring "*sufficient tension exist between the object and the name given to challenge the viewers' preconceptions of the objects, and draw them into speculative exploration.*" Participants make meaning here—in the space between the objects presented, the art systems' interpretation of them and the participants' interpretation of both. In exploring the tension between the meanings, Rokeby's work is also an exploration of the potential forms of perceptual emergence.

Discussion

The different artworks discussed here demonstrate different potentials for emergence. Perceptual and physical, intrinsic and extrinsic emergence have been characterised across them. There are also some surprising similarities between the works, in terms of emergence. In some there is a tendency to *switch* across levels of the parts and whole, while, in some others there is a *simultaneous* interaction at both the level of parts and whole.

Interaction Across Levels of Emergence

Participant behaviours identified in these artworks and studies vary in terms of their interaction 'scale'. In *A-Volve*, *Sentimental Sentience* and *The Giver of Names*, the participant fluctuates between operating at the level of the parts of the system, and having an overview of the whole. For example, in *A-Volve,* they draw to create a creature then move to the pool to watch and interact with the evolutionary system where their creature is now 'swimming'. Similarly in Penny and Schulte and Rokeby's works, they can interrupt or arrange an input respectively, then sit back to perceive the unfolding whole composition. In each of these situations the participant is *switching* between the level of the parts and the level of the whole. There is a tendency to *alternate* between the levels of emergence, while interacting with the work.

Behaviours identified in the other works facilitate a more *simultaneous* rather than alternating interaction with the emergent whole and parts. In *Body Movies, Text Rain* and *Autopoiesis* the participant is at both levels or scales of emergence simultaneously. That is, they are interacting at the level of the parts such as to 'collect letters along a limb' in *Text Rain,* or manipulate a shadow or a robotic arm in *Body Movies* or *Autopoiesis*, respectively. At the same time they are able to perceive the emergent whole this feeds back into—be it the animated collage they are creating, or the repulsion of a flock of robotic arms. In each of these cases the participant is interacting at *both* the level of the parts and the whole at the same time.

Relations Between Parts

Participant experience of these artworks is not only dependent on the parts that can effect an emergent whole, but also the manner in which those parts relate to one another. These relations can be influenced by participants but are, initially at least, determined by the artist in creating the works.

This chapter has presented a range of different relations between the parts. They are as diverse as the works and their aesthetics. For example, in *A-Volve*, the two-dimensional drawing interaction and AL rules impose constraints determining the scope for creature form and evolution (Sommerer and Mignonneau 1994). Rokeby's image analysis processes and choice of objects similarly inform the relations between those objects to render emergent compositions: silhouette and colour are core constraints for relations here. Lozano-Hemmer makes decisions about objects and people in space to inform the position of lights relative to architecture which, in turn, will affect shadow scale and participant play. The inclusion of a poem structures the way in which the letters combine in *Text Rain,* and ultimately influences the meanings made there (Achituv and Utterback (1999), Zimroth (1993)). In each case, the relations affect the capacity for interpretation and meaning-making. They are, in effect, the constraints or rules that bound the interactive art work and the participant's experience of it. They are also integral to each work's aesthetic, concept, and compositional whole.

Taboo

In two of these artworks perceptual emergence has coincided with taboo. The sexually explicit 'pussy' composition in *Text Rain* and the same-sex holding hands example in *Body Movies* are both instances of people engaging with the works in unconventional—unexpected—ways. It may well be that when social customs or conventions are transgressed we come up with new and surprising outcomes, as illustrated here. It may also be, more generally, that when rules are broken or transgressed, emergence occurs. Transgressing taboos may well be a creative opportunity for artists as well since, as David Rokeby describes in his interview with Lizzie Muller, it was when he saw someone construct a phallus with a thermos and some spheres and *The Giver of Names* interpreted this composition as such, that there was a shift in thinking and interest for him (Rokeby in Rokeby et al. 2007).

This chapter has provided insight into opportunities for emergence and increased understanding of what form it may take. The next chapter describes some of my own digital interactive artworks and the practice-based research approach that informed them. As is also shown, this practice directed me to the topic of emergence while the research informed my design for perceptual emergence. Following this discussion, in Chap. 6 I discuss evaluations of these artworks. These were analysed using theories of emergence and the TEIA and include participant descriptions of what their emergent experiences were like.

References

Achituv R, Utterback C (1999) Text Rain, interactive artwork

dangthephong (2010) Text Rain YouTube video, 1 min 32 s, 21C Museum Hotel in Louisville, Kentucky, USA. https://www.youtube.com/watch?v=_24diCvtAPM. Accessed 8 April 2016

Dietz S (2002) Ten dreams of technology, vol 35. The MIT Press, Leonardo, pp 509–522

Eco U (1962) The poetics of the open work. In: Bishop C (ed) Participation. Whitechapel, The MIT Press, London, England, pp 20–40

Jones C, Muller L (2008) David Rokeby, The Giver of Names (1991-) Documentary collection. The Daniel Langlois Foundation collection: DOCAM (documentation and conservation of the media arts), Montreal, Canada, http://www.fondation-langlois.org/html/e/page.php?NumPage=2121

Lieser W (2010) The world of digital art. Har/DVD edition. H.F.Ullmann Publishing Gmbh, Köln, Germany

Lozano-Hemmer R (2001) Body Movies Relational Architecture No. 6, interactive art installation
Muller L (2008) Towards an oral history of new media art. In: Daniel langlois foundation for art, science and technology. http://www.fondation-langlois.org/html/e/page.php?NumPage=2096. Accessed 13 July 2016
Muller L (2007) The Giver of Names: Documentary collection video-cued recall interviews, daniel langlois foundation for art, science, and technology. http://www.fondation-langlois.org/html/e/page.php?NumPage=2138. Accessed 11 April 2016
Penny S (2015) Emergence, agency, and interaction—Notes from the field. Artif Life 21:271–284. doi:10.1162/ARTL_a_00167
Penny S, Schulte J (1995) Sympathetic Sentience, artwork
Rinaldo K (2000) Autopoiesis, interactive artwork
Rinaldo K (2015a) Biography of Ken Rinaldo. In: http://www.kenrinaldo.com/. http://www.kenrinaldo.com/bio/. Accessed 22 April 2016
Rinaldo K (2015b) Videos Ken Rinaldo. In: http://www.kenrinaldo.com/videos/?video_id=1365. Accessed 22 April 2016
Rokeby D (1990a) The Giver of Names, interactive art installation
Rokeby D (1990b) Works: The Giver of Names (1990-) (in progress). In: David Rokeby. http://www.davidrokeby.com/gon.html. Accessed 18 Oct 2016
Rokeby D, Muller L, Jones C (2007) Interview with David Rokeby, 18 Sep 2007, Montreal museum fine arts, The daniel langlois foundation collection. http://www.fondation-langlois.org/html/e/page.php?NumPage=2130. Accessed 12 April 2016
Sommerer C, Mignonneau L (1994) A-Volve, interactive artwork
Sommerer C, Mignonneau L (2002) Modeling the emergence of complexity: complex systems, the origin of life and interactive on-line art, vol 35. The MIT Press, Leonardo, pp 161–169
Sommerer C, Mignonneau L (eds) (1998) Art as a Living System. In: Art @ Science. Springer, Austria
Stocker G, Sommerer C, Mignonneau L (eds) (2009) Christa Sommerer Laurent Mignonneau, interactive art research. Springer, Austria
Utterback C (2016) Text Rain Romy Achituv & Camille Utterback. In: Camille Utterback. http://camilleutterback.com/projects/text-rain/. Accessed 16 Oct 2016
Zimroth E (1993) Dead, Dinner, or Naked. Triquarterly

Chapter 5
Three Interactive Art Systems

Abstract This chapter describes three interactive art systems that were later found to facilitate emergent experiences. The discussion details my practice within a practice-based research approach. The three works are *+−now (2008)*, *Of me With me (2014)* and *Dichroic Wade (2016)*. Their form, technology and modes of interaction are very different, as are their creative, conceptual agendas. All are, however, primarily concerned with participant experience and emergence. As such, a key concern has been exploring the potential for perceptual emergence during participant interaction. Different approaches for facilitating perceptual emergence have been explored, including the use of models of physical emergence in the art system to effect perceptual emergence, an approach that draws upon both sides of the TEIA tree (physical and perceptual), simultaneously.

Practicing Practice-Based Research

This book is concerned with participant experience of art, specifically emergent experiences with interactive digital art. This focus comes out of my creative practice. It has also led to theoretical and evaluation research, areas which themselves have informed the creative practice.

As discussed in the first chapter, the approach taken here is practice-based research (PBR). In PBR, research is conducted around practice. In this case the practice is the creative practice of making interactive artworks. The pursuit of creative practical enquiry alongside research to generate knowledge outcomes has been investigated by a number of researchers (e.g. see Scrivener 2002a, b; Candy and Edmonds 2010). Practice and the research can combine in different ways, and a study of creative practice-based researchers by Edmonds and Candy proposed a framework consisting of practice, evaluation and theoretical research (2010). Here all three of these aspects also apply. The practice efforts consist of creating art works, while the research components constitute theoretical and evaluation research. And all of these interrelate in an iterative way.

The methods for making these works relied on prototyping and iterative approaches to software development (e.g. see Boehm 1986; Beaudouin-Lafon and

J. Seevinck, *Emergence in Interactive Art*, Springer Series on Cultural Computing,
DOI 10.1007/978-3-319-45201-2_5

Mackay 2003) as well as Schön's reflective practice approach (1983). Donald Schön was a philosopher and design professor who conducted case studies of professional practitioners, in practice. His research revealed how continual critical self-reflection on personal actions would facilitate self-learning about those actions and support their ability to handle unique and uncertain situations. He identified some key methods for reflective practice, including listening to *situation talk-back* and *reframing* (Schön 1983). Listening to situation talk-back acknowledges the practitioner's awareness of situations that are in flux. As we 'listen' to become aware of the changes in the situation, our understanding of that situation changes. That is, the new insight from the situation leads us to 'reframe' our understanding of it and requirements and dimensions are scoped out in a different way. This iterative, adaptive process has informed my creation of the three computer-based interactive art systems discussed here.

The interactive art systems created this way and discussed here are operational software and hardware systems. In addition to employing reflective practice methods, their creation also involves iterative software design. Here a computer system is created by iterating through stages of design, implementation and testing. Iterative design has also informed how the methods associated with reflection-in-action and grounded theory methods for data analysis (see the next chapter) have been integrated in this PBR effort—that is, through an iterative, spiral process of creating the art systems. This process iterates through the stages of planning and *problem framing* e.g. to come up with conceptual agendas for the work; sketching and software developing and employing *knowing-in-action* to create the work; evaluating and listening to *situation talk-back* to reflect upon the work personally, critically, as well as listening to others (through evaluation responses); and back to planning and *reframing* the problem, to revisit and evolve the conceptual structure behind the work.

Working with a conceptual structure is integral to my creative approach, as well as the PBR implementation described here. For me, this conceptual structure provides an aesthetic rationale or framework that informs decisions made during the process of making the creative work. It typically has some intuitive, expressive origin which has been developed into a range of related ideas. It is 'open-ended' in the sense that this set of organised ideas can take many forms and cannot be exhausted by any one artefact.

The conceptual structure evolves during the process of making; that is, it is reframed by the situation talk-back that is generated throughout the process of making. It is also informed by evaluation findings and theoretical insights that come from the other aspects of this PBR approach. In this way the conceptual structure facilitates a distance, effectively providing 'buffering' between those external influences, or 'voices' and the more internal, personal space of working creatively.

The three digital, interactive art systems described here stem from three distinct conceptual frameworks, and the discussion of each involves articulating that conceptual structure, or backbone, to the work.

+−*now* (2008)

+−*now* (pronounced 'plus min now') is an interactive artwork with sand as an interface (Fig. 5.3). Computer generated imagery is projected directly on the sand and on a screen behind it. The imagery tracks gestures in the sand and is projected into them in real time, qualifying the work as an instance of Augmented Reality,[1] while sand is the passive haptic interface and further characterises this work as an instance of Tangible Computing.[2] The work was installed at the Beta_Space at the Sydney Powerhouse Museum in 2008 for evaluations, as reported in the next chapter.

Conceptual Structure

The art system was informed by a conceptual structure that prioritises experience of the natural landscape. The preceding interactive art sketch *Glass Pond* (2005) was similarly informed by the same conceptual concerns as +−*now* (2008) allowing the exploration and evolution of a range of concerns for +−*now*. In many ways *Glass Pond* (Fig. 5.2) is a prototype for +−*now* (Fig. 5.3).

The concept originated during artist residencies in the iconic Hudson Valley area of the north eastern USA. The residencies at the I-Park enclave (2003, 2007) directed the artworks to look at physical and experiential aspects of landscape. In particular, personal experience at the site resonated with philosopher Martin Heidegger's idea of 'dasein' (Heidegger 1978)—when one feels highly involved or present in one's surroundings: more like 'being in love' than 'being in a car'. Interaction theory also contributed to this aesthetic program, namely the design for attraction and sustaining participants (Edmonds et al. 2006) and deep and shallow interactive experience (Norman 2002). These ideas would inform decisions for the visual and experiential qualities of the works. The first of these works, *Glass Pond* (2005) was evaluated in an exploratory study in a naturalistic setting, an arts

---

[1]The creation of this work has involved different computing technologies—specifically Augmented Reality (AR) and Tangible Computing. AR describes visual layering of digital data, though this can also be done aurally. +−*now* projects directly onto the sand. The shapes of coloured light fit into the marks made in the sand so that the coloured image registers directly with the gestural input. The shapes are generated and rendered as gestures are made, in real time. The overlay of a virtual image onto a real object, which is registered with that object and where this virtual image is computed in real-time, qualifies the colour image application as an augmented reality (AR) application (Azuma et al. 2001). The use of AR facilitates the liquid behaviour of the image: it can appear to follow a finger trailing in the sand and 'well up' in the sand.

[2]Tangible Computing aims to give "*… physical form to digital information, making bits directly manipulable and perceptible,*" leveraging the rich understanding we have of instruments, physical objects and architecture by adding information to these. These researchers aim to re-integrate these objects and their physical richness into HCI and our lives (Ishii and Ullmer 1997; Ishii et al. 2012).

studio at the Creativity and Cognition Studios (CCS), University of Technology Sydney. Findings include participant behaviours such as composing with the system, finding it unpredictable and frustrating, and emergent goals (Seevinck et al. 2006). When those findings were integrated back into the conceptual structure, reframing it, the concept of emergence came to the fore. Subsequent PBR efforts included theoretical enquiry into emergence as well other creative explorations. These would inform the interactive artwork +−*now*.

Subsequent to *Glass Pond* and the new interest in emergence, the conceptual structure iterated to focus on (1) the behaviour of light on the water and (2) ambiguity and illusion, as observed in nature. For example, in studying the landscape I found that I was able to interpret emergent shapes in the landscape, such as the diamond shapes that one can see in the 'knees' or aerial roots of the bald cypress tree as they protrude out of the water (Fig. 5.1).

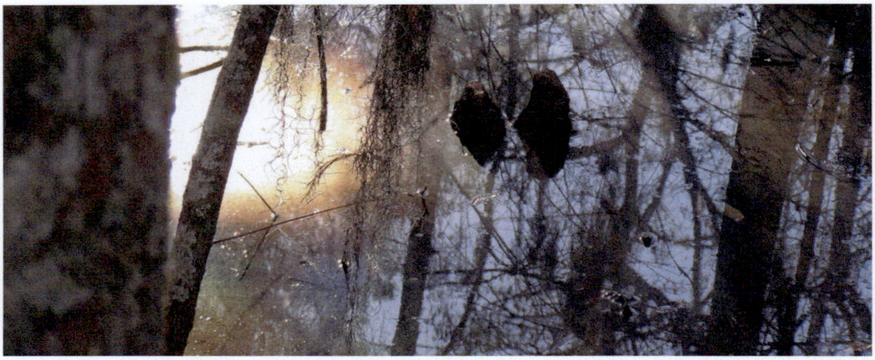

Fig. 5.1 Aerial roots from Bald Cypress trees combine with their shadows to create diamond shapes. Used with permission from the copyright holder, reproduced from Seevinck (2010)

A third aspect (3) was implicated in these landscape investigations: open-endedness. Diversity in form, detail and texture became evident on a micro scale, and this led to my reframing of my understanding of this place—and of nature in general—as 'open'. That is, this infinite richness and variation is due to its open-ness. Emergence, through its unpredictability and capacity for surprise, is also indeterminate and open-ended, while, of course, life is also emergent. The meeting point between nature, open-ness and emergence has continued to drive my creative efforts (e.g. Seevinck and Edmonds 2009; Seevinck 2013a). Furthermore the conceptual ideas around landscape, emergence and open-ness seemed almost serendipitous when literature on the artwork's interface—sand—came to light. Sand is used in psychotherapy and its origin there is attributed to *Floor Games*, the short story by Wells (1911). Wells describes a preference for wooden blocks as toys that are flexible enough to facilitate a range of imaginative play. Similarly sand is a versatile material that one can interact with in many ways. It is open like the simple wooden blocks Wells describes (Fig. 5.2).

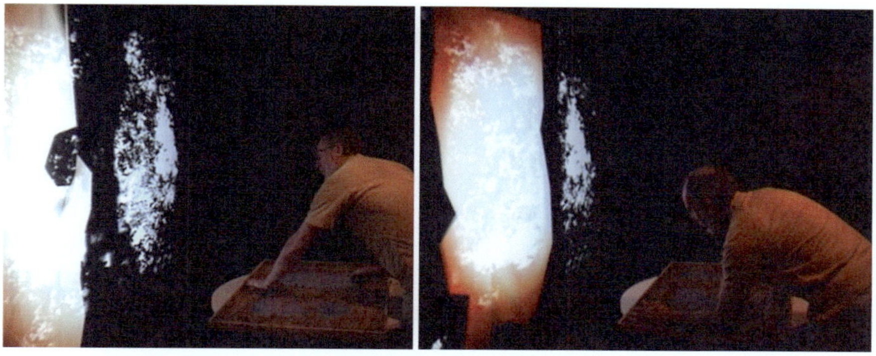

Fig. 5.2 In *Glass Pond* (2006) a *dappled light* background and a colourful *geo-forms* figure accompany a sand interface. Used with permission from the copyright holder, reproduced from Seevinck et al. (2006)

Experiencing the Work

+−*now* consists of colourful imagery projected directly onto fine white sand and responding to participant gestures in the sand (Figs. 5.3, 5.4 and 5.5). Additional monochromatic imagery is projected on a wall screen in front of the sand interface. The participant is free to move the sand around on the table and, through this mechanism, interact with the work.

+−*now* imagery responds to the speed and direction of a participant's gesture. This added sensor data is used to generate an 'echoing' behaviour that resembles the movement of water in the colour image and facilitates the interpretation of emergent shapes in the monochromatic image. This echoing behaviour results from the repeated rendering of shapes—that is, a stroke in the sand is made to layer several (transparent) shapes consecutively on top of one another. These are analogous to 'echoes' in the way that they repeatedly render the input data. The echoes outlive the input data, making it possible to superimpose a current gesture with one from a few seconds ago. The result is that one can interact with a history of one's gestures. Interacting with an image from a previous gesture is analogous to singing with an echo of one's voice.

The echoing behaviour differs between the colour and monochrome images. In the colour image the echoing creates visual 'waves' which give the impression of water (Fig. 5.4). In the monochrome screen image this layering of temporal gestures facilitates the interpretation of emergent shapes and compositions (Fig. 5.5). This is due to the layering of the shapes which add up in opacity to create areas of increased brightness, which can in turn be interpreted as new forms. It's a little bit like staring at the clouds and interpreting figures there. In this sense, it is also facilitating a reflective experience.

The ability to interact with a history of one's gestures means that you can improvise in time. That is, you can interact with a moment in the past as well as

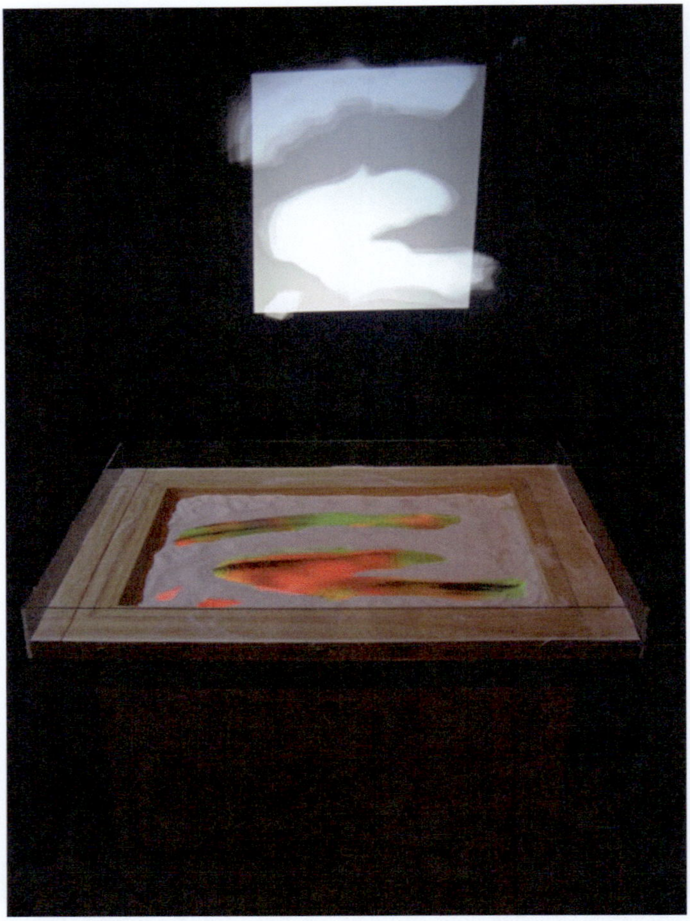

Fig. 5.3 +−*now* (Seevinck 2008) installed at the Beta_Space, Sydney Powerhouse Museum

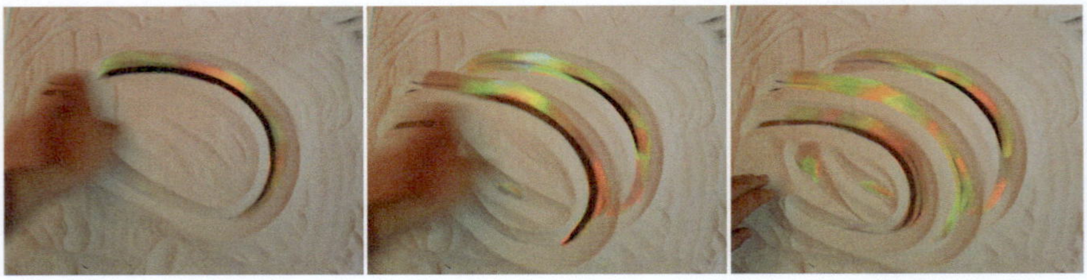

Fig. 5.4 Colourful trails follow gestures in the sand in real time in +−now (2008)

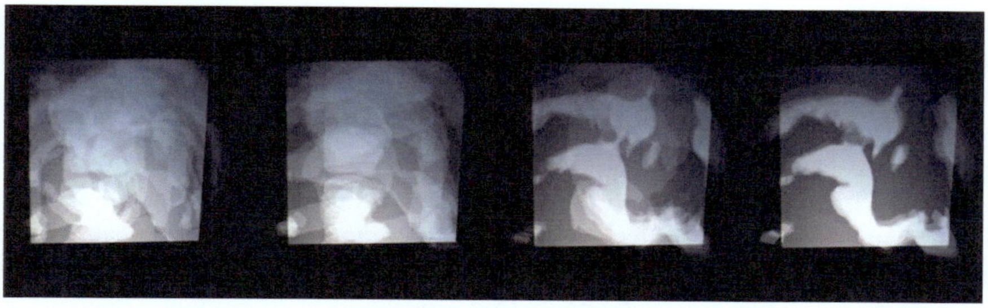

Fig. 5.5 In +−*now* (2008), interaction with the sand generates echoing layers of white imagery on screen, leading to the interpretation of new shapes or forms

building up imagery to appear in the future. These temporal aspects are what informed the title '+−now'. As discussed in the next chapter, some of these temporal interactions include the creation of animations as well as other more concrete and playful efforts such as the '*look stir and wait'* behaviour.

Design and Construction

The images respond to a sensor (video camera) located inside the glass-topped plinth, looking up at the sand to register clearings in the sand. In *Glass Pond* sand is the interface. The camera is positioned above the sand tray and informs the behaviour of two sets of imagery—*dappled light* (black and white) and *geo-forms* (white and red) as shown Fig. 5.2.

Glass Pond and +−*now* were both created using *Derivative Touch*, a real-time 3D graphics software API application programming environment (Hermanovic and Bairos 2000). The applications run at 60 Hz with real-time video sampling and manipulation of a live video feed from a digital video camera for vision tracking participant movement.

The conceptual agenda behind these works evolved to look at water and emergence, but attracting and sustaining participant interest also remained important. The *coloured* image works with the fine white beach sand to attract people to the work while generating immediate feedback for ease of understanding and engagement. It is quite different to the more ascetic *monochrome* imagery that is projected on the wall, and which supports the more reflective experience, sustaining participant experience. The imagery is intended to evoke a sense of movement of highlights on the water. The intention for the colour image to behave like water originates from the landscape and the conceptual structure. This is facilitated by modelling two aspects: the behaviour of light on water currents and the behaviour of waves.

Firstly, the behaviour of light on water currents is achieved through manipulating colour and light. A *Phong* shader (a specific surface shading algorithm named after creator Bui Tuong Phong and used for representing three dimensional computer graphics) was tuned to prioritise red and green colour and applied to the object. Red and green were chosen as these digital primaries are most readily absorbed by the human eye (over blue) and because they vibrate and contrast when perceived, making for a strong visual element. The Phong shader values were designed to have 'non-real world' properties such that the object can be seen to reflect red highlights, absorb all diffuse colour (creating a shadow) and emit green light (acting like a light source), all at the same time (Fig. 5.6). The peaks of the rippling geometry mesh can therefore become very bright, approaching white because as the digital primary colours (red, green and blue) combine, they add to white. The Phong shader also manipulates the transparency in the object. By enabling the participant to see through the ripples and echoing, overlapping 'waves' of shapes, the layered colour produces visual complexity. Additional transformations with noise are employed on the underlying geometrical mesh to refine the water-like behaviour. A recent history of shapes calculated and detected is also stored and played back. In this way, a stroke in the sand results in the creation of several shapes layered on top of one another consecutively, which is similar to the behaviour of waves washing up on the shore. The shader properties combine with the geometry properties and the scene lighting to create a colourful, transparent surface with distinctive highlights corresponding to the sparkling light on the water.

A similar approach to generating echoing behaviour is also used to generate this 'wave-like' behaviour in the monochromes imagery. Here, however the image prioritises transparency. That is, as layers overlap (informed by participant gestures now and in the past, and to a lesser extent by the random deformations) more opaque, white areas become apparent. These areas appear brighter, and as they visually 'stand out' they can be interpreted as new shapes. That is, the layered transparent areas can be perceived as new emergent shapes or compositions. The ability to interpret two four-sided polygons as emergent shapes in Fig. 5.7, frame **d** illustrates this.

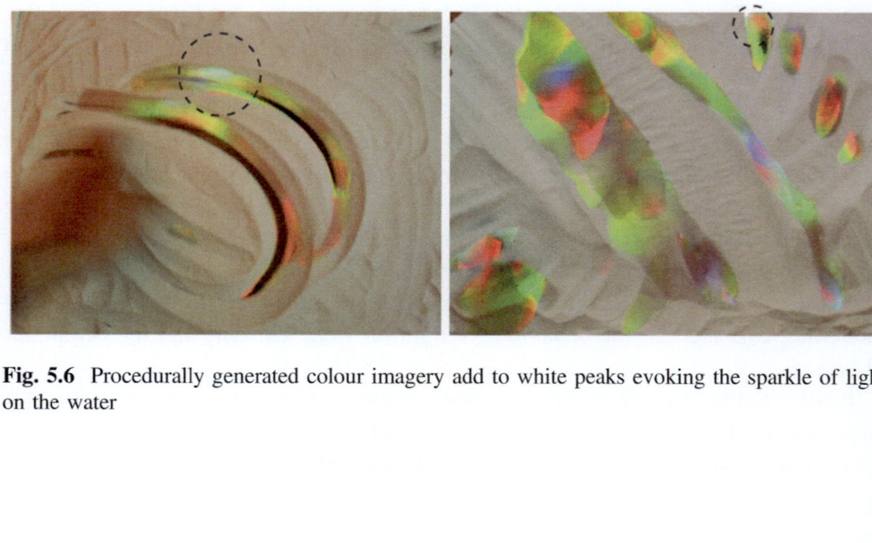

Fig. 5.6 Procedurally generated colour imagery add to white peaks evoking the sparkle of light on the water

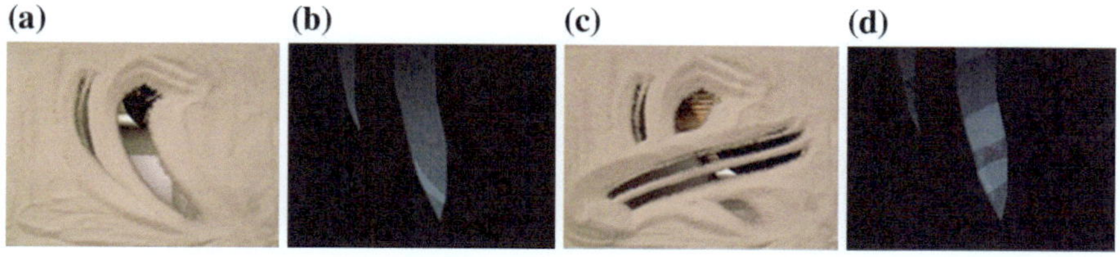

Fig. 5.7 In +−*now* a gesture in the sand (**a**) creates a shape (**b**). Another gesture (**c**) intersects with (**a**) to create brighter areas and new shapes (**d**). Used with permission from the copyright holder, reproduced from Seevinck (2010)

Novel Method for Creating Emergent Shapes

The construction of the new shapes in +−*now* draws on emergent shape research in the design community. This community has expressed an interest in instantiating emergent shapes because it can facilitate creative design. The community also features research efforts into the methods by which emergent shapes can be created using the computer. These have been described in Chap. 2. One of the approaches to creating emergent shapes decomposes a source image into an intermediate representation. This decomposition can be based on line or area. In +−*now*, a novel approach to decomposing using area is taken. This is the use of opacity and a history of participant gestures, as above in Fig. 5.7. That is, gestures in the sand result in corresponding transparent shapes being rendered on the screen. The transparent shapes are layered, overlapping with one another. The areas of overlap between these transparent layers are more opaque and stand out visually as brighter areas. The two brighter shapes that appear in frame d of this figure are new forms. They are made up of layers of transparent shapes produced from the gestures. The transparent shapes add together to create the bright, new shapes. The bright shapes in frame **d** can be considered as something new that wasn't directly implied by its context, and as wholes that are greater than the sum of their parts. The parts are the layers of transparent shapes. The whole is an emergent shape. These emergent shapes are classified as *extrinsic perceptual* emergence. They are similar to the new heart shape that emerges from the intersecting teardrops in Fig. 1.2.

Of me With me (2014)

The second art system discussed here is *Of me With me* (2014). It is an interactive computer-based art system that facilitates an emergent drawing experience through a tablet and stylus with custom software for real-time computer generated imagery. The interaction surface and monitor are inclined to facilitate drawing by someone with a wheelchair, as is appropriate for this projects collaborators (see Fig. 5.8). It

(a) (b)

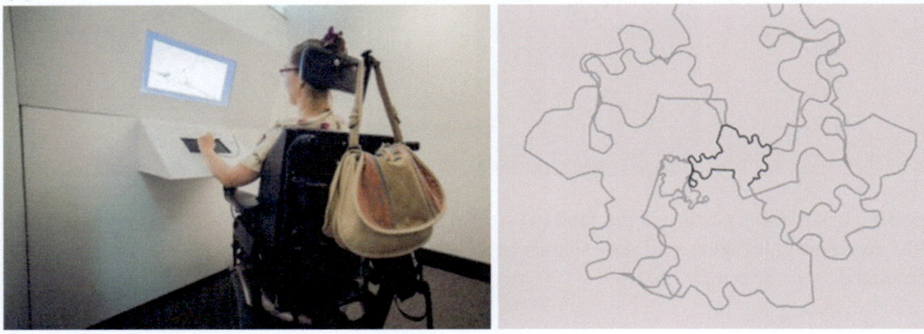

Fig. 5.8 **a** A participant interacts with *Of me With me* (Seevinck 2014b) at the Redcliffe City Gallery, Australia 2015, to draw a *black mark* which, in turn, generates echoing imagery (*grey lines*) dynamically and in real time. **b** Photo by Anthony Hearsey, images used with permission from the copyright holders

was installed at the Redcliffe City Gallery in early 2015 for naturalistic evaluation of participant experience (Seevinck 2014a, b; 2015a).

The work comes out of a collaboration with artists and staff at ArTel, a community arts studio program at the Cerebral Palsy League support service. This is an Australian non-profit organisation supporting people with cerebral palsy (CP) (CerebralPalsyLeague 2011). CP is a neurological disease that affects people physically. It can cause muscle atrophy and spasticity and often people with CP are wheelchair-bound. Some can speak while others need a head pointer or eye tracking to express themselves. The artwork (and project) concern drawing and visualising mark-making. It also investigates transferring the understanding of emergence in one area to facilitate emergence in another domain. Here the physical emergence model of the Koch fractal curve has informed a creative, interactive drawing experience for project collaborators and, ultimately, the participants of the final interactive artwork. As is shown, the mechanism of emergence provides a unique response to the moral and conceptual imperatives that came about for me in this project: *what if my every movement required a monumental effort? How then would I be creative?*

Conceptual Structure

The painter's brushstroke is unique, like a signature. This assertion has informed this project to explore visualisation of the unique drawing gestures of collaborating community artists and, through this, to work towards facilitating greater agency. The project was thought to give insight into the unique expression of their, the community artists' mark, in order to generate some ideas for the creation of a digital interactive system. We collaborated from August 2012 for approximately eighteen months to exchange ideas and concepts which would inform the overall *Iterative*

Drawing body of work. This included collaboratively drawing, including *action painting* with wheelchairs. A digital interactive sketch, *Iterative Intersectioning* (Seevinck 2013b), and the final interactive artwork system, *Of Me With Me* (2014), were also produced.

Wheelchair Action Painting A first step in the project was looking at how the artists currently work. At the ArTel studio pencils and brushes remain the primary means to the artists' mark-making, although these are used in very different ways. A pencil can be held in-hand, taped to a head pointer (where the artist can better control their head than hands) or taped to an elbow with the additional support of a CPL carer's steadying arm to mitigate tremor and spasms. All artists had a wheelchair, however, and given the project's focus on gesture in art, action painting came to the fore. Action painting was practiced by Abstract Expressionist painters around the 1940s to 50s. This loosely defined group of painters emphasise expression and emotion, rather than the considered application of colour or form. In many ways, action painting is concerned with the process of making marks rather than the finished work itself. This concern with process made for a good fit with this project's emphasis on mark-making. The interest led to an early group exploration of wheelchair-based action painting. Here a paint roller was attached to the back of a wheel chair and the artists were invited to drive their chairs (most could) across the floor to paint or make marks on it. A video camera caught the imagery from above (Fig. 5.9a).

At first the wheelchair action painting did not provide much insight for the project, because the expressiveness of the wheelchair seemed limited. However, the effort prompted me to explore their drawings as a fellow, albeit digital, artist. I traced curve segments from the video imagery and followed medical imaging techniques to generate a three-dimensional CAD model from these curves (See, for

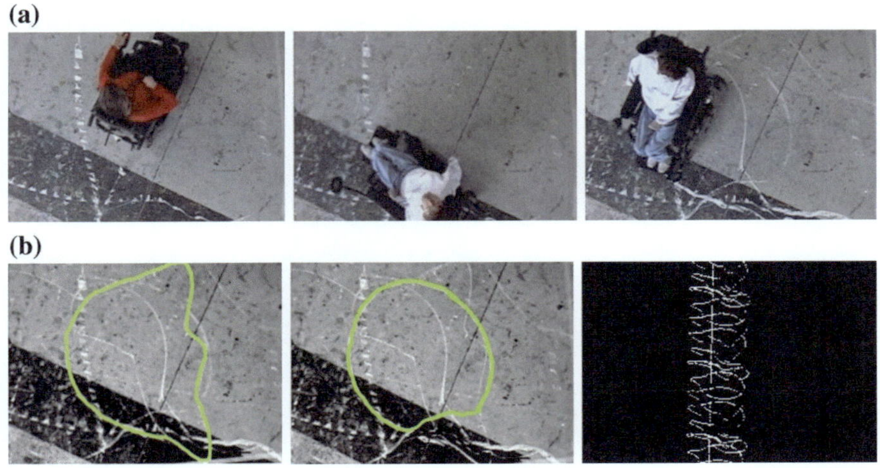

Fig. 5.9 **a** The 'action painting' sketch used paint rollers attached to artists wheelchairs. **b** Curves were extracted from these paintings (*green lines*) to extrapolate three dimensional geometry

example, McKenzie et al. 2003). This is illustrated in the bottom row of Fig. 5.9. The significance of this effort lay in the process that it hinted at: the idea of 'drawing into drawings.' This reframed my understanding of the project because it offered a means for conversing and collaborating with each other. A meaningful exchange and creative artefacts could potentially result from our shared drawing process.

Shared Drawing As I saw the ArTel artists continue working on their personal compositions I realised the value of the pencil and brush. This, combined with the new shared drawing approach, informed another implementation of this process. I asked my collaborators to draw or paint circles so I could explore a subsequent creative contribution to them. After some exploration of what this might be, I decided to layer a selection of each participant's curves to create a new image. I printed these compositions and returned them to each artist. They then acted on them themselves. In this way we passed the drawings between each other.

This process of shared, collaborative creation of a drawing is not new. In the early 1900s Surrealist artists, most likely Andre Breton, introduced the *Exquisite Corpse*. In this drawing 'game' an artist would start by drawing the head of a figure then fold the page to hide their drawing before passing it to the next person, who would draw a subsequent part (e.g. torso), folding it over and passing that along, and so on. The process would continue and each person would contribute something in sequence, while unaware of what came before. Eventually the paper would be unfolded to reveal a composition of a figure—part man, woman, animal perhaps, but definitely surprising and new to all.

The collaborative drawing process here is similar. A new composition is created here too, from interaction between myself and the community artists as we pass the drawing between each other. While we can see what the other has done, we cannot control it. This shared drawing process became embodied in these graphic forms. As a result, our creative efforts became distributed across these objects as well as all of us. Some of the imagery created through this iterative drawing process is pictured in Fig. 5.10.

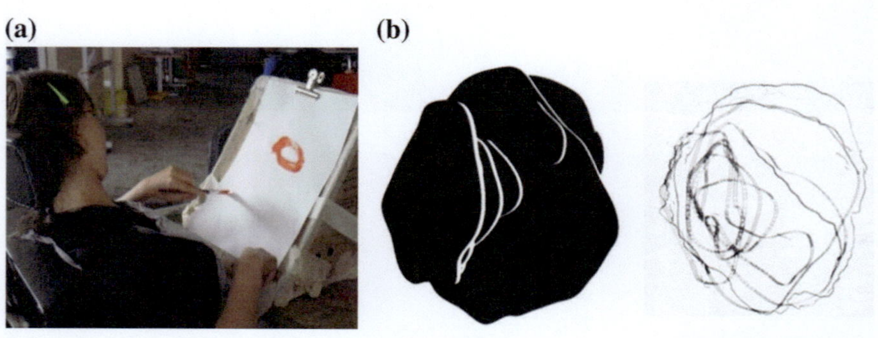

Fig. 5.10 **a** Artist Elizabeth Saunders paints an initial figure for the iterative drawing process shared with Jen Seevinck. **b** Final drawings created through this collaborative process (Reproduced from Seevinck 2013b)

This type of 'conversational' interaction would, eventually, go on to inform the interactive experience and form of the final digital artwork.

What if my every movement required monumental effort? How would I be creative? This process of collaborating was not, however, without its flaws. For one thing, each person's effort to draw into the work would take time and waiting, which started to lead to disengagement. Collaborator and artist Robert Oakman expressed his extreme distaste for the waiting—waiting for carers to assist him generally as well as waiting for help in working creatively at ArTel. The printing process itself is extensive, and the ArTel community artists often required carers to assist the production through the many stages from drawing through to final ink. Artists including Robert would be waiting for them to trace his drawing, carve it out of acrylic sheet, or see how his choice of colour would look on paper, once a carer had put it through the press. I started to see the extensive impact of the physical disability on the creative experience in other ways: I noticed how much concentration, strength and at times tenacity would be required to make a mark in the first place. Cerebral palsy is a physical disability that can lead to difficulties in speech, movement and posture (CerebralPalsyLeague 2011). Avoiding involuntary movement as well as making the movement in the first place are significant efforts; creative sessions often only last an hour or so at a time, and compositions themselves will take months to complete. Facilitating more opportunities for creative activity and creative feedback became an important moral as well as aesthetic driver.

Perceptual from Physical Emergence: Mapping Across the TEIA

An answer came from a physical model for emergence, the Koch curve. In this iterative mathematical function—a fractal—an original line is broken into even sections as well as copied and scaled. The scaled copy then replaces each segment and the process repeats, or *iterates*. A complex outcome is generated. In this project this is used as an approach to guide the treatment of the collaborating artists' gesture to make a line. Here the participant's line is sampled and this becomes an element for recursively copying it. As shown at left in Fig. 5.11, a participating artist's curve can be sampled, scaled, and divided into sections, and each of those sections can then be replaced with the scaled version. The original mark remains, though it has been manipulated into a new composition. An illustration of how this approach renders in the final interactive artwork *Of me With me* (2014) is shown at right in Fig. 5.11. Here the artist's gesture is in black with the fractal 'echoes' in a lighter tone.

The image generated in this way can be considered both physical emergence and perceptual emergence. It is an unanticipated new form that has appeared from the initial mark made by the artist, but which was not directly implied or predictable

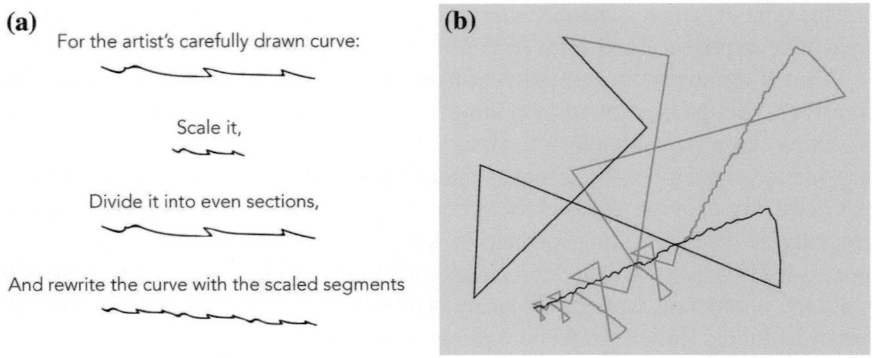

Fig. 5.11 The self-replicating quality of the Koch fractal informed the visualization process in *Of me With me* (2014b). **a** A visual explanation of the software, **b** a single still image created by a participant. Here the *black line* is the participant gesture while the *grey lines* are the scaled echoes

from that first mark. For instance, the image at right (Fig. 5.11) has visual structure, a sense of being a whole that is more than a simple sum or grouping of the different parts that make it up. This is because each copy of the original artists mark is rotated according to the original mark, but also in a way that relates to all the other marks. Similarly the scaling and transforming of all these copied marks is neither meaningless nor independent of one-another. Their interaction is informed by rules —those of the software instructions.

This design approach draws upon the TEIA. It utilises understanding and models for emergence from one domain (mathematics and computer sciences) and uses this to generate emergence perceptually, in the eye of the observer, the predominant understanding of emergence in design research. The approach demonstrates a capacity to map from the one side of the TEIA to the other, moving from the physical sciences understanding of emergence and model of the fractal to effect perceptual emergence and creative experience in the artwork participant.

The approach taken here retains the artist's mark, yet generates a new image or composition. It amplifies the artist's voice. As an approach, it stems from theoretical enquiry into emergence. It has also, however, developed from my practice. That is, the iterative exchange of drawings as discussed above as well as sketching procedurally and interactive prototyping, as shown next, have informed this work.

Design and Construction

The above conceptual and theoretical explorations ran in parallel with software development explorations. In 2013, a prototype interactive system was created (Seevinck 2013b). Here one begins by drawing a curve and then selecting a zone for generating the echoes from that curve. The selection is made by moving a square selection zone around the screen. Copies of line segments inside the cube selection zone are rendered off to the side, in real-time, and by moving the volume, different possible forms can be viewed. The process involves editing, or curating, one's curve in addition to drawing it (Fig. 5.12 and Seevinck (2015a, Fig. 7)). While promising, this prototype had some concerns, including the then cost of the proprietary Derivative software used and the hardware it necessitates. The final installation (e.g. see Figs. 5.8 and 5.13) was developed using the free and open source API, Processing (Fry and Raes 2001 see also: https://processing.org). As a two-dimensional graphics implementation it has a lower demand for computer rendering power, making it much more suitable for the community arts and disability sectors who typically have limited financial resources.

The software works to track the stylus position and populate an array with positions for X and Y coordinates of the stylus, in real time. These positions inform a line for rendering on the screen. As the participant drags the stylus across the surface, subsequent positions are sampled and added on to the array. That is, the generated line includes these new positions as well. The length of this line is, in part, determined by the length of the array, itself a factor of hardware capability.

The implementation involves copying the array itself as well, in order to translate, scale and rotate the recurring, smaller curves, or 'echoes'. These transformations occur in object space before the copies are returned to world space and rendered back alongside the original mark. Translation destinations are calculated by sampling from the source curve (breaking it into a predetermined set of span

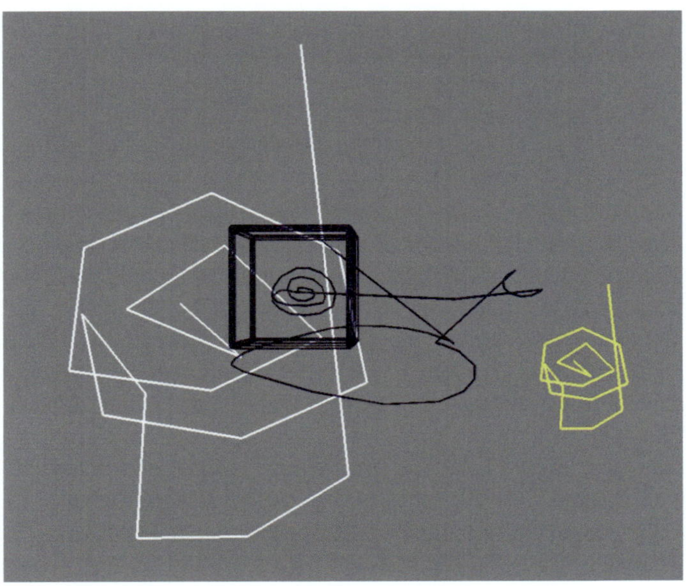

Fig. 5.12 In early work for the *Iterative Intersectioning* interactive art prototype (Seevinck 2013b), a participant's curve (*black line*) can be curated by moving a cube volume across it to generate scaled copies (*white and yellow*)

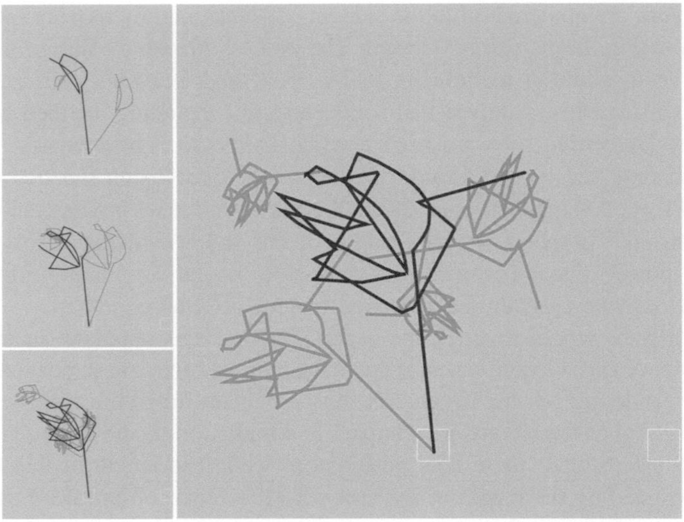

Fig. 5.13 The *Of me With me* (Seevinck 2014b) system runs in real-time so that the iterating curves, including their position, size and rotational values are continually changing. A participant's directly drawn lines (*black*) and the 'echoing' fractal imagery of system (*grey lines*) are simultaneously rendered

lengths). The result is that there are several versions, or copies, of a participants line created at once; and these lines include past positions of the stylus as well since prior XY coordinates have been stored in the array.

Experiencing the Work

In the final work, participants draw with the stylus and the positional, angle and speed of gestural movement data of the stylus informs the on-screen visualization.

The interaction in the final work, *Of me With me,* is 'flatter' than in the preceding interactive sketch. Here all aspects of the drawing are visualised immediately and there is no selection or curation involved. This facilitates simpler use, but it is also a meaningful difference as the new system affords an uninterrupted 'flow' of experience.

That is, the immediacy of this feedback promotes an uninterrupted and sustained participant experience. While the cost of this is the loss of 'curating' or 'exploring' one's past gestures and curves, the benefit is immediate play with your line and an intricate, patterned mirror of your gestures. That is, this new work is more focused on the drawing experience rather than a final image that may be created. While the interface also includes two metal buttons for resetting and saving images, it is not necessary to use these to interact meaningfully with the work. The intended emphasis of this work has been on the experience of drawing.

Its useful to note that the speed and direction of the participant's gesture directly affects their image and experience. That is, moving slowly with the stylus will generate a dense, closely packed grouping of visual echoes, since the points stored in the array are temporally sampled at a constant rate, but the stylus is only travelling a small distance. On the other hand, moving quickly with the stylus will populate the echoes widely across the screen. In terms of the participant's experience it means that there is much more than the final outcome being sampled in this gesture analysis: *speed* and *direction of movement* also contribute to the experience and the rendered composition as a whole.

The approach taken here has meant that the 'voice' of the artist, their unique mark and expression, is a significant part of the final image. In many ways the work amplifies the 'voice' of the artwork participants and project collaborators—my fellow artists at ArTel. It also has the potential to reveal something to them about the more intangible aspects of how they draw, the movement behind their gesture. The work facilitates understanding to emerge for the participant, and the nature of that insight is left to the participant.

Distributed Creativity

The iterative drawing body of work and interactive art system *Of me With me* seeks to amplify the creativity of participants while stemming from a conceptual process that emphasizes dialogue and employs emergence. The collaboration is a creative conversation between community artists at ArTel, the art studio run through Cerebral Palsy League non-profit organisation, and myself, an electronic artist. The conversation and collaboration was creative in the exchange of ideas and drawings between each other. Moreover, as we would take turns to act on those drawings or artefacts, the creative effort became *distributed* across those artefacts and ourselves. As with 'distributed cognition' where, for example, it is not just the pilot that lands a plane safely, rather the co-pilot, air control tower and guidance instruments all playing a role (Benyon 2010), here the creative effort can similarly be considered as distributed across all of these agents. Put another way, as our process and conversation became embodied in these graphic forms, the creative process came to exist across both the people doing the shared drawing and the drawings themselves.

I would characterise *Of me With me* in the same way, as similarly distributing the creative experience across art work, participant, and any images that the participant may have been saved. This is due to the nature of that work in facilitating co-drawing. It is also based on the concept development that informed it—the preceding co-creation of drawings that first pointed towards a distributed creative experience for us project collaborators. In this work I would therefore consider the creativity to be distributed across participant and interactive art system *Of me With me* in the same way as it was distributed across myself, my iterative drawing collaborators, and those print-based works themselves (Figs. 5.9 and 5.10).

Lightworks (2015–16)

The last case study is a part of the *Lightworks* series of art systems. This is a body of work concerned with using light in a 'painterly way', as a direct means of creating the imagery. That is, rather than being generated in a computer and projected, imagery results from the direct physical manipulation of light from a light source (using reflections and transmissions). This focus on the concrete, material aspects of the work (here, light) is consistent with a Constructivist approach to art-making. The two artworks that constitute this *Lightworks* body of work both share this aesthetic. In terms of interactive behaviour they are both also much more *influencing* than *responsive* works, as was the case in the last two case studies.

Light Currents (2015)

Light Currents (2015b) is the first art work in the *Lightworks* series. It is an architectural installation and site-specific, ambient work for a heritage-listed building on the Brisbane River in Australia. This building previously generated the city's power and is now a theatre for international performing artists.

Light Currents comprises a horizontal aluminium frame with an internal stainless steel wire web. This web suspends dichroic glass triangles, at angles, throughout. Dichroic glass is mineral coated glass that has been baked in a vacuum chamber. It is so called because it reflects one colour (e.g. blue) and transmits another (e.g. orange). The glass pieces are threaded into the steel wire web with white plastic fixtures, designed and printed for this purpose. The wires are agitated by servo motors in response to people's presence, and to changes in the weather outside. A bright theatre light above the work facilitates light reflections and transmission with the moving glass pieces. As people enter the space and the wind on the river changes, these light images shimmer and move gently.

Concept, Construction and Behaviour The concept and form of this artwork are driven by a juxtaposition of movement. Currents and tides on the Brisbane River are, in many ways, evocative of the tidal movement of theatre audiences coming and going from performances. This characterisation of the place was both at a landscape level and immediate to the building. It informed decisions about data sensing requirements. It also informed the visual form of the work. This was to look at the behaviour of light on the water, something that I had worked with previously but wanted to explore some more.

After exploring the concept as well as materials, I settled on theatre lighting and the dichroic glass to best create bright colour and light in this space (which received both daylight and artificial lighting). Data and behaviour were to combine sensing the presence of people close to the work (through a Passive Infrared (PIR) sensor) with changes in wind speed on the Brisbane River (through weather updates sent via the internet). Further exploration and testing resulted in continuous lengths of stainless steel wire rope, tautly spun, to suspend the glass. Servo motors were also wired into this steel 'web'. In the final work, sensor data would direct the servo motors back and forth rapidly to send small movement pulses along the wire, thereby generating vibrations and small movement in the glass. In this way I was able to create the desired shimmering reflections.

One servo was used for the PIR data (for people, or participants, in the space) and the other servo was used for responses to changes in the weather, as detected with internet data updates. Both are wired to the entire artwork's wire web since the vibrations will travel the length of the wire. However, each tends to be more apparent in its immediate vicinity so that PIR movement affects the centre left of the reflected imagery and wind speed affects centre right. The system data inputs and outputs were controlled using python code running on a Raspberry Pi microcomputer. In essence, it is a physical system that provided constrained turbulent, organic movement in the reflected light, initiated by the servo motors and their sensor input (see Fig. 5.14)

In *Light Currents,* concept, material and implementation combine with sensed data to facilitate a site-specific response that embodies an understanding of that place. Put another way, the use of highly intense and pure light and colour provides engaging visual form for the audience, an attractor. In bringing together the local wind data and the audience's immediate personal presence with the visually poetic reminder of the 'dance' of light on the water, the audience is able to interpret connections between the outside and self, or between data and self. In so doing, the work seeks to facilitate an emotional connection to the work and to nature.

Dichroic Wade (2016)

Dichroic Wade (2016a) is the second artwork created in this *Lightworks* series of works. As with *Light Currents*, it responds to human presence and site-specific weather data through sensors and wireless data updates that trigger servo motors to agitate suspended dichroic glass pieces. It is also an ambient media installation, or form of 'media architecture'. *Light Currents* started me thinking about the layering of data and physical place and what this might mean for visual form, *Dichroic Wade* continues this enquiry into the hybrid space (data-physical) we increasingly occupy. However there are other, including significant formal differences between the works as well. *Dichroic Wade* is distinctive in terms of form, transparency and behaviour.

Firstly, in terms of form, the suspended arrangement is vertical rather than horizontal. Here glass pieces are combined into modules consisting of four tiles. Four columns of modules hang side by side in the work. Two lights and three servo motors are positioned above the columns. The top of each column is connected to a servo motor. A wall-mounted plinth contains the motors, lighting and sensing components as well as a timber scaffold from which the glass pieces are suspended. The presentation is also much 'lighter', visually. Lasercut acrylic triangles, vinyl

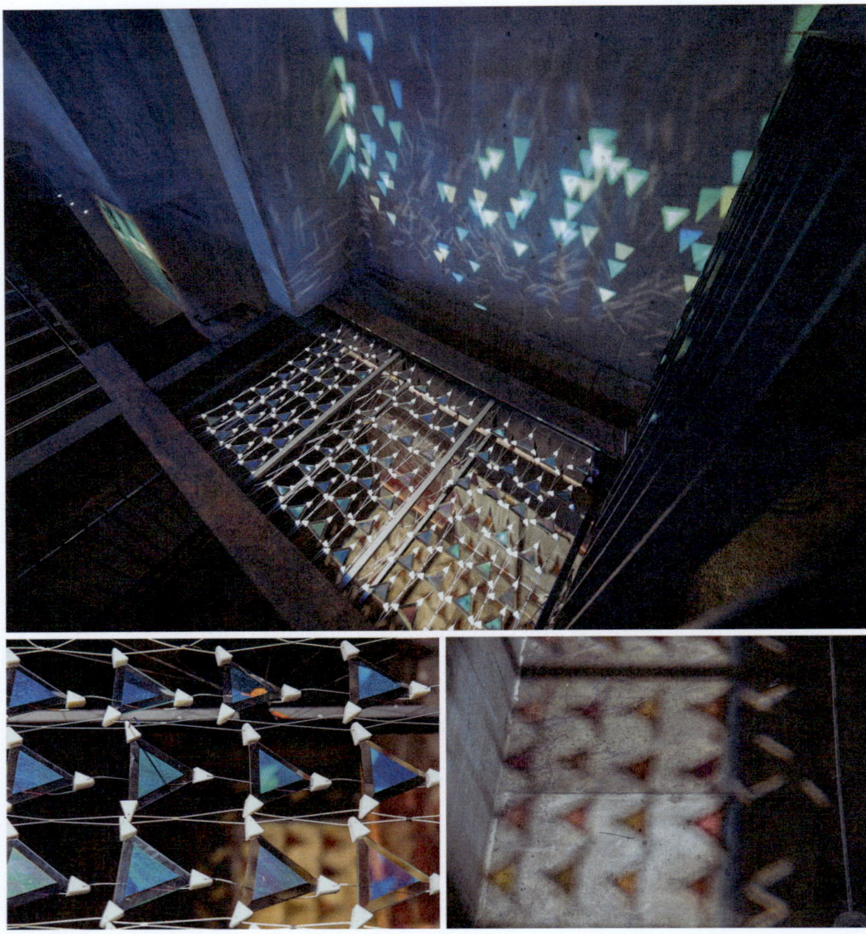

Fig. 5.14 *Light Currents* (Seevinck 2015b) installed at the Brisbane Powerhouse Theatre. The movement of theatre goers and wind on the river drive servo motors to vibrate a steel wire web suspending dichroic glass tiles. Photos by Anthony Hearsey 2015, used with permission from the copyright holder

line and tubing are used to connect the glass triangles to each other and the servo motors in lieu of the steel wire and white plastic connectors. The result is a kaleidoscope of coloured light on the walls, floor and ceiling (Fig. 5.15).

A prototype version of *Dichroic Wade* was installed at the Asia Pacific Design Library on the Brisbane River in March 2016 for evaluation studies. The study findings, discussed in the next chapter, reframed the concept, and the work was changed. The final piece *Dichroic Wade* was exhibited in the Art.CHI 2016 exhibition in San Jose, USA in May 2016. At this time the work also received an Honorary Mention award from the ACM CHI conference committee (Seevinck 2016b).

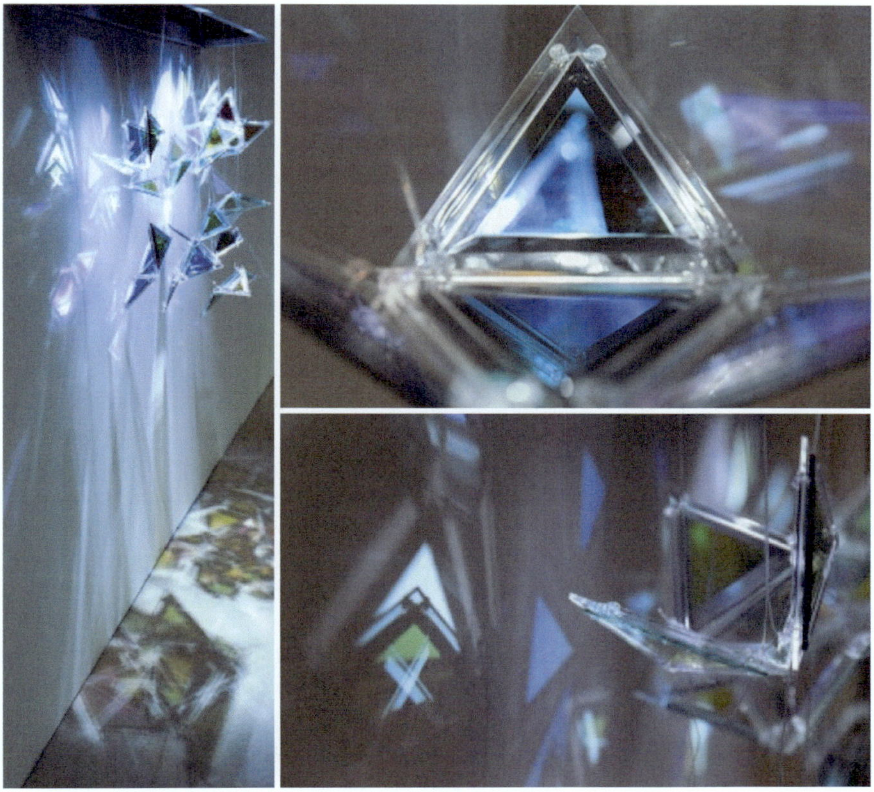

Fig. 5.15 *Dichroic Wade* (Seevinck 2016a). Dichroic glass transmits one colour and reflects another. Photos by Anthony Hearsey 2016. Used with permission from the copyright holder, reproduced from (Seevinck 2016b)

Hybrid Space and Interaction

The concept in this work iterated with theoretical enquiry and evaluation feedback from the prototype study. That is, while the work was initially concerned with a layering of two physical spaces—the wind and river outside with the people inside—this changed to include broader questions of data visualisation and hybrid space while I was in the process of framing the work for San Jose and the San Francisco bay area where CHI would be hosted. *Dichroic Wade* became a way of looking towards new ways of understanding the information space that we inhabit in a way that is more meaningful than a 'personal hotspot', or other wireless internet connection. The artwork both responds to you physically and is influenced by the ambient data networks (here transmitting weather information from outside) that surround us continually. It aims to ask us to go beyond utility and rather engage visually, experientially and aesthetically to connect data meaningfully to the real world. The treatment of light and colour that is directly physical or concrete, as it is in *Light Currents,* is one aspect of the work that reminds us of our bodies. The light is also dynamic and organic in its behaviour, further enhancing the immediate physical experience of the work (and data it conveys). That is, the different sources of data and intersecting patterns of colour and light may suggest visual forms and behaviours to the viewer, and in interpreting these emergent patterns and meanings the work can sustain interest. It may be that by engaging creatively with the plethora of data and our surroundings we can work towards meaningful experiences. The project is an opportunity to immerse oneself in data that is typically present in the background, but which has been brought forward here into one's physical surroundings and given distinctive visual form.

Evolution of Design and Construction The wall plinth contains all electronic and powered components: servomotors to vibrate the columns of glass tile below, a motion sensor for audience presence at the installed artwork, a Raspberry Pi2 microcomputer with wireless internet, and bespoke LED lamps. Python is used with the Raspberry Pi to interpret incoming internet weather data and control the movements in the servo motors when that motion is sensed. Custom alternative lighting had to be developed to facilitate something similar to the brightness of the theatre lighting used previously but at lower cost and with more portability. High-intensity CREE LED technology was sourced and I combined these with narrow beam collimating lenses to focus the light. The focused beam that resulted approaches the intensity of daylight, facilitating bright colour from the work despite ambient lighting conditions.

Sensing was the biggest technical difference between prototype and final installation. In the prototype system a PIR sensor would inform the movement of servo 1 (left). Weather changes would trigger servos 2 and 3 (centre and right). Since each servo acted only on those glass units close by, this meant that only the left side of the work would respond to participants in the space while the centre and right glass pieces would always only visualise the weather. These servos would agitate the columns of glass continuously. The amplitude of servo agitation is proportional to the wind conditions reported by the Australian Bureau of Meteorology and updated every couple of seconds. In the final work, weather data from a local weather station at the San Jose University was sourced. This would drive servos at each end of the work, or, if no participants were sensed, all three servos would behave corresponding to the wind conditions outside. The prototype sensed people's presence but evaluation feedback showed some problems with participants understanding that the work would respond to them. These findings informed a reconsideration of the design to change the sensor technology used. An ultrasonic depth sensor replaced the PIR sensor in *Dichroic Wade* to facilitate more information about movement in the environment. The artwork's behaviour was also changed for a more differentiated experience.

Evolution of the System Behaviour and Interaction Experience In the prototype version the quality of participant movement was highly variable: the PIR sensor would be activated by any detection of movement. This, combined with the turbulence of the weather data and the pendulum movement that typically ran through the system, affected participant understanding of the responsiveness of the work, as is explained from the evaluation findings in the next chapter. Those evaluation findings from the prototype installation and study informed the subsequent changes to the work.

The most significant change subsequent to evaluation findings was to replace the PIR with the ultrasonic depth sensor. This was intended to facilitate a more differentiated and responsive interaction for the participant, as follows. Triggering at various distance thresholds, this new configuration could respond to a person's approach to the work, i.e. rotation angle and frequency would change in proportion to participant distance to the work. Getting closer would increase the turbulence of the columns and their pendulum movement. The light reflections and transmissions also increases with one's approach, creating a sense of 'wading' into the work. After an approach and when standing directly in front of the work, choreographed behaviour was also triggered. In this 'crescendo' behaviour all the columns of glass would increasingly agitate over a few seconds. They would then stop altogether, and just the natural pendulum movement would continue as the physical system came to rest. These added behaviours are intended to balance the open-ended character of the work. They were also implemented in response to the evaluation findings from the prototype study discussed in Chap. 6.

Both *Dichroic Wade* and *Light Currents* combine input (data) from the outside world with participant sensing. In both cases, particularly the recent work, there is also some inherent turbulence or harmonics in the transmission of motion waves through the physical system itself: steel wires vibrate while pendulums swing to become turbulent or settle into harmonics. With all of these influences on behaviour, this body of work is much more open-ended and unpredictable than the other two case studies. These works also facilitate a different relationship between participant and artwork than the previous works did: here this is much more influencing than directly responsive, though *Dichroic Wade* does facilitate some immediate action response (through its implementation of the depth sensor) in addition to its ambient visualisation of weather conditions. These art systems are explorations into physical complex systems to see what opportunities might exist for emergent experiences and influencing participant interactions.

Direct Lighting The reflections of light from the triangular glass tiles facilitate an effect similar to that of light reflecting from the surface of water currents. There is, therefore, a distinct relationship between the external data source rendered here and the choice of material to facilitate this visualisation. The *Lightworks* body of work also explores direct lighting to create imagery. That is, rather than relying on computer graphics for dynamic visual imagery, here colour, line, shade and movement are created with physical, concrete elements and the light, directly. The coloured lights seen here are the result of light reflected and transmitted from the glass tiles, similar to the coloured light produced when the sun reflects light off the same glass tiles or passes through them. In contrast, video projectors position a range of other objects between the light source and the final image that we see. For example, in an LCD projector a line of dichroic mirrors channel the incoming light to reflect each of red, green and blue beams, which are then moderated through computer controlled LCD screens before being recombined by a dichroic prism and finally focused with the projection lens. In each of these steps the light is transmitted, reflected and absorbed, resulting in loss of light intensity and ambient spill. The 'black' in projected imagery attests to this ambient spill. Here the use of dichroic glass in combination with high lumen light sources (theatre lighting or, as in *Dichroic Wade*, CREE LED lamps) does however facilitate extremely bright, high contrast imagery with very pure colour. The reflected light and colour these can produce is comparable to that of daylight shining on the glass. In environments with ambient lighting this combination of dichroic glass and LED provides an opportunity to literally 'paint' light in a way that provides a much brighter and stronger visual outcome than projected light sources, such as LED projector technology, are currently able to provide.

The concern with light on the water is not new. Sparkling light on moving water currents informed earlier work *+−now* (Seevinck 2008). Here, however, these concerns have also informed the choice of physical materials and technology—glass and lighting technology—as well as the form of the work. In summary, the light reflections in this body of work are driven by a contemporary aesthetic enquiry considering light as a material and concrete element. Like the painter understands their paint and canvas, here the focus is on exploring and understanding the essential nature of light; it is treated as a real, concrete element to be explored and manipulated.

Conclusion

The three case studies discussed here have been created over about 10 years. They range in interface and technology, from tangible computing and augmented reality through to concerns with data visualisation and to use of microcomputers. They range in their means of image generation as well as abstraction, from procedural graphics using computers and projectors to create images, through to physical computing and materials to manipulate light directly and concretely, showing increased concern with those concrete elements of art rather than representational imagery. All three have conceptual structures to inform the art outcomes, where starting points such as landscape or collaboration evolve through practice and iterative reframing to drive the final work.

The concept of emergence features throughout this process of making, reframing, and thinking. In *+−now* (2008), an initial desire for facilitating aesthetic experience that is like nature in terms of being deep, wide, open and rich in its variety, led to the concept of emergence. That work and accompanying research helped inform the TEIA framework, presented in Chap. 2. Emergence has informed my creative enquiry ever since. The next case study artwork, *Of me With me* (2014), is a response to questions that came about through a creative collaboration with community artists who happen to have cerebral palsy. The conceptual agenda that evolved from that project directed the work towards explorations of drawing gesture and creative experience. This agenda, combined with an exploration of the TEIA and a means to amplify the artist's mark through creative experience of drawing, was generated using physical emergence modelling. Finally, the *Lightworks* art systems began with a concern for place which developed into a concern for hybrid place. Input and data from the world beyond the participant expand the sphere of these works. The physical properties of materials—from the vibration of steel wire through a web to the chaotic movement of a pendulum—further increased the complex behaviour of the work. Very open-ended systems resulted. In this last body of work the relationship between the work and the participant is also much more *influencing* than *responsive*. Complexity and openness can facilitate emergence, and the evaluation of the *Dichroic Wade* prototype (Chap. 6) discusses occurrences of perceptual emergence, namely where people were making meaning when interpreting the combined data visualisation of weather and personal interaction.

The next chapter reports on evaluations for each of these case studies. As shown, a range of different types of emergence as listed in the TEIA have been found.

References

Azuma R, Baillot Y, Behringer R et al (2001) Recent advances in augmented reality. IEEE Comput Graph Appl 21:34

Beaudouin-Lafon M, Mackay W (2003) Prototyping tools and techniques. In: Jacko JA, Sears A (eds) The human computer interaction handbook fundamentals, evolving technologies and emerging applications. Lawrence Earlbaum Associates Inc, New Jersey, pp 1007–1031

Benyon D (2010) Designing interactive systems: a comprehensive guide to HCI and interaction design, 2 edn. Pearson Education Canada

Boehm BW (1986) A spiral model of software development and enhancement. IEEE Comput 1988 (11):22–42

Candy L, Edmonds EA (2010) The role of the artefact and frameworks for practice-based research. In: Biggs M, Larsson H (eds) The Routledge companion to research in the arts. Routledge, New York, USA, pp 120–136

CerebralPalsyLeague (2011) CPL Corporate Brochure

Edmonds EA, Candy L (2010) Relating theory, practice and evaluation in practitioner research, vol 43. The MIT Press, Leonardo, pp 470–476

Edmonds EA, Muller L, Connell M (2006) On creative engagement. Visual Commun 5:307–322

Fry B, Raes C (2001) Processing. Aesthetics and Computation Research group at MIT Media Lab

Heidegger M (1978) Being and time. Blackwell Publishing

Hermanovic G, Bairos R (2000) Touch designer. Derivative Inc., Toronto, Canada. https://www.derivative.ca

Ishii H, Ullmer B (1997) Tangible bits: towards seamless interfaces between people, bits and atoms. In: Procedings SIGCHI human factors. ACM Press, Atlanta, Georgia, United States, pp 234–241

Ishii H, Lakatos vid, Bonanni L, Labrune J-B (2012) Radical atoms: beyond tangible bits, toward transformable materials. Interactions 19:38–51. doi:10.1145/2065327.2065337

McKenzie F, Hussein R, Seevinck J, et al (2003) Prostate gland and extra-capsular tissue 3D reconstruction and measurement. In: BIBE '03 Proceedings of the 3rd IEEE symposium on bioinformatics and bioengineering. IEEE, Washington, DC, USA, pp 246–252

Norman DA (2002) The design of everyday things. Basic Books, New York, USA
Schön DA (1983) The reflective practitioner how professionals think in action, 1995th edn. Temple Smith, London, England
Scrivener SAR (2002a) Characterising creative-production doctoral projects in art and design. Int J Des Sci Technol 10:25
Scrivener SAR (2002b) The art object does not embody a form of knowledge. In: Working papers in art and design, vol 2. Working Papers in Art and Design 2: Working Papers in Art and Design
Seevinck J (2008) +−now, interactive artwork
Seevinck J (2010) Tracing moments, vol 43. The MIT Press, Leonardo, pp 312–313. doi:10.1162/LEON.2010.43.3.312
Seevinck J (2013a) Concepts, water and reflections on practice, vol 46. The MIT Press, Leonardo, pp 494–495. doi:10.1162/LEON_a_00652
Seevinck J (2013b) Iterative Intersections. In: Do EY-L, Dow S, Ox J, et al (eds) Proceedings of the 9th ACM conference on creativity and cognition. ACM Press, Sydney, Australia, pp 425–426 doi:10.1145/2466627.2481237
Seevinck J (2014a) Emergence and artistic visualisation. In: Nguyen QV, Wu Y, Bednarz T, Huang T (eds) Proceedings of the 7th international symposium on visual information communication and interaction (VINCI 2014). ACM Press, pp 165–170
Seevinck J (2014b) Of me With me, interactive artwork
Seevinck J (2015a) Emergence in interactive artistic visualization. Int J Softw Eng Knowl Eng (IJSEKE) 25:201–230. doi:10.1142/S0218194015007555
Seevinck J (2015b) Light Currents, interactive art installation
Seevinck J (2016a) Dichroic Wade, interactive art installation
Seevinck J (2016b) Dichroic Wade. In: CHI EA '16 Proceedings of the 2016 CHI conference extended abstracts on human factors in computing systems. ACM Press, New York, NY, USA, San Jose, USA, pp 3889–3892 doi:10.1145/2851581.2891094
Seevinck J, Edmonds E (2009) Open in art, nature and emergence. ACM Press, Melbourne Australia, pp 365–368. doi:10.1145/1738826.1738898
Seevinck J, Candy L, Edmonds E (2006) Exploration and reflection in interactive art: glass pond. ACM Press, Sydney, Australia, pp 143–150. doi:10.1145/1228175.1228202
Wells HG (1911) Floor games. E-Book available through Project Gutenberg. http://www.gutenberg.org/ebooks/3690

Chapter 6
How the Work, Works

Abstract This chapter presents evaluations of three case study interactive art works, described in the previous chapter. The evaluations are focused on participant experiences of emergence: that is, *perceptual* emergence. Perceptual emergence was defined in Chap. 2 and classified in the TEIA, but when it comes to people interacting with an artwork, *how would we recognise it if it occurred?* And *what would an emergent experience would be like?* The studies discussed here demonstrate how evaluation and qualitative research methods, including the TEIA and specially created emergence coding tools, can be used to detect emergent participant experiences. A number of data samples are also presented, providing insight into participant experiences of emergence. Characteristics include open-endedness, with '*infinite variation, like looking at the stars*', depth, like a '*story within a story*' and creativity, as in the drawing experiences with *Of me With me* (Seevinck, 2014). The evaluation findings illustrate three of the four types of perceptual emergence from the TEIA: referenced extrinsic, referenced intrinsic and concrete intrinsic perceptual emergence. Other, non-emergent behaviours were also found, such as the generic ways in which people engage with interactive art. Identifying emergent and non-emergent behaviours alike can scope out some dimensions for participant experience of interactive art, pointing us towards new ways of understanding this area.

Approach and Methods

Systematic investigation into participant interaction with four art systems was conducted: *Glass Pond* (2005), *+−now* (2008a), *Of me With me* (2014) and a prototype version of *Dichroic Wade* (2016). These were in the form of evaluations that draw on qualitative social science methods, but within a Constructivist epistemology. That is, knowledge is understood as being partially constructed by us throughout understanding and interpretations of the world. Our cognitive faculties play *"some role in "making" the objects or facts in the area in question"* (Sidelle 1996). A Constructivist approach resonates with the research (and creative practice)

J. Seevinck, *Emergence in Interactive Art*, Springer Series on Cultural Computing,
DOI 10.1007/978-3-319-45201-2_6

conducted here, since these are concerned with participant experience and perceptual emergence, both of which are subjectively interpreted qualities.

Along the same lines we can understand experience as something which people construct in context. As such, and given the inherent complexity of this type of experience, field studies were considered most appropriate (Preece et al. 1994). The naturalistic settings of artist studios, galleries, museums and a design library were therefore used for the evaluation.

The nature of emergence also informs the evaluation research design. Firstly, emergence is a surprising quality, and secondly, some types of emergence are perceptual and hence subjectively interpreted (as articulated in Chap. 2 and classified in the TEIA). Instances of emergent experience should be volunteered by participants and described in their own words. Thus the best type of data is verbal accounts of participant experience accompanied by a visual record. An open-ended, exploratory approach is also helpful as emergent experience is largely unknown. Exploratory studies support the generation of understanding and rapidly scoping out a research area. Two exploratory studies were used in the *Traces* body of work.

Non-intrusive data collection methods were employed throughout, as is also consistent with the emphasis on facilitating an experience of the artwork. These included video recording of participant interaction with the work, and discussions with the participants afterwards to prompt them for their opinions or experiences during interaction. The exact methods and data vary across the cases, and are detailed in each section. In all cases the evidence collected includes audio and video recordings.

The approaches to data analysis vary, moving from anemphasis on inducting concepts from the data as in Grounded Theory methods to a more theory-driven approach as in thematic analysis, in which an understanding of that theory directs the research. Specifically, Grounded Theory methods (e.g. Glaser and Strauss 1967; Strauss and Corbin 1998) were used for the first two investigations to generate an understanding of participant experience of emergence. Grounded Theory methodology is a 'bottom up' approach, aiming to 'discover' theory directly from the data (Glaser and Strauss 1967). The Grounded Theory methods used here include memo writing, open coding, and consulting external literature and research. This external literature concerned emergence and interactive art, but its inclusion followed an initial data-driven activity of reviewing data, so as to avoid 'tainting' my interpretation of it.

Thematic analysis, a more generic yet also theoretical approach to analysis, was used in the evaluations for Cases 2 and 3 (Richards 2006; Braun and Clarke 2008). While codes and categories were still induced from the data similar to the approach taken in applying Grounded Theory methods, these investigations were much more focused on identifying aspects of emergence. Enquiry was guided by the TEIA, along with the mapping and emergent criteria coding schemes that came out of prior Grounded Theory analysis efforts. Here the analysis is 'sensitised' to the *"theoretical or analytic interest"* rather than being 'bottom up' driven by concepts in the data. My approach also follows Braun and Clarke to focus on potential instances of emergence through *"this form of thematic analysis (which) tends to provide less a rich description of the data overall (as is similar to Grounded Theory), and more a detailed analysis of some aspect of the data"* (Braun and Clarke 2008).

Evaluation for +−*now* (2008a) and *Glass Pond* (2005)

The interactive art system +−*now* and its preceding interactive sketch *Glass Pond* were both evaluated. Findings from the first, exploratory study of *Glass Pond* resonated with characteristics of emergence, and in effect pointed to the concept of emergence for further practice and research. It also informed +−*now*, itself evaluated through both an exploratory study and a main study. The PBR approach around these two artworks therefore involved a total of three studies, and findings from the studies would inform the practice. While all three studies are discussed here, the primary focus of this section is the third, main study, +−*now*. However, the findings from *Glass Pond*, along with its role in the practice-based research cycle, make it worth brief discussion.

Emergence and the *Glass Pond* Study *Glass Pond* was an early interactive art sketch evaluated in an exploratory study in an arts studio. The evaluation aimed to rapidly scope out an understanding of participant experience and, as is consistent with its conceptual structure, find out if any reflective and exploratory behaviours and experiences occurred during interaction with the work. The study protocols and data analysis have previously been reported (Seevinck et al. 2006). Findings confirmed that these behaviours and experiences occurred, but there were other outcomes as well. These reframed the concept behind the work to focus on emergence. Key outcomes included discovering that some participants would compose interactively with the artwork and come up with goals during their interaction (emergent goals). Many also said they had inadequate control of aspects of the imagery. The sense of participant control became an issue because unsatisfying experiences could lead to disengagement from the work. From an artist's perspective, however, I also did not want to the interaction with the work to be like that of an instrument or tool. Exploring the notion of control (and lack thereof) was eventually found to be possible through the emergence framework. This allowed me to reframe it in terms of unpredictability, a characteristic of emergence. I also facilitated feedback for participants in the subsequent work, +−*now*, by drawing upon interface design strategies (see for example the *Golden Rules* in Shneiderman et al. 2010). In all, there were three findings from this study that are core to this project: emerging participant intentions, composing behaviours, and sense of control. All three aspects coincide with the concept of emergence, which would go on to inform the conceptual structure. The creative practice became concerned with creating emergent experiences of interactive art systems. The interactive art system +−*now* was created in response to this brief. As mentioned, it would be evaluated in an exploratory as well as main study. Participant experiences of emergence—perceptual emergence, as it has been articulated in the TEIA—were found in both cases.

***+−now* Exploratory Study** This study aimed to find and explore the nature of any instance of emergent experience in the artwork *+−now*. This involved a field study conducted at my studio with one participant, Sophia, an artist and peer. As a professional, visual artist in her sixties, she was selected for the evaluation because she could also provide aesthetic insight into the work. Data collected was researcher notes from observation of her interaction with the work and from a subsequent open-ended interview in which she was prompted for her opinions of the work and asked for comments on her interaction. The whole session lasted about 30 minutes. The study and findings have been previously reported (Seevinck and Edmonds 2008b). As discussed there, Sophia perceived new shapes during her interaction with the work *+−now*. In particular, these were found to constitute 'dynamic compositions'. Dynamic compositions were identified during this study as where many individual newly detected shapes were visually 'read' in unison, combining to create the impression of a single composition. Furthermore, Sophia interacted with the dynamic composition over time; that is, she changed her behaviour and the composition interactively. Two such dynamic compositions were found, but this discussion will focus on the 'heartbeat' she identified. Here Sophia would make an arc-shaped mark in the sand with her fingers, wait for the system to respond and then make another, mirrored, arc adjacent to the first. She repeated this gesture a number of times, alternating between the arcs and varying their size. Her hands hovered slightly above the surface between each stroke and she appeared to be working rhythmically to layer the imagery. Each stroke was followed by a series of visual 'echoes' that intersected with each other and the preceding gestures. By continuing to draw the mirroring arcs, she sustained a fluctuating image that appeared to 'beat.' She described her interaction as *"it's a kind of pulsating, repeating thing. I like that…"* A recreation of this heartbeat image is shown in Fig. 6.1. Sophia's behaviour and the findings from this study prompted the subsequent main study of *+−now*.

***+−now* Main Study** A larger study of the interactive artwork *+−now* was conducted in 2008, in order to understand people's experience of it and to learn if other interpretation-type behaviours, such as the heartbeat dynamic composition

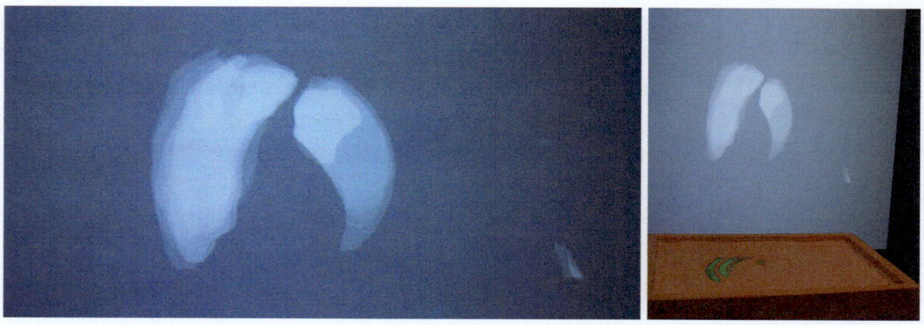

Fig. 6.1 Recreation of the 'heartbeat' composition created by a partisticpat during interaction with *+−now* installed at Beta_Space, Australia (Reproduced from Seevinck and Edmonds 2009)

found with Sophia, would recur. This main study was conducted at Beta_Space in the Sydney Powerhouse Museum. Beta_Space has been designed as a near-naturalistic setting. As such it supports the study of complex interactions as in the experience of artworks (Preece et al. 1994). Beta_Space has also previously been used for field studies such as the evaluation of participant interaction with the interactive art system *Iamascope* by Sidney Fels (Costello et al. 2005). In this main study of +-*now,* data was collected from 42 participants, male and female, aged between 18 and 60. Some participants were invited but most were volunteers who were visiting the museum venue where the work was installed. During the evaluation session the participants interacted with the artwork +−*now* on their own, while being video recorded. This interaction typically lasted about 10 minutes. When the participant had finished, we would go to another space where they described the video recording of their interaction. They were asked to help me, the researcher, interpret this video recording of their behaviour. This 'post event protocol' facilitates understanding what occurred during the interaction session without intruding on the event. In the process, participant and researcher jointly view the video recording and the participant is asked to *"provide a commentary on what they were trying to do"* during that viewed moment of interaction (Preece et al. 1994). The video was paused, rewound or fast-forwarded to facilitate discussion of points of interest. A semi-structured interview prompting them for their opinions followed last. Recordings of the post-event protocol, audio-visual data and interviews were subsequently reviewed for integrity and transcribed. The result was 30 individual participant interaction sessions, or 'profiles', with clear and complete data sets.

Bottom-upCoding The data collected in this study was analysed using Grounded Theory methods (Glaser and Strauss 1967). The aim therefore was to work towards a coding scheme from +−*now* data, induced by that data.

Data was compiled in NVivo qualitative data analysis software (QSR 2010). Each profile was reviewed in depth and annotated. Annotating involved identifying items of interest. Examples of topics that were identified during the main study are shown in Table 6.1. Displays were constructed to visually organise and help categorise the annotations. Participant interaction sessions were decomposed into chronological listings of events and topics, and network displays were created in NVivo.

During the process of constructing a display, similar items were grouped together into higher level categories (e.g. see Miles and Huberman 1994). As more and more of these displays were constructed, each new topic was compared to the existing categories. This process ensured that the categories were representative of the data. It also surfaced new categories. By the time the 15th profile had been modelled visually no new categories were appearing. Glaser and Strauss explain this tendency in analysis as category saturation (Glaser and Strauss 1967).

Coding schemes were induced from the data collected. In the first instance this could build on the saturated categories assembled during the displays, or other items identified as similar in the data during stages of annotating. Similar items were grouped together into a larger, broader category, or 'code'. External literature was then consulted and used to inform some codes. These were drawn from other

Table 6.1 Example topics identified as being of interest in the +−*now* main study data

Topics	
Past experience reference	Feeling thinking
Pattern in sand	Making something
Light pattern(white)	Goal or thoughts
Light pattern(coloured)	Unplanned action
Assessing the system	Sand interaction
Moving pattern or shape	Perceive shape
Recreate interactive experience	Joy
Two hands swirling in sand	Process of perceiving shape
Maximum colour, colour gratification	Sound
Perceiving shapes changes behaviour	Even out the sand
Interact with imagery through sand	Hand down
'Completely blank the screen so I could start from afresh'	Wall image

studies into participation with interactive art. The use of external literature is consistent with a Grounded Theory methods approach, so long as it follows after the "*analytic core of categories has emerged*" to avoid 'contaminating' the researcher's understanding of the data (Glaser and Strauss 1967). For instance, work from Costello et al. (2005) and Bilda et al. (2006, 2007) contributed codes about the participant's body, included under the master code 'Body' in Table 6.2.

Analysing for Emergence

Other additional stages of analysis were alsoinvolved to identify participant experiences of emergence. Thesestart with identifying and applying *Object* sub-codes, follow on to code the data corpus in terms of emergence criteria codes using an emergence mapping scheme, and, finally, determine the type of emergence that occurred (if any) by drawing on the TEIA. The following examples of +−*now* evaluation data demonstrate this process.

Identifying Object sub-codes In +−*now* three groups of *Object* sub-codes were identified. The first of these describes the interface that the participant interacts with. Any instance where participants have engaged with the sand interface in some way was therefore coded under the *sand* sub-code. The second type of element identified relates to an experience of the artwork as a whole. This is *image*, a code applied to all mentions and occurrences of virtual computer-generated imagery of the work in the data, i.e. any interaction or discussion of the coloured light on the sand and/or the monochrome imagery on the screen. The last sub-code, *ObOther* (short for '*object – other*'), is used to capture mention or engagement with other aspects of the artwork installation, such as the signage, pedestal interface, etc. These codes are listed in Table 6.2.

Table 6.2 The composite coding scheme combines codes induced from the main study data with external literature

Master code	Sub-code	Definition of Sub-Code and how it is used
Thought	Association	Association or lack of association, analogy, metaphor, past experience, participant has given it a name
	Start	How the event started e.g. cause (if any), goal, goal-less intention
	Emotion	Feeling
	IS	Interesting item/sum of things
	-IS's include	
	Shape	A shape or composition has been perceived and described as such by participant
	Figure out	"Reach an understanding of."
	Neaten	"1. Tidy or carefully arrange."
	Clear	"4. Free of obstructions or unwanted objects"
	Play	"Engage in games or other activities for enjoyment rather than for serious or practical purpose"
	Explore	"1. Travel through (an unfamiliar area) in order to learn about it."
	Compose	"1. Create (a work of art, especially music or poetry). 2. Constitute or make up (a whole). 3. Arrange in an orderly or artistic way."
	Reverse	"2. Make (something) the opposite of what it was"
	Reflect	"Think deeply or carefully about"
	Perceive	Perceive a feature of the work; "Become aware or conscious of through the senses"
	Other	
Object	Image	Either coloured light or wall screen or both
	Sand	
	ObOther	Pedestal interface, sensors, signage, museum context, people etc.
Misc	Repeat	"Occur again in the same way or form"
Body	Bmodel	Interact with the sand, touching it
	Bmove	Move but not touching sand
	Bhold	Sustain a movement or pose
	Bdust	Dust hands off
	Gstate	Describe general state for example feel cold, warm
	Gender	

Definitions in quotes are taken from Oxford (2006)

The *sand* and *image* codes capture the key aspects of a meaningful experience with *+−now*. Identifying these aspects in the data is a means to identify possible engagement with the aesthetic experience of the work. In this way, the coding facilitates distinguishing engagement with aspects that are core to the art system versus those that may be outside of the designed experience of the art system.

Identifying the *Object* sub-codes was a matter of critiquing the artwork on its own to identify what the composition is and what the *parts* that make up that composition might be. Evaluation data also informed the understanding: those elements that participants repeatedly engage with, explicitly identify, perhaps touch, are the elements that contribute to their overall experience. The granularity of this effort was managed to ensure that the elements identified could contribute to a meaningful experience of the art work. For example, for interaction with +−*now* it is expected that people would need to engage with both the sand and some aspect of the imagery to be considered to have engaged with the work at all. Awareness of the signage or the sensor was not, however, necessary. Conversely, if they only engaged with the sand and no digital imagery then I would not have considered them to have engaged with the aesthetic experience of this work.

The elements identified in this stage of analysis assisted subsequent analysis using the emergence criteria codes. This is because, as is discussed in the emergence mapping scheme, these elements could map across to the '*parts*' from which a new emergent behaviour might surface.

Emergence Coding Subsequent to coding the data for interesting behaviours or events, a coding scheme for emergence was introduced. This coding scheme was created in 2008 and is based on the theoretical literature and discussions of Chaps. 2 and 8. Characteristics for emergence presented there (*new, parts* and so on) and in the TEIA are included in this coding scheme as sub-codes (see Table 6.3). These were applied using a mapping scheme.

Mapping Scheme for Emergence The mapping scheme was developed to facilitate data review in terms of emergence. It facilitates 're-coding' from the key composite codes across to the emergence coding scheme. Re-coding with the mapping scheme makes it easier to view the data given the intertwined and complex facets of emergence. This approach was particularly useful during the analysis of +−*now*, as this was the first time that I had reviewed data explicitly for aspects of emergence.

Table 6.3 The coding scheme for emergence

Master code	Sub-code	Definition of Sub-Code and how it is used
Emergence criteria	New	"Not existing before; made, introduced, or discovered recently for the first time." Qualitatively new to what was there before, for example named
	Un-Pred	Relates to the spontaneity of the event and whether it is predictable or unpredictable
	Whole	"A thing that is complete in itself."
	Parts	"A piece or segment which is combined with others to make up a whole." For example the sand or the affordances of the sand, where the sand is a part of the whole work
	Feedback	"The modification or control of a process or system by its results or effects"
	Ref-Conc	Either refers to an event or does not; as in "existing in a material or physical form; not abstract"

This draws on the theories discussed in Chap. 2. Definitions in quotes are taken from Oxford (2006)

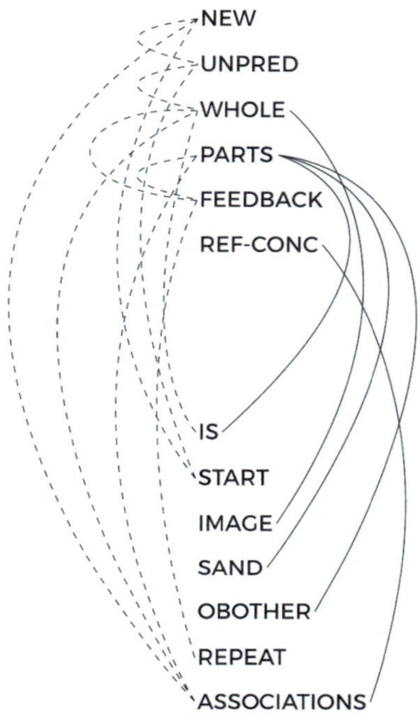

Fig. 6.2 The mapping scheme for emergence. Here the emergence criteria codes (top) are checked against composite codes (bottom) from the evaluation of +−*now*. A solid line means that the emergence criteria code applies, while a broken line means that this mapping is a possibility that requires further assessment in context

The mapping scheme involves reviewing coded material to see it can 'map' across to emergence criteria codes (Fig. 6.2), explained in detail below. By reviewing data events in this way it is possible to determine if that event is, in fact, emergent. If it is then it is subsequently classified using Table 6.4.

The application of the mapping scheme involves reviewing instances where any of the key composite codes have been applied: *IS, Start, Repeat* and *Associations* as well as any instances of the *Object* subcodes—here *Image, Sand and ObOther*. That coded data is then revisited in context and it is checked against its corresponding emergence criteria code: *New, UnPred, Whole*, *Parts*, *Feedback, Ref-Conc*. The selective mapping of these key composite codes to emergence criteria codes is shown in Fig. 6.2. As also shown in Fig. 6.2, there are two kinds of mapping processes relating the coding schemes: equal (solid line) and indicative (broken line). Thus where a code such as *start* indicates that the emergence codes *new* and *un-pred* may be applicable, this needs additional interrogation of the data and context to find out if it is, in fact, so. Its usage and meaning would be checked against the definitions of *new* and *un-pred* (Table 6.3) to see if they would correctly describe this data event. Where the context supports reinterpretation of the item as something that was not, for example, planned, but is instead new and unexpected to the participant, this item would then be re-coded as *new* and *un-pred*. On the other hand, where a general code such as *IS* equates to the emergence code *parts*, the definition of the first code necessarily implies the second code (an event coded as an 'Interesting Sum' by definition implies that it is made up of one or more *parts*).

Table 6.4 The types of perceptual emergence classified in the TEIA

Code	Feedback (Feedback from whole to parts?)	Ref-Conc (References something or is it a new construct?)
Concrete extrinsic perceptual E.g. A melody	No feedback	Concrete
Referenced extrinsic perceptual E.g. The interpretation of the heart shape in Fig. 1.2, or the interpretation of other iconic emergent shapes from overlapping rendering of gesture in *+−now*	No feedback	Referenced
Concrete intrinsic perceptual E.g. New gameplay strategies such as bluffing in Poker	Feedback	Concrete
Referenced intrinsic perceptual E.g. The interpretation of emergent shapes during a feedback process such as the heartbeat animation in *+−now*, and the interpretation of shapes whose meaning is changing from feedback of their interpretation, during the design process of the lotus bicycle	Feedback	Referenced

These differ in terms of two emergence criteria codes: feedback and ref-conc

The mapping system also correlates emergence criteria codes internally; that is, some emergence criteria codes may imply instances of others, depending on the context surrounding that event. Thus there are two stages of coding for emergence criteria: (1) from key composite code to emergent criteria, and (2) from emergent criteria to emergent criteria codes.

Checking for Emergence All the emergence criteria are identified through this mapping process of Fig. 6.2. Four of the emergence criteria codes are essential for a clear instance of emergence: *whole, parts, new, unpred*. These embody the definition from Chap. 2: *"when a new form or concept appears that was not directly implied by the context from which it arose. This new 'whole' is more than a simple sum or grouping of its parts"*. Where these four codes are not co-present, the event or object under consideration is, in this data analysis process, considered to be non-emergent. For example, behaviours that were properties of the parts rather than the collective whole, or usual and expected behaviours often found during interaction with interactive art systems, are considered to be non-emergent. These 'other' behaviours that were found are discussed later in this chapter, but include things like 'figuring out how system works', which is not new but rather common to many interactives, and 'tidying up', which is not concerned with a whole that involves the artwork but rather is an artefact of the sand itself.

Classifying the Emergence Finally, where an event was found to be a clear instance of emergence, it is then useful to determine what type of emergence that is. This stage of classification tests for an additional two emergence codes: *feedback*

and *ref-conc*. This positions the event in terms of the TEIA, identifying it as one of the four kinds of perceptual emergence (Table 6.4).

Summary of theProcess In summary, the process of analysing the data for-participant experiences of emergence began with (1) a bottom-up coding of the data to identify any interesting events, things or behaviours – anything unusual that stood out as discussed and illustrated above (e.g. see Table 6.1). The elements that make up the artwork as a *whole* were then (2) identified and listed under the *object* master code. A composite coding scheme specific to that art installation was generated from these efforts (e.g. see Table 6.2). The data corpus was reviewed for instances of key composite codes that could be re-coded for emergence. Where this seemed possible, an emergence mapping scheme was applied but within the context of the data ((3), see also Fig. 6.2). This worked to re-code a selection of the composite codes to emergence criteria codes (Table 6.3). Where an event was described with the necessary emergence criteria codes, this indicated a likelihood that the event was an instance of emergence. After (4) checking it for emergence against the definition, the type of emergence was identified by reviewing the TEIA (also in Table 6.4). This process is demonstrated in the following discussion of data analysis and findings from the +−*now* main study.

Emergent Experiences

The analysis process just described revealed a total of 25 instances of emergence in this data. This was in 16 of the 30 participant interaction sessions, just over half of the people. No emergence was clearly evident in the remaining 14 cases. It should be noted that each event was only classified once, for example as either *referenced, extrinsic perceptual or as referenced, intrinsic perceptual* types of emergence, and not both. Where an event contained two types of perceptual emergence, the clearest instance instilling the most confidence was selected.

The most common form of emergence found was the referenced extrinsic perceptual emergence type in the TEIA (see Table 6.4 and Chap. 2 for a detailed discussion). It typically occurred where an emergent composition was interpreted as a result of overlapping rendered shapes. As was discussed in Chap. 2, this class of emergence occurs (a) when there is reliance on it being perceived or interpreted by someone to exist—that is, it is perceptual. The second condition for this class (b) is that the emergent *whole* must not affect the *parts*—that is, there should be no *feedback* between the levels of the *whole* and *parts*. This means that the emergence is *extrinsic* to the system. Lastly, (c) when the emergent *whole* refers to something else, it is classified *referenced* emergence.

Easter Island Faces An example of an emergent composition was when participant Charlie perceived 'Easter Island faces' towards the end of his interaction with +−*now*.

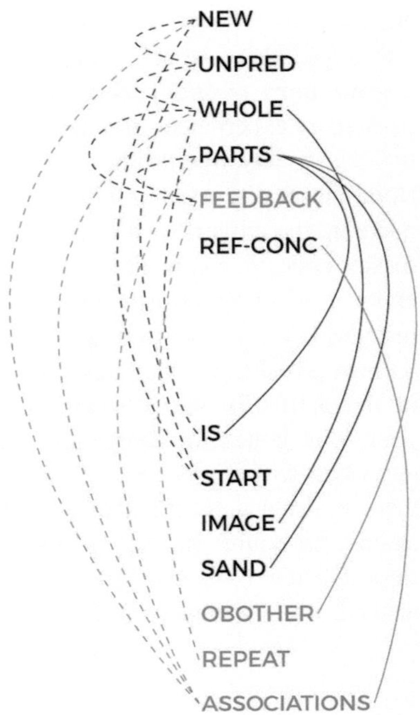

Fig. 6.3 The mapping scheme is used to re-code Charlie's perception '*Easter Island faces*' in terms of emergence criteria codes

> CHARLIE "…And I think I also looked up on the screen again, because after I did that it started to making this sort of shapes I guess, that I hadn't seen before of making these faces so it started looking like the ah, ah, heads on Easter Island, you know the statues. … I thought that was a bit interesting."
>
> RESEARCHER "Where's that, are they here or—?"
>
> CHARLIE "Yeah, they're coming now to the display, start pressing play. As I made these patterns they all have, see them, see them basically up there—here's the statues. Fair enough you know, the eye, the nose, the mouth down here." (He points out the features).

The first, bottom-up pass at coding Charlie'sinterview identified a number of key codes around this instance where he perceives 'statues' of the 'heads on Easter Island'. These are *IS, Start, Image, Sand,* and *Association*. These codes were then reviewed through the re-coding process. That is, the emergence mapping scheme was applied. As explained above, this involved checking emergence definitions (Table 6.3) and the context of the data. For example, as is clear from the data excerpt, the 'statues' image was not planned by Charlie, but was instead something *new* and unpredictable (*unPred*). The mapping process along with resulting emergence codes is shown in Fig. 6.3. Since the critical aspects of emergence were satisfied and the data context confirms this is an instance of emergence, the next step involved determining what type of emergence has occurred. In this step, the list of emergence criteria codes are checked against the classification table for instances of perceived emergence.

Charlie did not act on this '*Easter Island faces*' composition to change it, subsequent to seeing it and therefore there was no *feedback* from this emergent *whole* (the '*Easter Island faces*' composition) back into the *parts* (the *sand*, *image*

Table 6.5 The *Easter Island faces* imagery perceived by Charlie

Code	Feedback	Ref-Conc
Concrete extrinsic perceptual	No feedback	Concrete
Referenced extrinsic perceptual	*No feedback*	*Referenced*
Concrete intrinsic perceptual	Feedback	Concrete
Referenced Intrinsic Perceptual	Feedback	Referenced

This has no feedback and is referenced, classifying it as referenced, extrinsic perceptual emergence

shapes, that make up this emergent composition). In other words, this newly interpreted composition does not affect its *parts*. This lack of feedback from the *whole* back into the *parts* means the emergence is *extrinsic* to the composition and it is classed as *extrinsic perceptual* emergence. Lastly, by virtue of referring to the stone statues, it is classed as *referenced* emergence.

As shown in Table 6.5, the presence of the reference but lack of feedback means that the 'Easter Island faces' event is classified as referenced, extrinsic, perceptual emergence.

An additional 10 instances of participants interpreting emergent compositions were also found and some data extracts that describe these are listed in Table 6.6. The next section describes a second type of emergence that was found during data analysis: referenced intrinsic perceptual emergence.

Table 6.6 Data samples for Referenced extrinsic perceptual emergence from the main study of interaction with +−*now* (Seevinck and Edmonds 2008b)

Participant, behaviour	Data excerpt
Naomi, *psychological ink diagram*	"…It was kind of like an ink diagram. (Laughs) A psychological ink diagram. I didn't intend it to be like that but it kind of ended up being like that."
Naomi later in the same interview, *Tadpoles*	"… It was sort of like little tadpoles or something"
Rania, *Flames of light*	"I wasn't looking at it in particular I was just looking around and I happened to see these things here, these flashes of light appearing… …So I'm trying to clear it out of the way, and just seeing what those, umm, like 'flames of light' whatever they were, were doing. RESEARCHER "Flames of light, did you say?" "Yeah, they looked kind of like flames of light to me."
Joey, *Shooting stars*	"…You can see on that screen now (pointing to wall screen) see you get these shooting, shooting, almost like shooting stars, moving across the screen. I hadn't seen that before and I thought it was pretty interesting."
Arthur, *Face*	"…I think here I'm thinking that it's doing an eye, sort of a face…there is the eye… and the face"

Referenced Emergent Behaviours

A second type of emergence was also identified in this data: referenced intrinsic perceptual emergence. These were behaviours that resembled or *referenced* something else in the world. For the sake of brevity in this study this type can be called 'referenced emergent behaviours'.

This type of emergence is characterised by both *referencing* something in the world and through its reliance on *feedback*. That is, it involves a dynamic feedback process between the emergent *whole* and its constituting *parts*. This is different from the previous example of '*Easter Island Faces'* and that type of referenced, extrinsic, perceptual emergence where there was no feedback. Feedback means the emergent quality occurs at both the level of the emergent *whole* and at that of the *parts*; that is, it is *intrinsic* to the emergent system.

While the emergence discussed here is *intrinsic* rather than *extrinsic*, it is nevertheless similar to the emergent compositions discussed in the preceding section. This is because both are *referenced*. That is, in both cases an association, metaphor or analogy is relied upon for the experience or behaviour to exist. For example, an emergent composition may consist of a face interpreted in the imagery, thus referencing faces in the outside world. On the other hand, a *referenced* emergent behaviour might involve making a face in the imagery 'talk', by manipulating the sand interactively while watching it. This is like animation, yet also immediate and responsive, and as such it would be classed referenced, intrinsic perceptual emergence. In referenced emergent behaviours the emergent *whole* can be considered the participant's behaviour. The *parts* of this *whole* are the different facets of the artwork and interaction with it, all of which combine to create the emergent, *whole* behaviour. For example, the *parts* can include the emergent compositions that make up the image the participant responds to, transparent sub-shapes that overlap to create these emergent compositions, and the gestures that create these shapes and images.

Piano playing An example of a referenced emergent behaviour is when Anthony started to play the piano during his interaction with +−*now*. This is apparent both from the video recording where he can be seen to draw in the sand, and his accompanying description of his actions:

ANTHONY "…At this point I was listening for that god-damn song—um, and then this was me playing around trying to figure out—because I basically had a very rough keyboard at the top and I was trying to match this, the tune. And seeing what would happen if I did that."

RESEARCHER "Oh, so you're drawing a keyboard and you're—"

ANTHONY "…And then I'm trying to play. Not this piece of music which is playing now in the background but a different piece… I was just sort of trying to sort of play along and seeing what would happen there. And you can see the keys which I played a lot of became firmer on the screen.… I've played piano in the past.… I wasn't doing anywhere near correct fingering but I was just sort of playing along. (Pause.) And then … just below the keyboard. That's me thinking—that's me, because I've already made this very thick mark above it—and I'm thinking I've already done that—so I'm trying—it's actually meant to be

> the same note but just trying to re-emphasise it—this note I've played a lot.....Because it finishes—the piece finishes with the repeat—repetition of the high note. It's like, I want to make this a very obvious."

Anthony's piano playing behaviour was initiated by a song that he hears during his interaction with the work. The song is from an adjacent exhibit and a part of the museum's ambient sound environment. At first Anthony tries to work out the notes of the song by drawing a piano keyboard in the sand and tapping the 'keys'. This leads him to play along with the tune. He then emphasises the final note by creating an additional mark in the sand and line on the screen, underscoring the 'piano key' for that note. The sand 'keys' and the gestures that create them can be understood as *parts*. A group of these *parts* laid out on the sand is a keyboard, while the action of touching them again and again ('striking keys') he describes as 'playing' the piano.

The first, bottom-up pass at coding Anthony's session identified a number of key codes around this event, for example the *IS* of the piano playing behaviour, the *Sand* which is used to create 'keys', the *Image* representing these keys on the screen, and the *Start* of the event as being informed by his interaction with the sand as well as hearing music from an adjacent exhibition. These general codes were then reviewed through application of the mapping scheme and context checking. For example, as indicated by the *Start* code and clarified by the above data excerpt, the 'piano playing behaviour' was not planned, but is instead something *new* informed by the music and what he was already doing in the sand. The event was re-coded from these general codes and all emergence criteria codes were matched. This list of emergence codes was subsequently tested against the classifications of emergence in order to determine the type of emergence that had occurred. The result classified this 'piano playing behaviour' as an instance of referenced, intrinsic, perceptual emergence.

More specifically, as Anthony draws a piano keyboard in the sand and 'plays' it, this 'piano playing' behaviour is the emergent *whole*, and its *parts* are the transparent shape, sand 'keys', and the gestures that create them. The piano playing is an instance of perceptual emergence because it relies on the participant's interpretation of the transparent shapes to exist. It is referenced emergence because it refers to playing the piano. Lastly, it is intrinsic because each time he touches the sand to play a note or to emphasise a note, he is creating a shape for that key. Each shape he creates changes the keyboard composition and his subsequent action is informed by each slight change to the composition. Put another way, each shape he creates changes the condition of the *whole* and so changes the condition of the subsequent shapes or *parts*. Put another, more specific way: while his 'piano playing' is the reason for creating the shapes that make up that composition, those shapes also define this piano keyboard and the piano playing behaviour.

Some other examples of referenced emergent behaviours were also found. Some are similar to animating, as in the excerpts taken from Barry's and Joey's evaluation sessions. As shown in Table 6.7 Barry made a stick-man 'walk', and Joey came up with the idea to recreate an animation activity from his childhood while he was engaged in drawing.

Table 6.7 Data samples for Referenced, intrinsic, perceptual emergence from the main study of interaction with +−*now* (Seevinck and Edmonds 2008b)

Participant, behaviour	Data excerpt
Barry, *Stickman walking*	"See I've got a little stick man. He's got bow legs. And there he's look, he's walking. See that. He's moving (laughs)"
Joey, *Recreate animation from childhood*	"I was actually thinking 'what's something silly or fun that I could do in the sand?' I guess by that stage I was like, well, I think I sort a know how it works I think I'll enjoy it, muck around for a bit. Then I thought what could I do, what could I draw? …And I was just thinking of an image from way back and I was just trying to draw it on the sand RESEARCHER Oh ok so that's what that arc was about? "Well you'll see I continue on, its actually an animated shot of an old man with a bald head glasses… it didn't work very well"
Arthur, *River and mountains*	"Here I'm trying to do a river… (He's drawn a line in the sand) These are mountains (pushes sand bank up to side of 'river')"
Abby, *Rainbow in the sand and light*	Abby compared the light on the sand to a rainbow; describing it as "…so colourful it's like a rainbow…" She makes a rainbow in the sand and light

There are also instances of participants creating something in the work in response to a new meaning they have identified in their experience of that work – that is, where their new understanding of the work feeds back to that experience of the work to change it. For example, Arthur models a mountain and causeway out of sand to create a mountain and river for the coloured light. Interactively drawing while the work 'animates' through this drawing, and subsequently responding and changing his actions along with it, is another example of emergent behaviour. Similarly, Abby reflects on the resemblance of the coloured light to a rainbow, and this new understanding goes on to inform her subsequent action: the creation of a rainbow shape in both sand and light. Here the perceived 'rainbow colours' inform her behaviour to create a rainbow, feeding back into the work.

Concrete Behaviours

Lastly, instances of concrete intrinsic perceptual emergence or 'concrete emergent behaviours' for short, were also found. This class of emergence is similar to the class of referenced emergent behaviours just described, but differing because here there is no reference to anything. Here the emergent *whole* is also an emergent behaviour, and each of the *parts* that make up that *whole* is affected by this behaviour.

Similarly here the *parts* of a *whole* might be the *gestures* in the *sand* and *image* that constitute the behaviour, and this behaviour could then cause a change in the *gestures* and *sand* and *image*—for example, it might go from a slow to a staccato rhythm. In this way the emergent behaviour can be said to affect the *parts*; that is, the emergence is intrinsic to the system. However, unlike referenced emergent

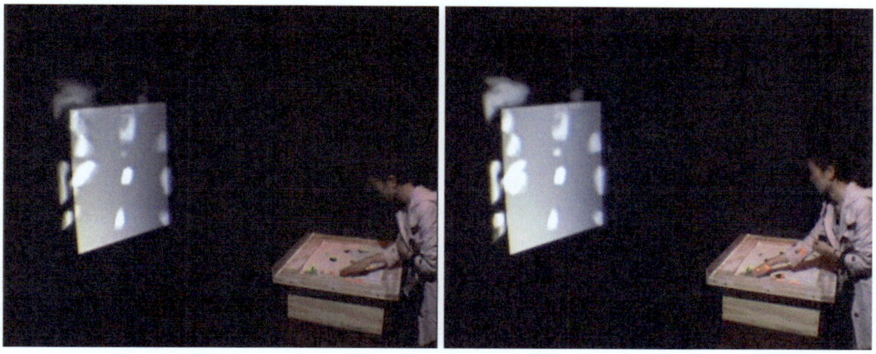

Fig. 6.4 Participant Numi interacts with +−*now* at the Beta_Space, to 'touch the colour parts' of light projected in the sand

behaviours, concrete emergent behaviours do not refer to anything; no analogy or metaphor anchors the interpretation. Instead the concrete behaviour is something local to this art system. Six clear instances of concrete emergent behaviour were identified. The first of these is detailed below with some data excerpts for three others.

Touch the Colour parts An example of a concrete emergent behaviour is when Numi interacted to 'touch the colour parts' (Fig. 6.4).

> NUMI "The colour on the sand, yeah, I touch the colour parts. So, I want to know the reaction if I touch the coloured parts."
> RESEARCHER: Oh Ok. So there was colour on the sand there and that's where you made the hole. (Laughter as NUMI and the RESEARCHER watch the video of her make more holes in the sand, seeming to follow where coloured light appears)
> NUMI: "…Whenever I touch the colour parts again and again, I can see there on the screen the part it becomes whiter, whiter, whiter. So…It's a little bit interesting to me. So quickly making circle again and again on the colour part…It was fun…"
> RESEARCHER: So you like that?
> NUMI: "Yeah. It was fun."

As shown in the transcript excerpt Numi repeatedly circled and touched areas of coloured light in the sand. The behaviour originated from her curiosity about the coloured light, which led her to touch the sand. As she subsequently made a small hole in the sand with her fingertips, she found that the corresponding spot on the screen became whiter. This interested her so that she touched the sand and coloured light again. Thus she repeatedly circled coloured areas on the sand, making the corresponding screen areas 'whiter and whiter'. The artwork's response to her interaction interested her and she found the experience to be 'fun'.

She would repeat the action of touching and circling the areas of coloured light, but it became more a means of sustaining this interest and fun, creating 'whiter and whiter' spots on the screen. In this sense this new behaviour changes the meaning and significance of the *images*, *sand*, and her *gestures*; that is, the emergent *whole* is changing the *parts*. These *parts* have become integrated into a 'game-like' interaction and they are now something other than what they were before the behaviour started. There is also *feedback* going from the *whole* back into the *parts,* and this makes this behaviour an instance of *intrinsic* perceptual emergence. Finally, the behaviour is *concrete* because its meaning is inherent in this behaviour, relying on its own immediate, *concrete* nature rather than on a reference to something outside itself.

The bottom-up coding of this event identified this as an interesting item, or sum *(IS)*. Other codes were also applied: *Start, Image, Sand, Repeat* and *Association*. The mapping scheme and contextual understanding from reviewing the codes in context (described above) then led to re-coding the event to all of the emergence criteria codes. This list was subsequently tested against the classifications of emergence and, since it involves feedback and a new construct (i.e. the value of *Ref-Conc* is *Concrete*), the 'follow lights' event was classified as an instance of concrete intrinsic perceptual emergence.

Circles in the Sand Another example of concrete intrinsic perceptual emergence, or concrete emergent behaviours for short, was when Zahara was drawing circles in the sand.

> ZAHARA: So I was just trying to circle the part who is coloured…
> RESEARCHER "Umm… What, do you mean a circle, or—?"
> ZAHARA: "Yeah, there is some part with colour (she points to the sand table on screen) and I just circle it… (She points to where she's clearing a circle on screen)"

Like Numi, Zahara also interacted with areas where the coloured light falls on the sand. She began her interaction with the work by lightly smoothing over the *sand* with her hand and then drawing circles around the coloured *parts* with her index finger. Up to six areas were circled in this 'circles on sand' behaviour. Despite the similarity of this behaviour to Numi's, the participants exhibited these behaviours independently of one another.

Stir Wait Look Another example of concrete emergent behaviour is when Sarah was found to swish the sand, then pause and look towards the monochrome image on the wall:

> SARAH "I'm looking at the screen—see another bird. (Laughs) Just here—that's the beak there, and that's the body. (Starts swishing again)…It's kind of a delayed re-action isn't it, when you stop swishing the sand around… Ah, it, um—ah, I be-came aware of it and I, I liked to look for the shapes in it after I stopped. (Pauses, looks at screen for a while, then swishing sand again) That's why I stopped for a while."

This behaviour was repeated up to five times. She describes herself as looking for shapes and patterns and summarises the behaviour as *"I'll make patterns in the sand and then look up here and see what you've (I have) made."*

Stir Wait Feel Similar to Sarah was when Ted interacted with the sand. His interaction was, however an emotional one:

> TED: "(it) just draws those emotions out of you" and "there's these things where you're starting to go 'okay, now I've got it' to something, and the first time I got it, it made me smile. I stood and I stopped and it made me smile."

> … And it was like I was 6 years old, looking in a kaleidoscope and just—you know that feeling when you look at stars. Like you go to the country and there's millions of stars and you just look up and it feels wondrous and eternal and deep and complex and are they there, are they not—because of that and it's like looking in leaves moving and all those things I was talking about but there's that magical depth..
> And that infinite variation. And you just—(pause) they're almost things you can't create. You can manipulate water to do it, you can splash and splash and splash and you see the ripple patterns, but you can't draw it, you can't paint it, you can't even really speak it.
> "Because what you need to see is, you need to see that image and it just draws those emotions out of you. And that was when I really got a sense of joy and I realised that it's not about sand painting …It's actually—a different, quintessentially different experience. You're trying to make infinite patterns and then create stillness within them… and then you see this random pattern. And even though it's delayed, if you continue the same movement there's this correlation between that and the complexity of movement and it's, it's lovely."

Ted interacted with the sand to *"create a movement"* and then pausing and *"watching the feeling come"*. As shown in the data excerpt, he compares his experience to that of looking at stars. He describes the work as having a "*magical depth*" with "*infinite variation*" which "*just draws those emotions out of you*", including the joy of smiling. These other aspects start to allude to the concept behind the *Traces* body of work, and its concern with the open-ness and the richness of the natural world. Openness is also a characteristic of emergence. Ted's description of an infinite variation seems to evoke an experience of emergence. It also has design implications for creating with emergence as discussed in the *Insight for Emergent Interactions* chapter.

Non-emergent Behaviours

Additional interaction behaviours that are not emergent were also identified in the data. These were interesting events that were identified in the data, coded and found to be non-emergent. This would be for one of two reasons—either the behaviour did not reflect engagement with the work, or it was deemed generic.

In the first case this included events where participants were not actually engaging with the work as a *whole* but rather just relied on a *part* of the artwork. For example, some mark-making behaviours in the sand such as doodling, writing, drawing and erasing were observed during participant interaction with +−*now* but later found to be independent of any consideration of the digital imagery. Because they related only to a part of the work and not all of its elements necessary for a meaningful experience of the whole, they were found to be non-emergent of that artwork. Participants who were only clearing the *sand* without paying attention to the *imagery* were engaging in a behaviour that can be attributed directly to the *sand*, a *part*, not the artwork, as a *whole*. As such it is not describing emergent experience with that artwork (here it is actually just a reflection of the affordances of sand). However, where the behaviour does involve interaction with the *whole* artwork then it may well be emergent. For example, in Barry's drawing of a man in the *sand* which he continually amends to make it walk, the mark making behaviour is an artefact of the *whole* artwork rather than of just one part (the sand) because he is watching the *imagery* and figure walking on screen, while he is manipulating the *sand*. On the other hand, when people would shake the *sand* from their hands, or pat it down to, in their words, 'tidy up', this again did not concern the artwork as a *whole*. Rather, this behaviour is just an artefact of a *part* of the artwork (the *sand*). Put another, more general way, this behaviour is non-emergent because it relies on attributes of the *parts* of the artwork rather than it as a *whole*.

The second type of non-emergent behaviour found was that which was not *new*. Behaviours that are, arguably, common to interaction with interactive systems and interactive art would not be new to interaction with +−*now*. This lack of novelty means they are not emergent. *Assessing*, *resetting* and *anthropomorphising* are three generic interaction behaviours that were found. Assessing or trying to figure out how the artwork works has been previously identified in interaction research (Costello et al. 2005) and as such it is not a new behaviour. Examples of people trying to figure out how +−*now* worked include drumming on the glass surface to see if sound affects the work, or marking the edges of the sand tray to identify the limits of the interaction space. Participants often articulate this intention quite easily, as stated by participant Anthony who says he was *"...trying to figure out how big a time delay was needed..."*

Participants were also found to reset the system. Participant Sully described his thinking while interacting as wanting to "start over" with his interaction. Once again this resetting behaviour is common to participation with interactive systems and this lack of novelty means it is not emergent. Lastly, the anthropomorphising behaviours were interesting but subsequently found to be non-emergent. They were originally identified using the *Reference* code. For example, one person described his actions where he was clearing the sand as "*quieting the system*", while Barry said he "*smothering*" the light and Numi described her intention as wanting to make the artwork "*happy*".

Summary

The studies of *Glass Pond* and +−*now* demonstrate how evaluation research can be integrated with practice and PBR generally. Study findings have directed enquiry towards emergence as a concept and fleshed out what it might mean for participant experience. The main study of +−*now* showed the work has a capacity for facilitating emergent experiences as well as illustrating what these might be like for participants. Three out of the four types of perceptual emergence in the TEIA were found here. The most common was participant experience of Referenced extrinsic perceptual emergence, such as recognising faces or shooting stars in the work's imagery. Referenced intrinsic perceptual emergence and Concrete intrinsic perceptual emergence were also found to occur. Ted described an intensely open-ended type of experience during his interaction: a *"magical depth"* and *"infinite variation"* similar to looking at the stars. This experience accompanied a concrete emergent behaviour and is both relevant to the aesthetic intention of the work as well as having some implications for design, as are discussed in the *Insight for Emergent Interactions* chapter.

Non-emergent behaviours were also identified and are equally useful for understanding interactivity and design. For example, awareness of generic interaction behaviours can inform the design decisions made by artists and practitioners. It is useful to reflect that in all evaluations participants were found to interact creatively. These include making a heart beat in the exploratory study of +−*now*, and a range of creative behaviours from piano playing to animating to chasing lights in the main study. As discussed in the descriptions of this body of work in Chap. 5, this project has been concerned with participant efforts to actively create compositions during their interaction with the work. From the examples shown here, this turned out to be the case. Creative interaction was also of interest in *Of me With me*, discussed next.

Evaluation for *Of me With me* (2014)

The interactive drawing application and art system *Of me With me* (Seevinck 2014) is the last part in the *Iterative Drawing* body of work, which involved collaboration between myself and community artists at Cerebral Palsy League. As explained in Chap. 5, this project involved workshops and collaborative drawing. This informed a conceptual structure and the interactive artwork Creative participant experiences and notions of shared drawing were core to the work. They were addressed with *physical* emergence—specifically, a type of 'fractal drawing'. This evaluation is, however, focused on the participant experience of emergence i.e. *perceptual* emergence.

***Of me With me* Study** This artwork was installed in a partitioned area within the Redcliffe City Gallery in 2015. The evaluation approach was very similar to that of +−*now*. A naturalistic setting was favoured, since the experience of art is contextual. Similarly observations and interviews were used. Unfortunately post event protocols were not possible due to limited space at the gallery. Interviews with participants after they had interacted with the work for a time were, however, useful, because these interviews were conducted in front of the work and participants could re-engage with it to demonstrate any activities they recollected, if they chose to. The interview questions concerned the artwork set up and general impression, and directed discussion towards what the participant did, thought and felt while interacting with the work. As such the participant would often be asked, *"can you show me what you mean?"* which they were then able to demonstrate and discuss. The interview discussions and preceding participant interaction were recorded on video. Since the artwork facilitates the creation of drawings and saving these, those images also informed the evaluation.

Ten evaluation sessions with male and female adults, physically abled and not, constitute this project's dataset. The audio data was transcribed and imported into NVivo software (QSR 2014) along with images saved from the interaction sessions and video recordings of the participant interaction. Participant profiles were compiled, collating this data per participant. Given the focus on emergence and that relevant theories had already been developed in prior work, thematic analysis was used.

Analysis

The analysis approach taken here is a form of theoretical thematic analysis that is influenced by an external theory from the outset, rather than the primary emphasis on being bottom up and data-driven, as is the case with Grounded Theory approach (Braun and Clarke 2008). Here theory sensitises the researcher in their analysis of the data, directing their enquiry (e.g. Patton 2001). In this study the theories and concepts surrounding emergence are used. The approach draws on my experience in identifying emergence in prior evaluation studies and the emergence analysis tools created there. The coding processes followed generic thematic analysis practices while being focused on themes surrounding emergence theory (e.g. Richards 2006; Braun and Clarke 2008).

As with the previous case study, the data was also reviewed for interesting events, things or behaviours. Any events, effects or activities that could be considered distinctive were highlighted. For example, where participants described a specific experience, event or effect, or used an analogy or metaphor to name something, it was of interest. Distinctive events were sought out across the data as these could, upon further analysis, be found to be emergent. These were coded as *Interesting Sum (IS)*. The context around these instances in the data was also reviewed and any instances of a selection of 'key' codes were sought out in the data. These key codes draw on the previous case study, but they also include some specific codes for this artwork and study. These are the *Object* sub-codes. The key codes and definitions are listed in Table 6.8. Column three also lists an example of data from this study that has been coded this way.

As with the previous case study, identifying *Object* sub-codes facilitates clarifying what interaction behaviour is needed for a meaningful engagement with the artwork. As such it involves identifying the elements that make up the artwork as a *whole*. In the artwork *Of me With me*, the elements that make up the artwork experience are considered to be the black marks that the participant draws and manipulates directly (sub-code *Black Mark*), the system response that animates this line length (sub-code *Movement*), and the grey marks that are the fractal echoes of that first mark (sub-code *Grey Marks*). Of course the stylus, tablet, screen and so on also inform the experience, but for this study these are sufficiently coded under sub-code *ObOther*. The black mark is the equivalent of sand from the prior case study, i.e. the participant's direct input. Movement and grey marks are both aspects

Table 6.8 Key codes in the *Of me With me* (2014) study are listed and defined

Code	Definition of code	*Of me With me* data example of code
Interesting sum IS	Interesting sum, event, or effect identified in data	"Sound wave with resonance surrounds"
Start	How the event started	Playing around… the grey lines made her think of harmonics
Object/ Grey marks	The grey marks that are rendered with the fractal algorithm in response to the participant's direct, black line	A sound wave composition was interpreted consisting of the lower and higher harmonics (grey lines) and the…
Object/ Movement	System generated movement rendered as a part of the system's rendering response	–
Object/ Black mark	The black marks a participant makes when moving the stylus	… the main sound (black line)
Object/ ObOther	The stylus, table, installation plinth, peoples voices etc.	ObOther—there were no other aspects outside playing a role
Repeat	Misc. from dictionary definition in now study understood as "occur again in the same way or form" and helps to identify behaviours and feedback	The interpretation of grey lines as resonance harmonics led to her drawing sound drawings
Associations	From Thought master code in +−*now* data analysis "association or lack of association, analogy, metaphor, past experience, given a name	In naming the image she associated it with a visualisation of sound waves

These draw on the prior study codes as well as those from this dataset. Corresponding examples from this data set are listed in the last column

of system response and part of the designed artwork experience. They are generated based on the black mark. As such, and given their nature, I consider that engaging with these grey marks or the movement of the black line (such as when it was described as 'vanishing') constitutes engagement with the artwork as a *whole*. I have identified these aspects based on understanding the work (discussed in Chap. 5) and from reviewing participant evaluation data.[1]

Emergent Experiences

Analysis of the *Of me With me* study data revealed three instances of emergent behaviour. This includes Olive's interaction with the work when she created drawings of sounds (Figs. 6.5 and 6.6, Table 6.8). The *IS* that first identified this as

[1]This same process of interpreting the artwork and analysing using key codes and *object* codes was employed in the analysis of the third case study, *Dichroic Wade*. As discussed there, the *object* sub-codes for that work relate to the glass pieces and the reflections or transmissions of light.

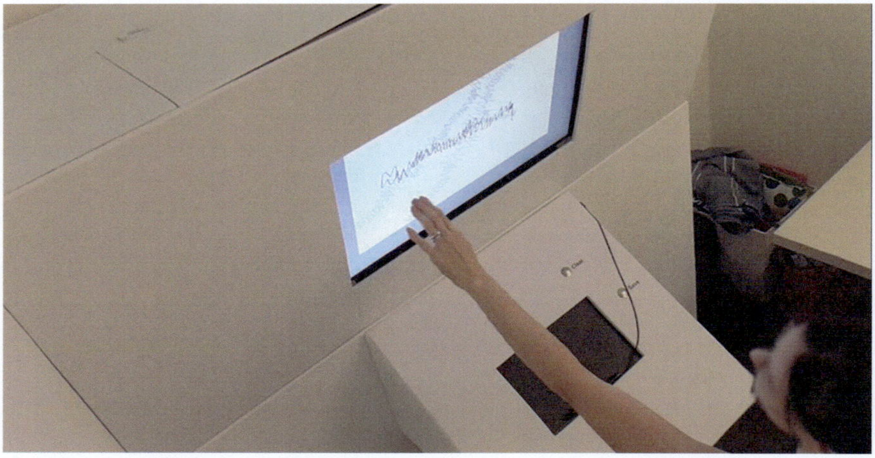

Fig. 6.5 During her interview, participant Olive points out lines she considers to be 'harmonics' from her drawing of 'resonance surrounds'

Fig. 6.6 The mapping scheme is used to re-code participant Olive's '*sound drawings'* in terms of emergence criteria codes

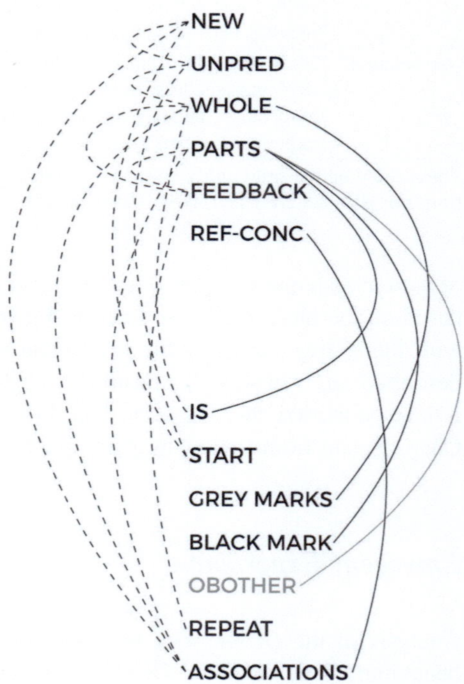

something to consider is when Olive described drawing a *"sound wave with resonance surrounds."* In her words: *"I started playing around you know, drawing something that might have looked like a sound wave or something like that. Then I decided to start drawing musical notes. And that looked kind of cool, like an experimental score or something."*

Subsequent discussion during the interview revealed that this drawing effort was also informed by what she saw during the interaction: *"I was sort of thinking about the grey areas sort of being like harmonics."* This data tells us how the event started and was subsequently coded under the *start* code.

Data analysis further revealed that this interpretation of the grey lines informed her subsequent interaction with the work to create a sound image. She re-created this image for the interviewer, discussing her thinking in the process:

> RESEARCHER: Oh yeah? Show me?
> OLIVE: (After drawing lines) So, they're not very good sound waves (laughs) but … yeah, it sort of, you know, creates all these others around.
> RESEARCHER: Ahhh …
> OLIVE: A fairly noisy composition obviously (laughs)
> RESEARCHER: So, can you tell me about the grey lines here and the black line. Like, can you tell me about the different lines here?.. Or what were..?
> OLIVE: "Yeah. Like, maybe like I see that as being like your main sort of picture was coming through. (Points to black line) And then you had like the resonance surrounds. This might be like your higher resonance sound and these might be your lower resonance sounds around that. (Points to grey lines surrounding black line)"

Olive's sound drawing was coded under the *Grey Marks* code for the resonant harmonics she points out, and under the *Black Mark* code for her direct line drawing, the '*main sort of picture coming through*' or initial sound wave (Table 6.8).

Mapping and Classifying Emergence

The analysis process involves two more stages. These are firstly, where instances of the key composite codes are mapped into emergence codes, and secondly, if emergence is found, determining what type it is.

Firstly, the emergence mapping stage aims to understand whether or not the event can qualify as emergence. The emergence codes represent key characteristics of emergence and, if they are satisfied, indicate that an emergent event has occurred. The mapping into emergence codes involves recoding key codes in the data and returning to the data source to review it in context in order to ensure the recoding is accurate. For example, in order to qualify as emergence, an event must be '*new*'. In Olive's sound drawing interaction the codes *ne*w and *unPred* may come about from an instance of the *start* code; however, this needs to be verified by revisiting the data. From reviewing that data (above) it can be seen that her interaction was informed by the relatively aimless and unplanned action of 'playing around'. It was also prompted by the work itself: the grey lines that she interpreted as harmonics.

As such, her behaviour can be considered new and relatively unpredictable, unplanned by her and unforeseeable by others. This means that the *start* code can be mapped across to *new,* as shown in Fig. 6.6. Similarly *grey marks* and the *black marks* also map across to *whole* and *parts*, while her reference to sound waves which was coded under *association* maps across to the *ref-conc* code.

The *feedback* code is also prompted here, informing her interpretation of the grey lines to change her thinking about her interaction, and 'feeding back' so that she subsequently draws a sound wave. In perceiving this drawing as a *sound wave with resonance* surrounds she is acting on both black and grey lines, *parts* to make up the composition as a *whole*.

From this assessment, and the emergence criteria mapping above, Olive's '*sound drawing'* behaviour is understood as *new*, unpredictable (*unPred*), and a *whole* that is made up of the *grey marks* and, of course, the *black line* that initiates these. As such, they describe an emergent event that occurred during interaction with this artwork. Furthermore, as the emergent event also involved *feedback* between the participant and her (changing) behaviour, that is changing the black lines in response to her understanding of the grey lines, this emergence can be understood as *intrinsic*. Finally, through her reference to the visualisation of sound waves, it can be characterised as an instance of *referenced* emergence. In conclusion, therefore, this example would be an instance of *Referenced, intrinsic perceptual emergence*, or *referenced emergent behaviour* for the sake of brevity. The mapping of Olive's key code values to emergence criteria codes is shown in Fig. 6.6.

Another two instances of emergent behaviours were found during this study. These interaction behaviours were described by the participant as '*stamping*' and '*chasing*'. Both were unexpected mark-making behaviours.

Shirley *Stamping* points During our discussion Shirley showed me a new way of drawing which she described as 'stamping' (Fig. 6.7). This involved putting down discrete points across the screen that the drawing algorithm would then connect with lines. She developed this way of drawing in response to 'things vanishing':

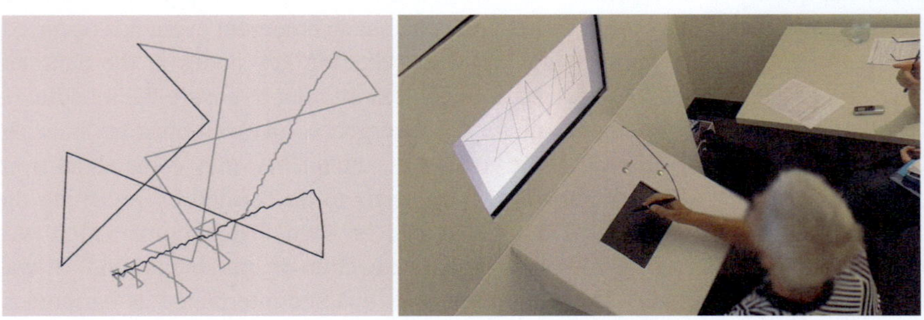

Fig. 6.7 Participant Shirley '*stamps*' points to make long lines and avoid the '*vanishing*', then makes small movements to effect the 'shadows' (the *grey* marks)

SHIRLEY: But I don't understand why all the other stuff has vanished. (Drawing lines, the end of the black line disappears as she continues to draw) Is it… now it's started… gone! I can't figure that one out. I did earlier; I tried writing my name…
RESEARCHER: Mmmm?
SHIRLEY: (laughs) and it goes everywhere (laughs)
RESEARCHER: And what did you think of that?
SHIRLEY: Um…. it's okay. It's not…. (pause, looking at line and drawing) That one seems to be going backwards. (Laughter) It's ah… want to try that again. (Pause. Laughs) All the shadows go everywhere….
RESEARCHER: Does that frustrate you? Is it annoying? Is it feel, does it surprise you, do you like it? What do you think?
SHIRLEY: "I actually quite like it. But I would like it in different colours."

Shirley developed a way of drawing to respond to this 'vanishing': *"When you move, it just seems to vanish. And it will only stay if you start moving like this,"* she said as she stamped dots across the screen, lifting the stylus to make a single point each time: *"It won't if I stamp like that."* The marks she made in doing this are coded under *black mark*. The *movement* code was, however, also applied, given that Shirley was also acting in response to how the system rendered movement (e.g. *"That one seems to be going backwards"*). In this way she created a number of images which she says she would like to colour in on a paper printed copy of the drawing, since this is an activity she enjoys doing in her spare time. She saved a few images and we discussed the colours she might use. She also demonstrated how, subsequent to *stamping* these lines for colouring, she manipulated the grey lines to 'open up or spread out' the image she is creating, further engaging with the art system's capacity for movement.

June *Chasing* to close a shape Another example is June's interaction. She is an artist who draws as a part of her practice. During her interaction with the artwork she describes herself as having 'chased' her black line. That is, this event can be understood as both engaging with the 'black mark' and the 'movement' in the work, as was the case with Shirley. June demonstrates this by drawing a square, talking through her thinking about the activity as she does it:

JUNE: "I'm just trying to make it and it doesn't work like that. Well, not in the way…say I wanted to do a square… and it just, you see it turns the whole… the line just disappeared, you, you can't chase it, join it up (she sits again to explain something). It just keeps going…
RESEARCHER: Were you trying to chase it?
JUNE: I was, yes.

Chasing and *Stamping*: Referenced and Concrete Emergent Behaviours

Like Shirley's '*stamping*' technique for drawing, June's *chasing* behaviour is a response to the art system's characteristic behaviour—namely that older points in the participant's black line will 'vanish' or 'disappear' as they continue to draw.

These actions are prompted by understanding the artwork in this way—they were not planned activities but rather came about through interaction with the work. They are also not immediately predictable behaviours from viewing this artwork, or other artworks in general. The way in which they started can therefore be understood as new and unpredictable, two criteria for emergence.

Similarly, each of these actions is a composite of different *parts* that stem from the artwork and interaction. The '*chase*' action can be understood as constituting the movement (speed and direction) of the black line. Similarly the '*stamp*' action constitutes movement and direction of the black line in addition to the points themselves and the grey lines, which she also seeks to influence with this interaction. These different aspects can therefore inform coding the event in terms of a *whole* (*movement*) as well as *parts* (*black mark*).

Both are also instances in which *feedback* occurs—that is, as each participant interprets the work as either 'disappearing' or 'vanishing' they act on this new understanding to determine their subsequent behaviour, and feedback occurs. The '*chasing*' or '*stamping*' behaviour as *whole* affects the *parts*, in this case being the way in which the participant draws, from changing the quality and speed of the black line (June) through to simply placing dots down, as Shirley did. This feedback means that the emergence is *intrinsic*. Finally, their naming of their events indicates whether or not they associate their behaviour with something beyond the artwork interaction. June's description of her action is as *chasing* the line, and this use of metaphor implies a *referenced* behaviour, though it is difficult to be completely clear on this given there is slight hesitancy in her description (see transcription excerpt above). Shirley's description is, however, more easily classified, as it is specific to the act of making a mark and as such concerned with the *concrete* elements of this interactive experience. Arguably she has uncovered a formal dimension to the interactive mark making experience—perhaps a brush stroke like the 'stipple' that the impressionists could manipulate so well in their engagement with direct perception in art.

Summary

The emergent behaviours found during participant interaction with this work are all about drawing, and people would draw collaboratively with the system such as to create *resonance surrounds*, *stamp points* or *chase* a figure on screen to make lines. In each case it was about making a mark. These marks differed, like art does, in intention or meaning as well as gesture, ranging from ideas which are prompted then drawn, such as the '*soundwave with resonance'*, through to more expressive or formal, where it is about the act of drawing, such as '*stamping*' behaviour. While this was a small study of participant interaction it has still revealed insight into emergence for drawing: emergent behaviours as shown here can and do reveal novel ways in which we can make marks. As such, they may also point to new opportunities for creative and conversational interaction.

Other instances of emergence also occurred during participant interaction with the work, such as the interpretation of emergent compositions. These were not as many as expected, however, which may be an artefact of the data collection methods. That is, the fact that post-event protocols could not be used (there was not enough space for this in the gallery) made it difficult to prompt participant reflection on their interaction and experiences. If this method was to be used in a subsequent study it might be that more instances of emergence, particularly emergent compositions, could be found.

Evaluation for *Dichroic Wade* (2016)

Dichroic Wade (Seevinck 2016) is the second in the *Lightworks* body of work, as was discussed in the previous chapter. Conceptually these works are concerned with responding to a site and a sense of place there. This has entailed an 'opening up' of the art system to other inputs beyond the participant. Here, the site is fed into the work both aesthetically, through visual characteristics and through live weather data updates about the wind conditions outside. A prototype of *Dichroic Wade* was evaluated in early 2016. This was focused on the opportunities for meaning making, and specifically perceptual emergence, in participants with the work. It is presented below. Study findings informed the work, later installed as a part of Art.CHI 2016 in the USA, where it received an Honorary Mention award from the ACM CHI committee.

Dichroic Wade Study An evaluation of participant experience with a prototype version of *Dichroic Wade* was conducted in February 2016. The evaluation was conducted at the Asia Pacific Design Lounge at the State Library of Queensland in Brisbane. This installation location, like the Beta_Space used in the first case study and the Redcliffe City gallery in the second case study, was selected because it could provide a naturalistic setting given its public nature and art and design context. As such, it could support understanding participant experience of the work, which, while technically complete, was still in need of improved understanding by the artist of how audiences might experience it.

Fourteen participants, male and female and aged between 19 and 72, interacted with the work for durations ranging from about three to 30 min, with an average of around 5 minutes. Non-obtrusive data collection methods were used. These are indirect observation and interview discussions after the participant had interacted with the work. Post-event protocols (Preece et al. 1994) were conducted in a room behind the installation. Here the participants would describe what they were thinking while interacting, as prompted by video recordings of their preceding interaction with the work. The video recordings that were collected did, however, have some problems. This was because the detail and quality of light captured in the video image was limited due to the venue lighting and camera technology. As a result, interesting items that participants identified during interaction were in many cases not visible on the recording, and the discussion was therefore sometimes limited to events the participants recollected rather than being reliably prompted.

Seven clear examples of emergence were found out of the 14 interaction sessions with participants. They demonstrate a capacity for the work to facilitate emergence; however, as mentioned, there was an issue with the data collection: the limited efficacy of the post-event protocols may mean that there were other instances of emergence that were missed.

Analysis

The approach to analysing this data is similar to that taken during the previous case study. That is, interpretation and coding followed a process of theoretical thematic analysis (see, for example, Richards 2006; Braun and Clarke 2008), and once again the emergence mapping scheme and codes were employed. The data was reviewed and transcribed into NVivo (QSR 2014). Annotations and memo-making accompanied this process. 'In Vivo' coding also occurred during this time, in which aspects were labelled and categorised during the process of reviewing and 'getting to know the data'. The research enquiry was sensitive to aspects surrounding emergence and this oriented the analysis. For example, if the participant commented on being surprised during interaction with the work, or if I found their interpretation surprising (based on my understanding of the work as the artist or researcher), these events were noted down. Similarly, I noted any instances where participants described their behaviour through analogy or metaphor, where it became apparent that they did something more than once, or where such an event seemed unplanned.

Codes were subsequently applied to these events. These are listed in Table 6.9. The process of creating those codes and analysing this data corpus follows that of the previous study. Similarly, after that coding stage the data is 're-coded' using the emergence mapping scheme to help check for emergence. The type of emergence that it might be is then assessed. The application of these analysis processes to this data is exemplified in the following example of Yolandi's interaction with the work. Her experience is also included as an example for each code in Table 6.9, while the mapping is shown in Fig. 6.8.

Emergent Experiences

Of the seven instances of emergence found, four were referenced, extrinsic emergence, while the other three were intrinsic perceptual emergence. One example of referenced extrinsic emergence is Yolandi's interpretation of the work as *"trees with leaves moving in the wind"*, listed in Table 6.9 (see also Fig. 6.8). This is a situation where a composition was unexpectedly interpreted by the participant during her interaction with the work:

Table 6.9 Key codes in the *Dichroic Wade* (2016) study are listed and defined

Code	Definition of code	*Dichroic Wade* data example of code
Interesting item (IS)	Interesting sum, event, or effect identified in the data.	"A tree with leaves moving in the wind"
Start	How the event started	When participant was asked what she was thinking of when first approached the work, her impression of it was as trees in the wind
Object/Ref/Trans	Light reflections and transmissions	She sees colours and movement from the reflections and transmissions of light and colour in …
Object/Glass Triangles	Glass and acrylic triangles	… the moving glass triangles
Object/ObOther	Sensors, glass wall, reflections on that wall, people in space, signage, buses outside etc	None - there were no other reflections etc. outside aspects playing a role
Repeat	From dictionary: "occur again in the same way or form". Helps to identify behaviours and feedback	The interpretation did not lead to actions that were repeated or behaviours
Associations	From dictionary: "association or lack of association, analogy, metaphor, past experience, given a name	She associated it with nature and an actual tree moving in the wind

These draw on +−*now* study codes and those from this dataset. Corresponding examples from this dataset are listed in the last column

> RESEARCHER: "What were you thinking about now, when you first saw the work?"
> YOLANDI: Trees. Trees and wind with the leaves going like that (she flutters fingers. Then later on:) Look! (Points at monitor) you see, that is leaves! Look the wind—
> RESEARCHER: That's what you saw?
> YOLANDI: Oh yes… I found that fascinating because that movement on this lot is—(points to glass tiles on left side of installation) if you look at trees or leaves you see leaves move in the wind and suddenly the wind moves a little bit and not everything moves exactly the same. These move here a little bit, these go a bit faster. That's exactly what's happening here. So as a whole "I see a tree, maybe a science fiction tree because of the colours…"

Reviewing that event in the context of the data reveals that the interpretation came about when she approached the artwork (rather than having read about it, for example). Yolandi's interpretation of the work can therefore be considered spontaneous and novel, and the *start* code maps successfully to emergence criteria codes *new* and *unPred* (see Fig. 6.8). Similarly, she has identified the glass triangles (*Object* sub-code *Glass Triangles*) and reflections (*Object* sub-code *Ref/Trans,* see also Table 6.9) as contributing to her experience. When analysing this for

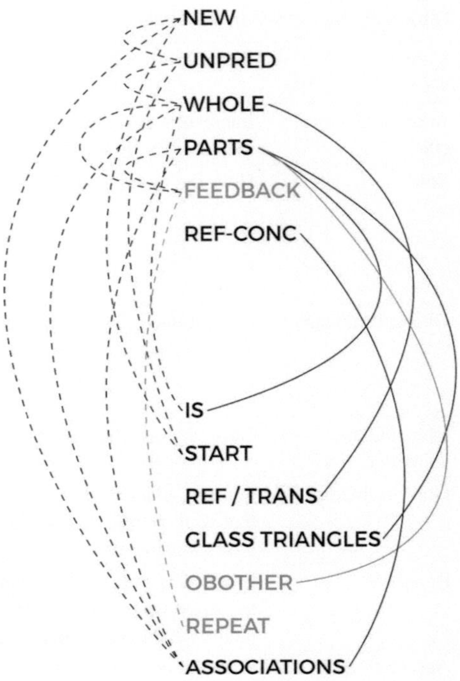

Fig. 6.8 Assessing for emergence: Yolandi sees a '*tree with leaves moving in the wind*'

emergence, these can be mapped across to *parts* and *whole* respectively. The overall description of this resultant experience is more than a simple sum, more than simply the group of reflections and triangle *parts*. Rather it is a "*tree with leaves moving in the wind*", a composition she has found and a '*whole* that is complete within itself'. There is no repetition in her actions and given her association with nature and trees, the *IS* will map across to *ref/conc* code.

Based on this analysis, including the satisfaction of key emergence criteria codes, this event is concluded as being an instance of perceptual emergence. More specifically, with its lack of feedback and its association with something (leaves, tree etc.), it is an instance of referenced extrinsic perceptual emergence, as is consistent with the TEIA requirements.

Other examples of referenced extrinsic perceptual emergence found during participant interaction are when Yolandi and another participant, Patricia, interpreted animal forms in the work. Yolandi perceived a bird in the work as shown in Fig. 6.9.

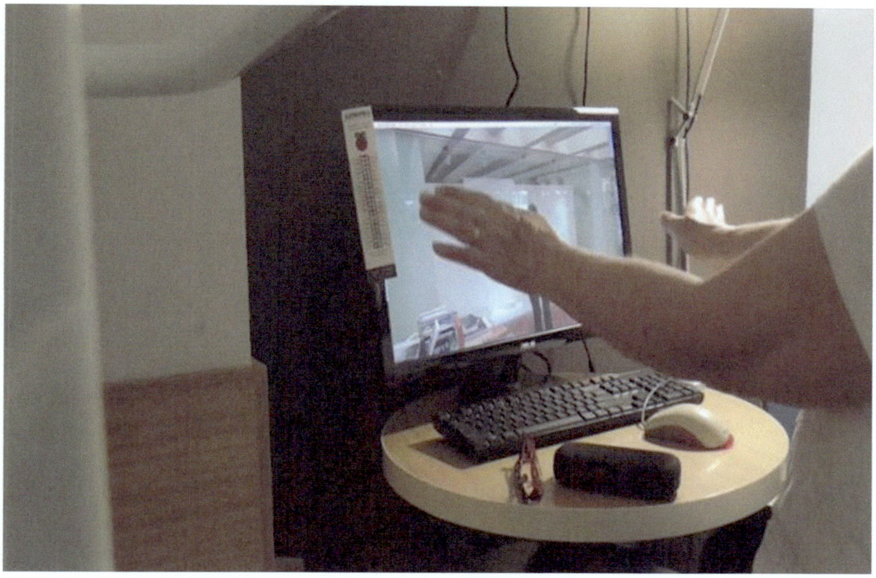

Fig. 6.9 During a post event protocol session for the *Dichroic Wade* study, Yolandi gestures to describe the form of a bird

Another participant, Patricia, saw a butterfly, as explained in the data excerpt from her post event protocol session. She subsequently goes on to describe the butterfly as comprising reflections and moving. This indicates her interpretation is of the entire work rather than a single part; that is, it is an emergent composition generated through the work as a *whole* and not just a property of one of its *parts*.

RESEARCHER: "Did you say a butterfly?"
PATRICIA: Yeah the shape was sort of like a butterfly…
RESEARCHER: So, can you point out the butterfly to me?
PATRICIA: Might be that one or… or it might be somewhere lower (points). Because it was, so like, the triangle was that shape (gestures with hands) and then it was like that (puts both hands out palms down in symmetrically opposed).

Referenced Emergent Behaviour*: I am the Tree*

In addition to these instances of referenced extrinsic perceptual emergence in which participants would interpret or perceive new compositions, there were also instances of altered or emergent behaviour during interaction. That is, there were instances of intrinsic perceptual emergence, namely where *feedback* occurs within the emergent *whole*. In these emergent behaviours a participant's interpretation of the work would go on to influence and inform a subsequent action by them. This action would then change their interpretation of the work and a feedback cycle would be established. Where the emergent *whole* feeds back to influence the nature of the *parts* that make up the system, it is an instance of *intrinsic* emergence.

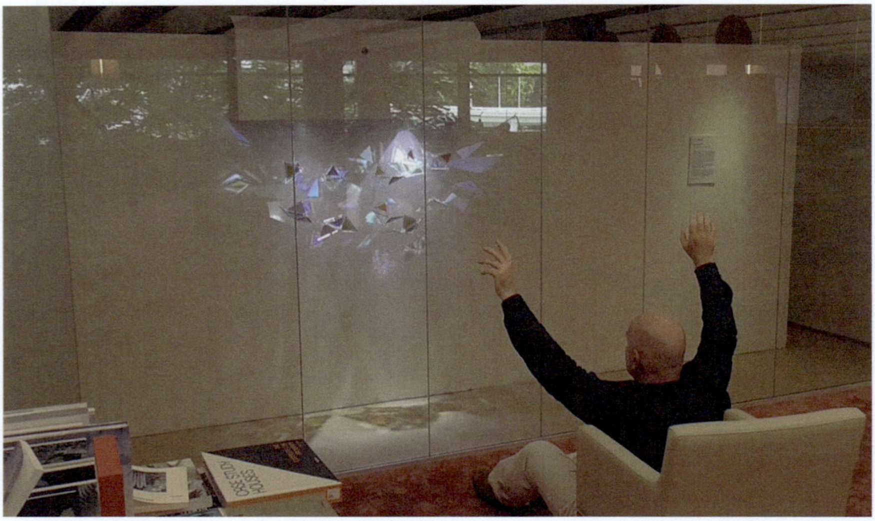

Fig. 6.10 Participant Tim interacts with *Dichroic Wade* and a tree behind him mirrored in the glass partition. Both are moving in response to wind conditions outside

One example of a *referenced* emergent behaviour was during participant Tim's interaction session (see Fig. 6.10). After spending approximately 20 minutes trying to figure it out by walking around in front of the work and pausing to watch, he pulled up a chair. Soon afterward he moved the chair slightly to sit on the floor in front of it. His interaction differs to the other participants in that he experienced the work in relation to the installation context. That is, he developed a behaviour and understanding of the work where he felt as though he was part of the artwork and part of a tree at the site. He described his experience as feeling as though he was influencing the movement of both the artwork and that tree outside.[2] Tim chose to focus on this combined movement of the tree outside moving in the wind, overlaid on top of the artwork that is moving in response to servo motors, prompted by wind speed updates outside. He explained that he was sitting on the floor to watch the reflections in the artwork as well as those of the tree outside. This position was better because his own reflection is no longer visible. He would raise his arms during this interaction period and described it as "*I'm being a part of the tree... so*

[2]This tree is located outside the building but visible through a window and mirrored in the glass partition that separates artwork from participant. While I did not originally intend for this tree to be a part of the artwork, I believe it was a meaningful addition to the work since it is consistent with the conceptual emphasis on site and because the tree moved with the same wind from the river as that which informed the artwork's movement. The tree is directly on the river, experiencing the wind movements that are similarly affecting the artwork. In one sense, the weather data visualised by the artwork are also visualised in the physical surroundings since the same wind would act on this physically real tree outside.

basically I can see the tree structure and part of the tree that's moving... (arms are raised during the interaction) *I'm the tree, I **am** the tree*."

Tim's experience was highly embodied. For example, at a later point he also described the tension he felt in his arms from having them raised as tiring but similar to what a tree's branches would feel.

The *"I am the tree"* experience developed out of a period of trying to figure out how the artwork works (about 20 min) which Tim also said was, at times, frustrating. However, he added that when he achieved this experience it was extremely joyful for him and, once he had reached that latter point, he did not feel as though he needed to be 'in control' of the work any longer since the *"feeling he is getting now is enough"*.

Concrete Emergent Behaviour

Two other participants, on separate occasions, were found to move along with the artwork reflections during their interaction with it. Each would see something in the work that would affect their interaction and this would, in turn, affect that which they are observing.

In the first case Phoebe was observed to move back-and-forth four times and then, shortly thereafter, move back-and-forth again. As in the discussion and data excerpts below, she was viewing the 'layers' of reflections, which she describes as resembling a '*story within a story'*. In the second case another participant Suzi describes how she would direct her gaze from one element to the next throughout the work to 'look through' and follow the reflections. Each is an example of concrete intrinsic perceptual emergence. Each situation features a *new, unpredictable* behaviour where the participant is engaged with the artwork as a *whole*. As is also shown from the below data excerpts and discussions, in both cases there is a type of repetitive behaviour that *feeds back* into participant understanding and subsequent actions, making it *intrinsic*. Finally, these participants were concerned with a direct, material experience of the work rather than what it might refer to or represent, and as such, these are instances of *concrete* emergence.

Layers Participant Phoebe described the artwork in terms of the reflections within and across the glass tiles. She later described the work as having depth *"because I feel like that encompasses all the layers and you kind of having to look at everything to see what's going on."* Our discussion during the post-event protocol session indicated that this understanding of layers of reflections informed her experience of the work, including a back-and-forth movement:

RESEARCHER: You said before there were lots of reflections going on. How did that make you feel? Was that just too much? Was it overwhelming? Or…?
PHOEBE No, it was cool. I thought it was kind of like a story within a story within a story. Like all these layers going on. Ummm…
RESEARCHER: So it worked for you?
PHOEBE: Yeah, I think so.

(And later on:) … I'm just moving back and forth.
RESEARCHER: So why are you moving around? Or are you not sure?
PHOEBE: No not really. I think… The only reason I can think of is maybe the angles of everything and just seeing and to direct ways of looking at it.
(And later on)
PHOEBE: umm well I felt like as the mirrors were moving I was also moving… a little too. Umm and that was initially because I thought it was me that was causing the mirrors to react. But then I think also just moving around I got different angles of the artwork and kind of, like, a different view of it

She says that "*moving made it more interesting for some reason*" and comments on how different angles provided different ways of looking at it. It is not unusual for people to move around when viewing an artwork, and ordinarily this would discount this behaviour as not new and therefore not emergent. Here, however, the movement has a specific character and meaning that is local to this artwork interaction. It is a back-and-forth movement that she repeated at least five times. It has a specific meaning to her which stems from interaction with the artwork—that of getting views of 'layers' of reflections and seeing a *story within a story*. Furthermore, this periodic back-and-forth movement followed on from a deliberate interaction to solicit a reaction from the work: *"initially because I thought it was me that was causing the mirrors to react."* This, however, changed as the intention became to get 'different views' of the artwork. This indicates that this behaviour was not planned and has instead emerged during interaction with the work.

Looking through Participant Suzi also describes a relationship between her physical movement and gaze across the work. She would step across to look at different parts, and this movement of hers would trigger movement in the work. However the movement of those parts also draws her gaze across the work.

SUZI: … as this one swings and swings a bit more, it makes that one swing a bit more… umm it sort of, I get drawn to one piece, and then as it affects the next piece it pulls me up to the next bit and I sort of see how this bit is connect - it affects - it is connected to that piece and like each small piece is actually part of a bigger piece.
(And later on)
SUZI: So I was not only looking at the reflections but looking through the pieces and seeing how the colour got pulled from light through pieces …and the palette that produces.

This latter comment suggests that engagement with the colour as well as the movement of the glass pieces influenced Suzi's movement and gaze. She explained this idea of the colour being 'pulled through' the glass pieces, as shown in Fig. 6.11.

Suzi's experience is informed by the moving light and colour. It follows on from trying to understand how the work works, or figure it out. This type of *assessing* behaviour is common to interaction with artworks and is not in itself new, nor, therefore, emergent (as discussed during the first case study and as has been identified by Costello et al. (2005)). During this session, however, her initial curiosity to understand how it works was replaced by an interest to instead know more about how the work could be experienced. This indicates that this behaviour, like Phoebe's movement above, was not planned, and has instead emerged during interaction with the work. She explains that she became focused on enjoying the work:

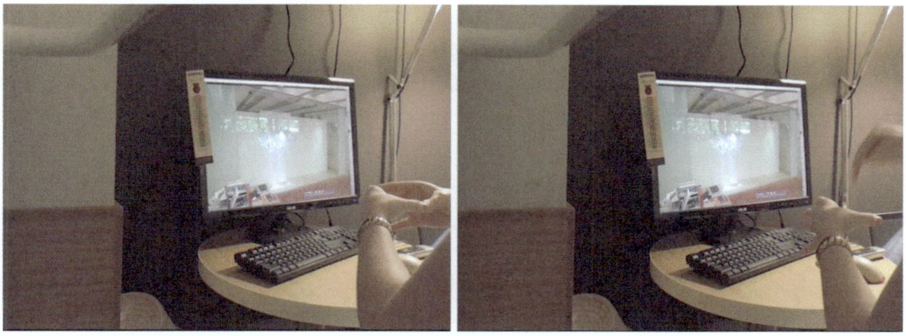

Fig. 6.11 During a video-cued recall session participant Suzi gestures to explain how colour is 'pulled through' the glass pieces

SUZI: Well I saw the sensor.
RESEARCHER: And here where you ducked down?
SUZI: I was looking at how all the strings connect together and then I thought no actually I want to keep the mystery there. Like I don't think I want to know how it works.
RESEARCHER: So you weren't just trying to figure it out?
SUZI: Yeah at first I wanted to, I did, and then I was enjoying it so much that I thought no I don't want to.
RESEARCHER: okay
SUZI: It's like when you see a magic trick and you think no I don't actually want to know how that was done because that was pretty cool.

Suzi explicitly identifies her experience as informed by colour and light rather than evoking a memory or relying on a representation to engender meaning. In this respect the experience articulated here is similar to Phoebe, who also focused on the layers of reflections. Both are concerned with a direct experience of the local, material elements of the work rather than what it might refer to, and can be considered *concrete* experiences of the work. Similarly, in both cases the participants enter a *feedback* loop with what they saw (the dynamic reflections, triggered by participant sensor and weather data) to change their movement, gaze and experience, which in response would change the imagery they were watching. As such, they are both examples of concrete intrinsic perceptual emergence.

Control

During the interview sessions participants were asked if they thought the system was easy or hard to interact with. All said that they thought it was easy, except for Tim. Interestingly, many of the same participants also said that they did not think their presence affected the work. While Suzi and Phoebe recognised they had some influence, complete understanding of what this was and how it worked did not seem to hold much importance. As Tim said of his own experience at the end, he no longer needed to *"feel in control of the work"*, since the feeling he was getting of 'being a tree' was enough. He did, however, change his mind, and admitted later on that he almost 'gave up' during his interaction in trying to control the work and not being able to. This, as well as participant understanding and, indeed, expectations of interacting with the work, indicated some issues around participant sense of control that would require addressing.

For instance, in the emergent behaviours found and listed above, the participants *did* think they were affecting the artwork, but they were not overtly concerned with controlling it. This could mean that increasing feedback of participant response could increase the work's capacity for eliciting emergent behaviour. Of course it may not, but a similar issue concerning lack of participant control was also found—and addressed—during the *Glass Pond* study, with strong outcomes of emergence in the ensuing artwork *+−now*. That design approach involved facilitating participant understanding and feedback. Here this was similarly identified as a necessary 'calibration' of the *Dichroic Wade* art system.

This understanding of control led to some changes to this artwork before its installation at the Art. CHI gallery in the USA. That is, the evaluation findings informed the creative work. These changes include replacing the PIR sensor with an ultrasonic sensor and including some more differentiated movement responses in the work, such as the *Crescendo* motif described in Chap. 5.

Reflection

Seven clear examples of emergence were found out of the 14 interaction sessions with participants. Mostly these were the interpretation of emergent compositions, such as the butterfly and flock of birds. Having better visual quality in the post-event protocol's video recordings may render more instances since, as discussed above, only some of the reflections and light transmissions were captured in those images and able to prompt discussion.

The three instances of *intrinsic* emergence that were found have been discussed above. The data also revealed some aspects of participant interaction, such as participant understanding of their influence over the system's behaviour. Tim described this as an issue of control. This finding informed some changes in the artwork including redesigned sensor and remapping of behaviours for its installation in the USA.

Reflection upon this has however also revealed that there is a difference in the type of interaction that the two *Lightworks* pieces engender. These works are more architectural and 'ambient environments' given the rendering of weather data which is more for background information processing than the typical interactive system which prioritises focused, foreground information processing.

On a related note, the inclusion of weather data means that these works are active without participant interaction. In this respect *Dichroic Wade* differs from the other two case studies: this artwork does not require someone to interact with it in order to exist. It may also be that one can see patterns of (weather driven) behaviour with the work, i.e. extrinsic perceptual emergence, without needing to interact with it. The fact that participants thought the work was 'easy to interact with', yet at the same time did not think they were affecting it, can indicate that their expectation of the work is similarly one of ambience.

These works are perhaps more appropriatelyconsidered *influencing* works, rather than the 'responsive', direct interaction with immediate feedback that we are used to in most interactive environments today. Retaining this character is also something that became a design agenda for *Dichroic Wade*. Some design implications for working with influencing interactives are discussed in Chap. 8.

Conclusion

These evaluations have shown what emergent experiences can be like. Theoretical qualities of emergence have featured throughout participant descriptions. These include a perceived lack of control and system unpredictability, such as participant feedback from the *Glass Pond* study (Seevinck et al. 2006) and more recently in the *Dichroic Wade* prototype. Participants' experiences can also be understood in terms of openness, such as Ted's description of "*infinite variation like when you look at the stars*" *(+−now*), and Phoebe's description of *Dichroic Wade* as having "*depth*" and a "*story within a story*". In many cases the participants perceived new and surprising images or compositions during their interaction with the artworks. In addition, creative interactions also occurred, ranging from co-creating compositions by engaging dynamically with these unpredictable and surprising systems (for example animating and piano playing in +−*now),* through to innovating in the action of mark-making itself (for example Shirley's *stamping* in *Of me With me*). Other emergent participant behaviours were also found, for example when people would initiate new playful behaviours from the combined affordances and qualities of the work as a *whole* such as chasing the surprising lights, or find new ways of interacting like moving through the depth of the (layers of) reflections.

Evaluation data can be coded for emergence, as has been demonstrated here. In this approach interesting items or 'effects' are identified within the data corpus and subsequently re-coded for emergence criteria such as how it started (using the *start* code to test for *newness* and *unpredictability*) and how the event may or may not engage with the experience of the artwork as a *whole* (using the *Object* codes to test for *whole* or *parts*). The TEIA further guides analysis in helping determine what type of emergence may have occurred.

Non-emergent behaviours are also useful to our understanding of interactive art. For example, they can show us how people tend to act around interactive artworks; that is, they can reveal generic behaviour. Three of these more predictable behaviours were identified here. These are trying to figure out how it works i.e. *assessing* the system; *resetting* the artwork; and *anthropomorphising* it. Another type of non-emergent behaviour that was found relates to instances where participants did not engage with the artwork as a *whole* but rather the construction of meaning was limited to just a *part* of the work. These non-emergent interaction behaviours are discussed in more depth in the last *Insight for Emergent Interactions* chapter.

Last Note on Evaluation

This chapter has provided evaluation guidance for understanding participant experience by illustrating the process with three artworks: *Dichroic Wade* (2016), *Of me With me* (2015) and +−*now* (2008a). Another two exploratory studies for +−*now* and *Glass Pond* were also briefly reviewed. Since the experience of an artwork is contextual, evaluations were conducted in naturalistic settings (for an artwork). Data collection also prioritised non-intrusive methods such as observation and interviews after the interaction had taken place. However, evaluating for participant experience is not without challenges. With the diversity of interactive artwork and practice there is no single approach that can work for all works or all artists. In some interactions, observation needs to capture gross body movement, and in others, fine fingers. These are differing demands for the technology and researcher, particularly given priorities for non-intrusive methods. Trade-offs necessarily occur, as has been the case with my latest study of *Dichroic Wade*. Here the data collection suffered because of what was possible in the field and the camera technology available. Similarly, space constraints at Redcliffe gallery meant that post-event protocols could not be conducted for the *Of me With me* study, which also impacted on the reflective accounts.

The chapter has illustrated an integration of evaluation research with creative practice. Here, the findings and insights from the evaluations provide '*situation talk-back*' to '*reframe*' creative thinking (Schön 1983). For me, the integrated PBR approach led to an interest in the concept of emergence in 2005. It facilitated deep conceptual enquiry alongside creative investigation. As such, it has directed forays into new territories—such as combining different, varied data streams within interactive artworks and facilitating open-ended interactions. Some insights from these practices and the research findings are discussed in the *Insight for Emergent Interactions* chapter, along with other implications for design.

References

Bilda Z, Candy L, Edmonds E (2007) An embodied cognition framework for interactive experience. Co-Design 3:123–137

Bilda Z, Costello B, Amitani S (2006) Collaborative analysis framework for evaluating interactive art experience. Co-Design 2:225–238

Braun V, Clarke V (2008) Using thematic analysis in psychology—qualitative research in psychology—Volume 3, Issue 2. Qual Res Psychol 3:77–101. doi:10.1191/1478088706qp063oa

Costello B, Muller L, Amitani S, Edmonds EA (2005) Understanding the experience of interactive art. In: Iamascope in Beta_Space. ACM Press, pp 49–56

Glaser BG, Strauss AL (1967) The discovery of grounded theory strategies for qualitative research. Aldine Publishing Company, New York, USA

Miles MB, Huberman AM (1994) Qualitative Data Analysis: An Expanded Sourcebook, Second Edition. Sage Publications, Thousand Oaks

Oxford (2006) Oxford English dictionary. Oxford University Press, UK

Patton MQ (2001) Qualitative research and evaluation methods, 3rd edn. SAGE Publications Inc, Thousand Oaks, USA

Preece J, Rogers Y, Sharp H et al (1994) Human computer interaction. Addison-Wesley, USA

QSR (2010) Nvivo 9. QSR international Pty Ltd, Doncaster, Australia

QSR (2014) Nvivo 10. QSR international Pty Ltd, Doncaster, Australia

Richards L (2006) Handling qualitative data a practical guide. Sage Publications, London, England

Schön DA (1983) The reflective practitioner how professionals think in action, 1995th edn. Temple Smith, London, England

Seevinck J, Candy L, Edmonds E (2006) Exploration and reflection in interactive art. In: Glass Pond. ACM Press, Sydney, Australia, pp 143–150. doi:10.1145/1228175.1228202

Seevinck J (2008a) +−now,interactive artwork

Seevinck J, Edmonds E (2008b) Emergence and the art system "plus minus now". Design Stud (Interaction Design Special Issue) 29:541–555

Seevinck J, Edmonds E (2009) Open in art, nature and emergence. ACM Press, Melbourne Australia, pp 365–368. doi:10.1145/1738826.1738898

Seevinck J (2014) Of me With me, interactive artwork

Seevinck J (2015) Light Currents, interactive art installation

Seevinck J (2016) Dichroic Wade, interactive art installation

Shneiderman B, Plaisant C, Cohen M, Jacobs S (2010) Designing the user interface: strategies for effective human-computer interaction, 5th edn. Pearson, Boston, USA

Sidelle A (1996) Constructivism and conventionalism. In: Borchert DM (ed) Encyclopedia of philosophy, 2nd edn. Macmillan Reference USA, Farmington Hills, pp 474–476

Strauss AL, Corbin J (1998) Basics of qualitative research: techniques and procedures for developing grounded theory. Sage, Thousand Oaks, USA

Chapter 7
Emergence in Depth

Abstract The preceding chapters have provided a foundation for emergence in interactive art. In this chapter the interested reader will find an expansion of the theoretical discussions presented in Chap. 2, facilitating insight into some of the debates and concerns surrounding emergence. As well as theoretical, however, the focus of this discussion is also illustrative and pragmatic, its aim being to find a useful understanding of emergence in the context of interactive art. I will begin with the challenge of explaining emergence. This involves reviewing reductionist through to deterministic and complex systems approaches. Digital art and computational models for emergence are also presented. The processes of perception that inform how we see are then reviewed. These can help us understand how designers perceive emergent shapes, as well as creative, visual thinking more generally. There is still much to understand when it comes to creative,perceptual emergence perceptual emergence and the physical emergence of our complex, natural world, but the application of deep understandings of emergence to interactive art experiences will move enquiry forward.

Introduction

This chapter builds on the characterisation, definition and overview of emergence presented in Chap. 2. As was broadly defined there, emergence occurs *when a new form or concept appears that was not directly implied by the context from which it arose. This emergent 'whole' is more than a simple sum of the parts*. This chapter provides more background to this definition, with its focus being on how it works in the context of interactive art. Specifically, given this book's focus, the thinking around emergence is pragmatic, emphasising two key elements. Firstly, computation in emergence is an important consideration given the prevalence of digital media in interactive art and the pioneering generative interactive artworks concerned with emergence (such as *A-Volve* (1994), *Autopoeisis* (2000) and *Sympathetic Sentience* (1995) discussed in Chap. 4). Secondly, as discussed in Chap. 2, creativity is a key aspect of emergence, and creativity and perception are

J. Seevinck, *Emergence in Interactive Art*, Springer Series on Cultural Computing,
DOI 10.1007/978-3-319-45201-2_7

themselves key aspects to participant experience in interactive art. The creative role of perception is therefore also discussed in this chapter.

To begin with, however, I will review the debate surrounding the 'explainability' of emergence. This debate, particularly through a reductionist critique, has undermined the concept of emergence as something material and knowable. Other thinkers, from physics and complex systems theory through to design, have, however, asserted the usefulness of emergence and provided some arguments towards resolving the issue.

Explaining Emergence

In 1889 the philosopher John Stuart Mill described two 'conjuncts of causes', identifying these as distinct phenomena in our world. The first case is where the "... *joint effect of several causes [is] ... identical to the sum of their separate effects...*" (1889) For example, where a series of dynamic forces are combined, the resultant direction of motion of a body they act on is the same as if the forces had acted separately one at a time. This view is, however, a deductive approach that can only explain and predict the behaviour of some phenomena. There are others which cannot be so simply 'summed'. These other types of conjuncts are where "... *agencies which are brought together cease entirely, and a totally different set of phenomena arise...*" Instead of a 'compounding of parts' there is a change in kind of the effect of the constituting parts. That is, this emergent phenomenon is a difference "*...between the case in which the joint effect of causes is the sum of their separate effects, and the case in which it is heterogenous to them...*" (Mill 1889).

The inability to explain such phenomena in terms of parts, that is, reductively, was problematic for Mill and others of his time. Alternative, 'holistic' approaches were seen as leading to mystical interpretations of these 'conjuncts of causes'. The efforts of Vitalism to explain the emergence of life are one example: Vitalist philosopher Henri Bergson described the distinguishing aspect between a live organism and a dead one in terms of *élan vital*, meaning 'vital essence'. This vital essence is an external entity that combines with the parts to form the whole, emergent phenomenon of a living organism (1978). However, with no further explanation offered, this can seem too much like magic.

The tension between holism and reductionism has caused much debate for emergence. Holism considers the interconnectedness of the parts, holding that they cannot exist independently but rather must be thought of in relation to their whole —a whole that may also include contextual factors. Reductionism, on the other hand, considers explanations in terms of the theories or properties of the constituting parts alone (Oxford Dictionaries 2010).

When he first identified these 'conjuncts of causes', Mill cited water as an example of an effect that could not be explained by analysing its constituting chemicals hydrogen and oxygen. Similarly the water also behaves according to different laws than those of its constituting parts. Science philosopher Ernest Nagel has, however, critiqued this example and position to argue that an emergent effect is only emergent relative to a theory that is unable to explain it in simpler terms. If another theory was found to explain this effect then it would not be emergent relative to this latter theory (1961). Therefore, while water's property of transparency cannot be deduced from theories about hydrogen and oxygen, making it emergent relative to them, theories of optics *can* explain the transparency of water. Relative to optics, water's transparent effect is not emergent (1961).

For Nagel, the difficulty of deducing or predicting the emergent effect is a matter of what is included in the various theories and their premises, and no quality can be deduced from a theory which does not somehow include or allow for it in its premise. Thus although water's transparency can be explained in the theory of optics, unless 'transparency' or a similar concept was included in theories of hydrogen and oxygen it cannot be deduced from those theories. Nagel considers this disparity a key point to emergence.

However, Nagel's position is also assuming that if we do not have a theory to explain the phenomenon today we will have one in the future. He is defining emergence as relative to our knowledge and, in so doing, he is also defining the concept as subject to our ignorance. This position has some problems: the assumption that we will one day be able to explain everything is, arguably, idealistic; furthermore, a reductive explanation of an emergent effect to simple parts still requires the emergent effect to guide it, and is thus self-defeating (Emmeche et al. 1997).

Contemporary physics also has some difficulties with reductionist approaches to understanding emergence. As physics professor and director of the New England Centre for Complex Systems, Yaneer Bar-Yam, states, "*Science has made great progress by taking things apart. What is left out of this approach is the problem of understanding relationships between the parts*" (Bar-Yam 2002). A complex systems approach seeks to explain emergence by discovering the "*new general principles-organizing principles over and above the known laws of physics*" (Paul Davies in Emmeche et al. 1997). Physicists from Stanford and Los Alamos National Laboratory, Laughlin and Pine maintain that observation and experiment are needed, given that deducing such higher order organising principles that inform emergent behaviours from underlying equations is generally impossible (2000). As philosopher Emmeche and his colleagues asserted, how do we know what to model at the level of the parts if we have not already observed and experienced it at the level of the whole? This latter, higher-order emergent quality will guide the investigation at the lower level to direct any deductive reasoning from first principles. The former remains necessary for the latter.

Simulation

The challenge of explaining a system's emergent property in terms of its parts do not, however, disqualify emergence as a valid area of enquiry. *Weak emergence*, such as that proposed by philosopher Mark Bedau, is one example of emergence that is consistent with reductionism. It can still be investigated and explained, yet retains its qualities of newness, surprise and a whole that is qualitatively different to its constituting parts. Bedau cites traffic jams—which seem to arise spontaneously and stretch back along roads—as an example of this scientifically useful, weak emergence. Here it is possible to trace through the series of causal events, step-by-step, that led to the congestion. "*Explaining the generation of a system's macro-behaviour by aggregating and iterating the earlier local micro-interactions over time I shall describe, for short, as crawling the micro-causal web.*" Computer simulations of artificial life and chaos theory are other examples of weak emergence (Bedau 1997, 2008).

This idea of necessitating 'crawling the micro-causal web' to explain the emergent phenomenon can also be understood as characterising emergence. That is, we have emergence when "*...there is no short-cut generative explanation of that macro-property that is true, complete, accurate and can avoid crawling the causal web.*" This more philosophical and less obvious point concerns the representation or description of something as a means to determine its capacity for emergence. Where we must trace through all the causal steps one by one in order to describe or understand the outcome, we can with more confidence assert it as emergent. On the other hand, if we can describe an outcome as a simple algorithmic sum, for example, then we do not have a greater 'whole'.

Simulation can play a key role here. Simulation has been cited as a means to differentiate degrees of complexity in systems. For example, systems scientist Vince Darley says that when simulation is the most economic approach to explain a phenomena, it may be complex enough to facilitate emergence: "*a true emergent phenomenon is one for which the optimal means of prediction is simulation*" (1994). Computer simulation can be a way to differentiate complex structures from other simpler constructions. There are, however, other aspects to the discussions around simulation in the computer that are also relevant here.

Determinism and Openness in the Computer

Computers, as finite state machines, are inherently deterministic[1] and bounded. Yet emergence has been characterised as unpredictable and open-ended. What, then, are the possibilities for emergence in the digital domain?

---

[1]A deterministic system exhibits a series of cause and effect operations. Each action causes a reaction, which is in turn an action on something else, causing it to react. Modern computers are understood as deterministic systems because they operate by executing small steps of instructions one after the other to calculate the outcome. The same starting step will always result in the same outcome. A simple example is a line of dominoes. Assuming no external forces or other influences (the system is bounded), if we topple the first domino we will topple the last domino because the first will knock over the second, that will topple the third and so on until the last is knocked over.

Determinism may initially seem problematic for the concept of emergence as it implies predictability.[2] This is not however the case—rather, determinism can facilitate explanation as well as unpredictability. In deterministic systems we can have emergent features that we can also explain. If we are able to trace the steps to its generation then we can explain it through its causes. Emmeche, Køppe and Stjernfelt call this '*explainable causality*' (1997). They and physicist Crutchfield (2003) cite Poincarés study of the '*three-body problem*', the collective motion of a sun, a planet, and a moon, and chaos theory as examples where deterministic systems, while explainable, are not necessarily predictable. Two celestial bodies, such as a planet and moon will follow a regular elliptical trajectory around their combined centre of mass. However, adding a third body—the sun, perhaps—changes the trajectories in unpredictable ways. There is much more sensitivity to initial conditions of orbit. Similarly we can look outside in the morning and we can tell if the weather will hold for the afternoon, but predicting rain for next week is not so straightforward. As Emmeche, Køppe and Stjernfelt have said, "*something which is unpredictable does not have to be unexplainable*" (1997), and the lack of predictability of an emergent phenomenon does not necessarily mean that it is non-deterministic.

The bounded, finite nature of the physical system does however constrain the type of emergence that might occur. That is, emergence within the computer, such as artificial life and other simulations, is limited to the finite domain of possibilities of the machine. Emergence that is constructed in the computer is described by Peter Cariani as *computational emergence*. An implicit limitation that Cariani identifies is its replicability and, as such, lack of surprise of creating something unexpectedly new. This is because any computer simulation will, provided we repeat the initial conditions, produce the same results. As researcher and artist Whitelaw puts it, "*...the same plant will grow time and time again from the same seed*" (2004). Emergence does not really occur because nothing new can result from the finite state machine. For Cariani, computer simulations such as AL:

> … do not change the formal and completely replicable nature of the process. Increasing the size of the simulation, adding new layers of simulation rules, simulating random or chaotic processes, or representing genotypes or phenotypes will in no way change the replicability of the simulation; hence these changes will be ineffective at transforming a previously non-emergent simulation into an emergent one (1991).

Emergent Effects on People

Computational emergence does, however, have emergent effects on people watching: there is still the opportunity for emergence in the mind of the observer as they comprehend the patterns and develop new understandings and insights. As

[2]Emergent phenomena may become predictable once observed, but are only ever predictable from the higher level on which they are manifest, not from the lower level of constituting parts (Emmeche et al. 1997).

Cariani goes on to say, simulations can"... *change the way we think and interact with the world. Rather than emergent devices in their own right, these computer simulations are catalysts for emergent processes in our minds; they help us create new ways of seeing the world*" (1991). Here the unpredictability and novelty that we expect of emergence is occurring within the participant-observer.

This idea of facilitating a subjective experience of emergence through computational means has been explored in the arts. AL artist and researchers McCormack and Dorin describe the potential of 'informationally open' systems. That is, the art system can be opened up to include a real-time feedback loop between a participant and the system, and the participant can experience interactive dynamics which are "*beyond the physical or virtual elements that compose the work*"(2001).

AL artists and researchers Sommerer and Mignonneau have also engaged with computation, emergence and openness in audience interaction. As we saw in Chap. 4, they work to facilitate open-ended and creative participant experience through employing the inherently creative aspects of AL. For them, the AL process in art is characterised to "*become like traces of living processes themselves*", creative beginnings of life which further describe artist engagement with emergence. Sommerer and Mignonneau describe audience interaction as "*continuously evolving levels of experience*" and the "*discovery of unexpected new paths*" rather than "*choosing between a variety of different choices and paths*" (1998). The experience emphasises creativity, unpredictability and finding something 'new'—all key characteristics of emergence. The work can also, however, demonstrate how a system can be 'opened up' by adding a participant to it in order to change some aspects of the computational emergence generated. For example, when participants draw an initial shape, this is transformed into a creature which, depending on how long it can survive, will reproduce and affect future additional shapes (Dietz 2002). The system behaviour is unpredictable insofar as we do not know what shapes people might draw or when, and this influences the creatures' form and evolution of creatures within the system. Participant involvement opens up the work, and the replicability and predictability of any computational emergence occurring within the artwork is mitigated, though this is limited to the extent of participant involvement that the system allows.

Adding real world sensor data to systems, such as people's movement through spaces (*Autopoeisis* (Rinaldo 2000)) or internet streamed weather data (*Dichroic Wade* (Seevinck 2016)), are other means to opening up systems and affecting the computational emergence within these. The changing configurations of Rinaldo's flock or harmonics in the oscillations in my work *Dichroic Wade* are some examples of the type of emergent patterns that may be generated. These are in addition to the subjective, perceptual emergence that is facilitated in the participant-observer perceiving melodies, dances and so on. The realm of possibilities does, however, remain computable and bounded in each case.

That is, the system as a whole cannot facilitate true emergence; only the added aspect of human interaction has that capacity for adaptation. As Whitelaw has pointed out, the need for adaptation means that adding an open domain such as a human being or the internet does not make it adaptive unless new sensors, effectors, internet communication protocols or similar are also evolving (Whitelaw 2004).[3] He describes Adrian Thompson's *Field Gate Programmable Array* as an example of a physical system that can facilitate adaptation and emergence. Here integrated circuits (IC) evolve directly on the hardware. The designs are "*...unconstrained by binary abstraction... making full use of the complex dynamics of their physical medium*" (Whitelaw 2004), as well as not needing to align themselves with any observer/programmer specified rules of operation. The array adapts semantically relative to the non-finite and non-discrete natural, physical world.

Summary

In returning to the earlier question on the possibilities for emergence in the digital domain, given the computer's inherently deterministic and bounded nature, it is useful to recall the context of this inquiry: interactive art. For the purposes of this book we can therefore answer this question as follows.

First, determinism can afford explainability and unpredictability for our participant-observer. We have seen that unpredictability can be sustained within an explainable system. In fact, this capacity for explanation is one reason why reductionism is not a necessary or useful approach to understanding emergence. Instead of trying to explain it in terms of its parts, it can be more useful to pursue empirical evidence and computer models, as well as the other tools that complex systems science draws upon. This is an area that specifically focuses on the relations between parts in order to understand emergent behaviours occurring across systems.

Secondly, where a participant is interacting with a computationally emergent system they can be seen to 'open up' that system. An opportunity for new and surprising meanings or perceptions will then come about within that open part of the system. This is, in fact, core to the creation of emergent experiences.

Simulation and creation of models can, when compared to evidence from the real natural world, facilitate understanding of those real world phenomena. This is a point towards the usefulness of emergence that is simulated in the computer as well as the potential that it provides for facilitating emergence in interactive, computer-based artworks. The new area of complex systems works with digital simulations to understand complex systems and emergence in range of domains—from biological life, the human brain, through to weather patterns. The following

[3]When adaptation occurs we are seeing something heterogeneously new occurring at another, higher level—the level of the whole. Whitelaw follows Cariani to identify adaptation as necessary for emergence (Cariani 1991).

section discusses complex systems and includes a basic model of a complex system demonstrating how that process can facilitate explanation and understanding.

Understanding and Modelling Physical Emergence

Through simulating life processes artists and researchers are computing patterns that help us understand living organisms. As we saw in Chap. 4, artists can generate emergence in the computer using artificial life (AL) algorithms, but there are other computational models for generating emergent patterns as well. The next section looks at the relatively new area of complex systems science which facilitates direct investigation of emergence in the natural world, through conceptual and analytical frameworks as well as experiments and computer simulations of processes.

Complex Systems

Complex systems study seeks to understand how parts in a given system relate to one another to generate collective behaviours. These parts can be the neurons that link together to form a brain, through to the interacting individuals that make up a social system. Where smaller scale parts 'self-organise', structures or patterns will emerge. The brain, social behaviours, a weather system are all considered patterns that come about from the interactions between people, neurons and air flow. In terms of complex systems theory, "*emergence refers to the relationship between the details and the larger view*" (Bar-Yam 2002). We can think of emergence here as the larger scale patterns that come about from the self-organisation of parts.

These patterns are 'wholes', structures that have come about through processes involving the local parts. Rather than being authored by a directing voice or set of instructions, as in an auto assembly plant where each part of a car is put in a specific place, here the parts direct themselves and we have a 'bottom up' self-organisation. The regular patterning of ripples of sand on a beach or the more intricate patterning of a living being like an animal or person demonstrate this self-organisation. Sand ripples such as those pictured in Fig. 7.1 are patterns that come about from the interactions of grains of sand with each other and water flow overhead (Hanes et al. 2016). They come about, in part, from the water picking up sand granules and bouncing them along the surface of the sand, which impacts on other sand grains to displace them as well, though for shorter distances. Those that are higher up will be more exposed and build up, and the crests self-organise. Similarly those lower down tend to be protected. In this manner, crests and troughs build up which provide the ripple pattern: the emergent structure that we perceive.

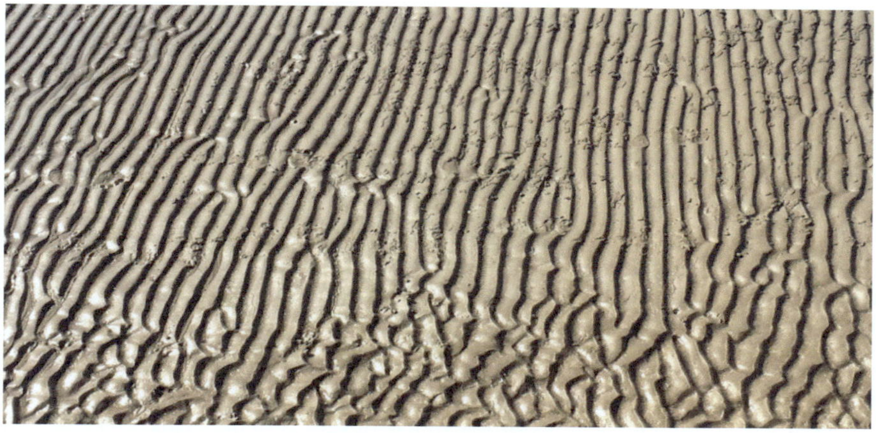

Fig. 7.1 Ripples in sand at the beach are an example of pattern formation in a complex natural system

A living organism is also a type of pattern. The first, single cell will go through a process of 'development' where heart, lungs bones and so on are all formed—once again with no plan or higher-order direction. There is no homunculus that grows in size and, as Bar-Yam asserts, neither is the cell DNA accurately understood as a blueprint or complete instructions. Rather DNA operates by 'telling' cells how to 'talk' to other cells and, through this self-organising process, the human being is created (Bar-Yam 2002).

Bar-Yam provides some examples of simple patterns of human behaviour to demonstrate this self-organisation. The 'local majority rule' shows how local communication and influence can drive pattern formation. In his example, a ring of young children are wanting to talk to their neighbours (one on either side) about buying either Pokémon cards (orange dot) or a beanie (blue dot). While they will each begin with their preference (line 1), if neither neighbour has the same interest they will change their mind so as to have someone to talk to, but otherwise will retain their initial preference. As time unfolds, 'patches' of Pokémon or beanie buyers will form and remain stable over time, resulting in patterning. Starting from the top row, each row is an application of the rule that when a child shares an interest with either neighbour it will retain that interest; otherwise it will change it to match the neighbour. Over five generations this local interaction between the units demonstrates how stable patterns can emerge (Fig. 7.2).

Patterns in animal fur are formed in the same way, although here we can think of the cells as releasing chemicals to their immediate neighbourhood that either activates or inhibits local pigment production. Spotted or striped patterns that occur are the result of local interactions that are activated, while at the same time there is an inhibiting longer-range interaction. Reaction-diffusion algorithms can be used to model these patterns in computer applications. They can simulate animal skin patterning as well as other biological processes. Computer graphics research has

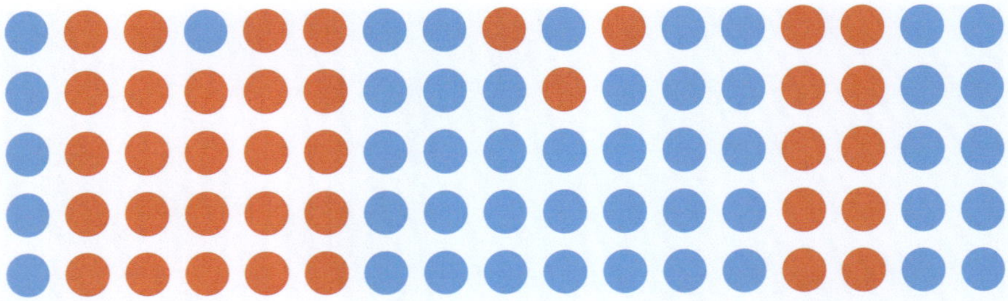

Fig. 7.2 Simple interactions between units starting from the *top row*, over five generations, will settle into a repeated pattern demonstrating the local majority rule as in Bar-Yam (after Fig. 8 in 2002)

rendered visual implementations of reaction-diffusion systems (Turk 1991; Witkin and Kass 1991; Lee et al. 1993; Pearson 1993) and graphics libraries and features are available to electronic and digital artists as well as researchers to create complex visual patterning. For example, the *Toxiclibs Simulibs* software class (Schmidt 2016) facilitates its implementation within the *Processing* API (Fry and Raes 2001) or the '*Reaction Diffusion VOP node*' (Animatrix 2015) extension for visual effects software *Side Effects Houdini* (Davidson and Hermanovic 1998). These are typically used to create animal skin and fur patterning and other real-world visual effects in computer graphics for film and computer games (e.g. see also Kim et al. 2015).

Neural networks and the brain can also be broadly understood along the same lines as skin patterning. Bar-Yam describes that if we think of the neurons in a network as connected through synapses which either 'excite' or 'inhibit' the one it connects to, and we think of the condition of each neuron in a network as being either 'active' or 'quiet', then a given active neuron, connected to another through an excitatory synapse, will be more likely to cause that connected neuron to also become active. If the connection is through an inhibitory synapse, the second neuron is less likely to become activated. Of course this is a more complex network than what we see with the animal skin patterning—here synapses can connect to multiple neurons and over greater distances than immediate proximity. But, says Bar-Yam, we can still talk about "*the pattern of firing of the neurons at one instant like the pattern of pigment at one instant*" (2002).

Studying the interactions between parts in complex models can help us understand the more complex patterns we increasingly see in our world.[4] As we've seen, tools can include conceptual understandings and analytical tools as well as models for simulation.

[4]Bar-Yam argues that society has become increasingly complex. The global conflict of the Cold War being replaced by a global economy and the relatively peaceful collapse of most Western dictatorships are among the evidence presented that our world is increasingly self-organising, moving to networks of control rather than singular loci of control.

Artificial Life

The broader domain of artificial life (AL) research and creative practice have involved modelling life processes through implementing computational models of evolution. As discussed in Chap. 4, AL has been used by artists to facilitate audience creative involvement and interaction—by involving them in the processes of creating artificial life (Sommerer and Mignonneau 1994) through to the generation of new aural compositions (Penny and Schulte 1995) and behaviours (Rinaldo 2000). In a formative paper one of the founders of AL, Christopher Langton describes emergence as key to the field and implicit in its methods:

> The "key" concept in AL is emergent behavior. Natural life emerges out of the organized interactions of a great number of non-living molecules, with no global controller responsible for the behavior of every part. Rather, every part is a behavior itself, and life is the behavior that emerges from out of all of the local interactions among individual behavors. It is this bottom-up, distributed, local-determination of behavior that AL employs in its primary methodological approach to the generation of life-like behaviors. (Langton 1987)

Langton follows the biological metaphor of genotypes (the genes in DNA) and phenotypes (the expression of those genes, in physical form) to articulate 'GTypes' and 'PTypes' in their systems respectively. By executing a GType's set of simple rules, global behaviours or structures can 'emerge' in the organism itself, the PType. The process is characterised as bottom-up and distributed on the local level, without direction from a higher order entity. "*Any behaviour at levels higher than the individual programs is therefore emergent*" (Langton 1987).

His well-known cellular automata *Langton's ant* is an example of a simple rule based model where a given square on a grid will start randomly as either black or white, but then proceed to affect neighbouring squares according to rules that include the current state of neighbours (when encountering a black square, flip it to white and turn left 90° and step forward; when encountering a white square, flip it to black and turn right 90° and step forward). Through iterations of these rules, black and white squares are populated across the grid. More interestingly, chaotic distributions of black and white will carry on but eventually an emergent attractor will appear: the 'highway' pattern at the bottom of Fig. 7.3. This visual pattern repeats and sustains itself across the grid as order overtakes the chaotic distribution of black and white squares. The highway was not in the initial rules or program for behaviour. Rather it is an unexpected, heterogeneously new behaviour and ordered arrangement within the system.

Another example of computer generated emergence is through Lindenmayer systems (L-Systems), models of branching structures used by botanists for understanding plant life. The branching is recursive and automatic. The models can reveal the emergence of patterns in nature (of those biological forms they are simulating) through iteratively executing the program rules (Prusinkiewicz and Lindenmayer 1990; Prusinkiewicz et al. 1996) as in Fig. 7.4.

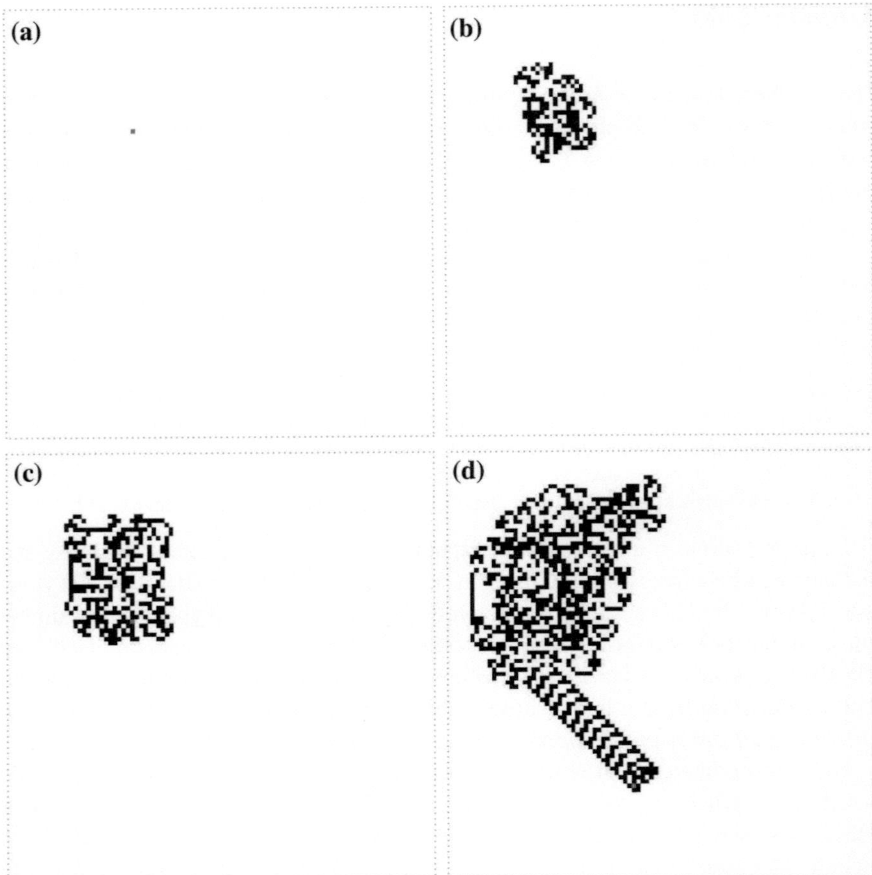

Fig. 7.3 Screen captures of Langton's Ant model programmed by Turner Bohlen. **a** Starting condition and model progress after approximately **b** 1000 steps and **c** 4000 steps. After **d** 10 000 steps the highway emerges (Bohlen 2016)

The structures of nature are described with algorithms that are self-similar and use 'rewriting' to change over time (Prusinkiewicz and Lindenmayer 1990). The snowflake curve pictured in Fig. 7.5 demonstrates the similarity between the whole and a part of the whole, and the process of rewriting that leads to this development over time. Mandelbrot describes this process for the generation of the snowflake, or Koch curve:

> Let us restate the basic principle of construction of the triadic Koch curve: One begins with two shapes, an initiator and a generator. The latter is an oriented broken line made up of N equal sides of length r. Thus each stage of the construction begins with a broken line and consists in replacing each straight interval with a copy of the generator, reduced and displaced so as to have the same end points as those of the interval being replaced. (Mandelbrot 1982)

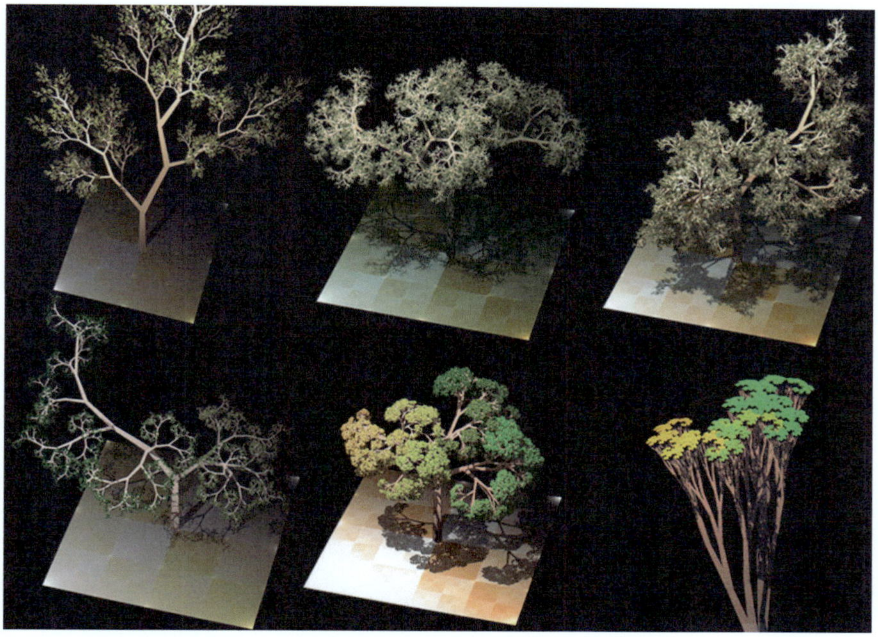

Fig. 7.4 Images of tree shapes generated using L-Systems. Created by Solkoll (2005, reproduced from Wikipedia)

Lindenmayer systems facilitate understanding of living processes and structures: the patterns of emergent natural forms. As a modelling process, they also provide "*...a methodology for constructing models according to biological observations and measurements*" (Prusinkiewicz et al. 1996). The computational processes of Lindenmayer systems, particularly in their application to computer graphics, can provide mechanisms for artists and designers to explore emergent forms or shapes as well as behaviours.

The rewriting process exemplified in the Koch curve above informed my own iterative drawing artwork, *Of me With me* (Seevinck 2014) discussed in Chap. 5. This interactive artwork was designed to amplify participant creativity and agency through mirroring, extending, their gestures. The creative, interactive experience was the core focus here, facilitated by the real-time interactive rewriting of a participant's incoming 'gesture' or 'generator' shape. That is, segments in their initial drawn line are extracted and replaced with generator shapes, where those generator shapes are, in fact, the participant's original curve. Example images created in interaction with this system are pictured in Fig. 7.6. As shown there, the participant's generator curve is black, while the rewritten emergent shape (echoing this part) is rendered as grey lines.

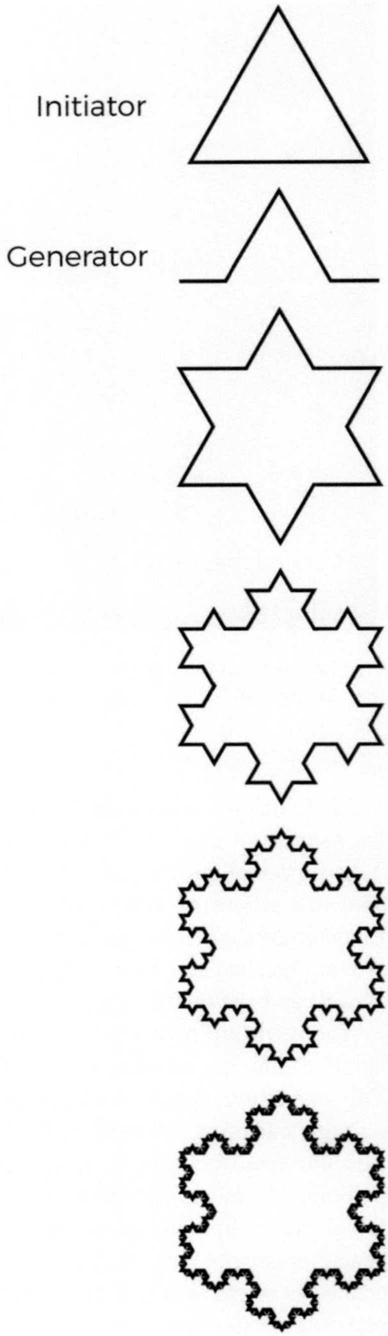

Fig. 7.5 The snowflake or Koch curve is constructed through rewriting with initiator and generator shapes (after Prusinkiewicz and Lindenmayer 1990)

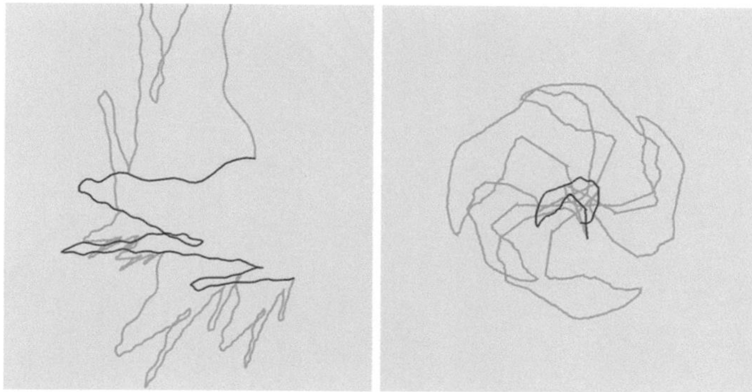

Fig. 7.6 Participant drawings from *Of me With me* (Seevinck 2014) illustrate how the rewriting processes for constructing the Koch curve have informed this artwork. Here participant gesture is the black line, or generator shape

Another example is *Turbulence* (McCormack 1994). Here the detailed visual and emergent forms generate using L-System grammars and develop over time (McCormack 2004a, b). Audiences interact with this work by triggering animations of the growth processes using a touch screen. They can see the unnatural, yet life-like artificial life forms appear to grow. McCormack and others have also worked in evolving L-system rules (e.g. Mccormack 1993; Hornby and Pollack 2001).

The simulated emergence in these images provides understanding and insight. We can learn about the emergence of tree patterns in nature and observe how simple interactions can effect complex and ordered outcomes. We gain insight into the workings of the natural world, from things such as the emergence of termite mounds through to the range of patterns that we have in nature. In art these processes of emergence can take on additional meanings and significances for us as well—from engendering creative behaviours as in *Of me with Me*, through to the uncomfortable familiarity of artificial life forms to challenge our assumed primacy as a species on the planet, as in McCormack's work (Fig. 7.7).

Emergence in the Participant

These computer processes are providing us with emergent understandings and perceptions. They facilitate a subjective experience of emergence in the participant-observer. This is internal to the person for whom the emergence is occurring. It is not physically manifest and in this way differs from an emergent physical structure. It is, however, relevant to the *perception* of physical structures and, as just discussed, core to our appreciation of computational emergence. This category of *perceptual* emergence is the second main type of emergence in the

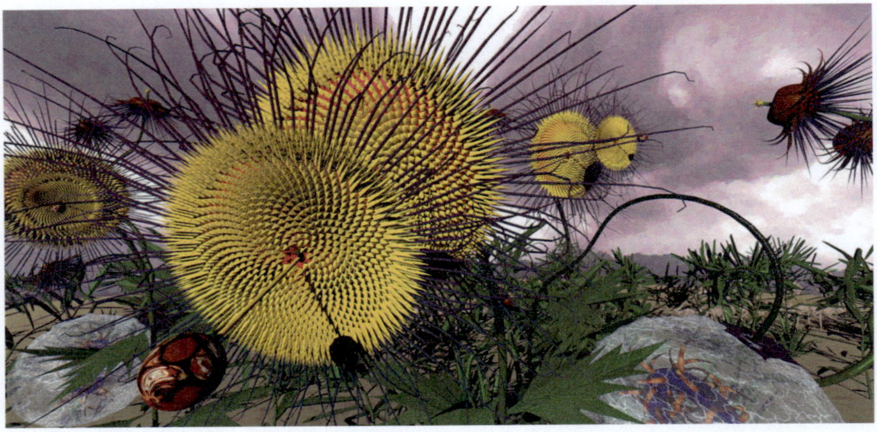

Fig. 7.7 Image from *Turbulence, an interactive museum of unnatural history* © 1994 Jon McCormack. Used with permission of the artist

TEIA (Chap. 2). There it was defined as reliant on being perceived by an observer to exist. This definition and area are explicitly focused on the subjective and creative experiences of emergence that the participants, artists and researchers of interactive systems can have. It is based on design research efforts in emergent shapes. This section discusses some of the research efforts in this area to flesh out more of an understanding of what these emergent experiences might be, and how we can create for them.

Perceptual Emergence

The perception of visual patterns is core to the understanding of creative, emergent features in both design research and visual thinking. It occurs in a number of areas between the eye and the brain. In his book on visual thinking for designers, Colin Ware draws on contemporary research in psychology and human perception to describe perception as a two way process. Light waves bounce off objects in the real-world to travel into the eye and agitate our photo receptors. Information registered in this way travels along the optic nerve to the forebrain in a so-called 'bottom-up' wave. Then, in a second, 'top-down information wave', information about what we are interested in travels from the forebrain back to the rear to direct our attention to relevant visual features and suppress the others, biasing our gaze to scan for what we are interested in (Ware 2008).

The first wave can be further understood in terms of three stages of visual processing. Initial physiological stimuli to the optic nerve prompts easy, quick feature processing of a select, few, visual aspects. These include form, size,

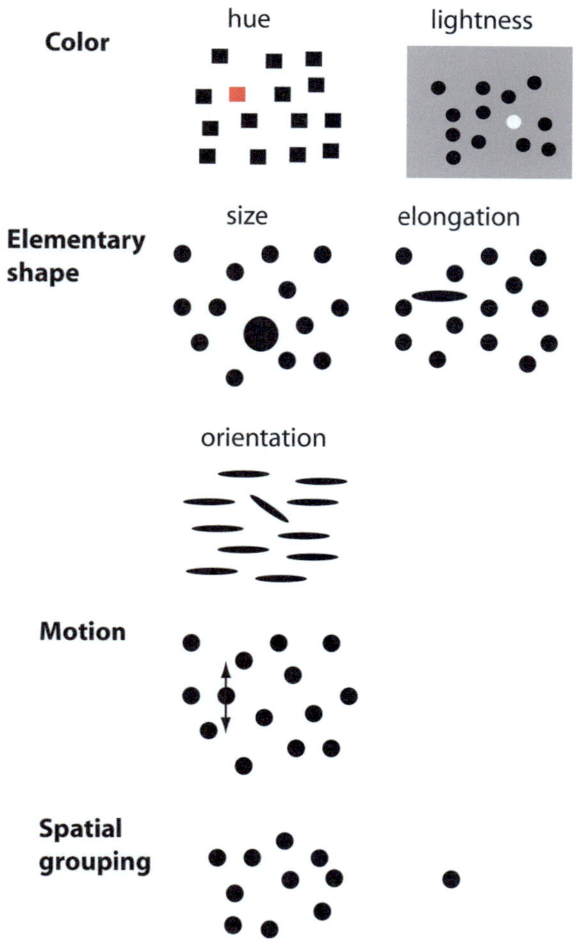

Fig. 7.8 *Basic Popout Channels* (Ware 2008). Used with permission from the copyright holder

orientation, colour, motion and three-dimensional spatial layout as shown in Fig. 7.8. Where a visual element differentiates from its surroundings in terms of one of these 'channels', it is very easy and immediate for us to detect. This information is processed by specialised neurons in the primary visual cortex, the part of the brain with the most neurons and highest capacity for processing signals from the retina. Typically there is just one eye movement that would be required to identify a difference in terms of one of these channels, making detection instantaneous. This differs from other searches which would take 5–10 movements and maybe a couple of seconds, greatly influencing the capacity for meaning making and visual thinking (Ware 2008).

These visual features then become organised and patterns can be identified, something which is a critical part of the creative process. Some aspects of Gestalt psychology and neuroscience can explain this intermediate stage of pattern[5] formation, which may include organising areas of similar texture or contours. The pattern processing informs the generation of a small number of visual objects which are held within our limited visual working memory. The objects constitute a selection of key details from the incoming visual information but they also rely on a set of associations that has been generated by our prior knowledge and experience. These objects are what we use to engage with the world. However, since our working memory is limited and only a few objects can be stored, we need to be frugal in this approach. The second top-down wave of vision processing prioritises our bottom-up processing efforts. That is, typically during our interaction with the world we would have a goal. This goal directs what we should be paying attention to. Information is therefore passed from the brain to direct the visual processes to concentrate on relevant bottom-up activities, as well as to 'highlight' or signal any relevant ones more strongly than the others. For example, if we're looking for red dots in an environment, those red dot detectors would be sensed more strongly.

Our processes of perception involve many facets. When we are engaged in a goal driven activity, the processes of feature detection will bias to serve this goal. When we are without a goal, there are distinct visual characteristics within our environment that will naturally take precedence given our physiology (e.g. we are more responsive to the pop out channels, not requiring much visual search or eye movement to identify those elements where they are distinct). These bottom-up perceptual processes include pattern formation, and this is where things get interesting in terms of creativity and emergence.

Perception and Creativity

Ware articulates the importance of the intermediate 'pattern finding' stage during the processes of perception: "*In many ways, the real power of visual thinking rests in pattern finding. Often to see a pattern is to find a solution to a problem. Seeing the path to the door tells us how to get out of the room, and that path is essentially a kind of visual pattern*".[6] Beyond problem solving, visual processing to identify patterns is an integral part of creative processes. As has been discussed in Chap. 2, the interpretation of emergent shapes is a core activity for designers that can facilitate the interpretation of new forms and design solutions. But how does this

[5]Here the term 'pattern' is used to describe an organised set of visual elements that we store during perception. This usage differs from the preceding usage in the context of complex systems.

[6]Here the visual information that is received by the retina from light reflected off the path is processed into a type of visual pattern along the early bottom-up processes just described. Further visual processing that imposes our experiences and prior knowledge on this to identify the 'path' object also constructs a pattern. Finally, the way in which we respond to this perceived pattern, such as by walking to the door, is also considered a pattern: *"A way of responding to a pattern is also a pattern, and usually one we have executed many times before…"*(Ware 2008).

occur? An explanation draws on this understanding of perception as an active constructive process, and one that comes into play with mental, or imagined imagery as well.

We can begin by revisiting pattern formation. This is, as previously described, the stage in which features and information from the retina are combined together and order is imposed, based on our experiences and prior knowledges, to define objects. This process of combining different features into regions or the same contour is called *binding* (Ware 2008). This is where the neurons sensitive to certain aspects are stimulated when that aspect, for example, edge detection, falls across the retina that activates them. A neuron becomes excited and, where its neighbours are similarly stimulated, the effect amplifies. As more and more neurons fire we are more likely to perceive that feature. Top-down information from the forebrain to bias attention also inform the process. This explains how our visual cortex works to identify those visual patterns (objects) that we perceive in the natural real world as well as recognise the ones we are looking for or already familiar with.

The perception of emergent compositions in *+−now* (Seevinck 2008) can be unpacked in terms of bright regions on the screen. The higher brightness of overlaid shapes is more visually distinctive and may 'pop out' visually, as shown in Fig. 5.7. They also work with adjacent areas of shade or colour and boundaries between them such that binding occurs. The interpretation of birds, a man walking or heartbeat (e.g. Fig. 6.1) are all examples of how prior experiences and understandings of the world has also informed the pattern formation. These examples of participant interaction with tart systems were described in Chap. 6.

Perception of Mental Images So far this discussion of the process of perception explains how we take stimulus to the retina to construct patterns and visual objects in our mind: how we see objects in front of us. But what about the objects or images that we do not see, that are not there? What about these so-called 'mental images'?

Perceptual activity theory (PA) argues that the same processes used in normal seeing are used in our perceptual construction of mental images (Thomas 1999). Experimental research has compared people's perception of both real and mentally constructed scenes. In the one study, people's eye movements were found to occur both when a scene is present, and when that (imagined) scene was not present at all. It also found that the eye movements between the mental and real images had some similarities. Another study used functional magnetic resonance image (fMRI) scans of people to compare their brains while they were perceiving real images and while they were perceiving mental images of the same content. This found that similar areas of the brain were triggered. "*They consist of activities without the external information*" (Ware 2008). The studies affirm the perceptual activity theory view that mental images are based on the same constructive mental processes that we use in normal seeing. Thomas further describes how according to perceptual activity theory, the "*…ways of looking (that we might use when looking at something)… get stored in visual memory and are reactivated as imagery*" (1999). The perception of emergent shapes might also be explained as a process whereby stored imagery is reactivated.

For design researchers and many others, the role of imagery and generally understanding creativity is of great interest. In a significant study of the creative sketching process, two architects and seven senior design students were asked to design an art museum using free hand sketching (Akin et al. 1997). They were video recorded and post event protocol interviews were conducted after the drawing session, at which time they were asked to describe their thinking while drawing. The researchers found the designers' drawings would be interpreted and refined through the process of drawing and that new conceptual, non-visual understandings would come about alongside the visual interpretation and manipulation of elements. The drawings work as a "'*perceptual interface' through which one can discover non-visual functional relations underlying the visual features*" (Akin et al. 1997). Visual features are created through the sketching process. These include both elements that the designer has intentionally drawn and also other embedded, implicit objects, namely emergent shapes. The study authors coded things like 'sculptures', 'areas' and 'parking' as these visual features, while something non-visual and more abstract like a 'view line' was coded as a functional relation. Objects could change meaning as well during the drawing process. In a subsequent publication the researchers Suwa and Tversky termed the process '*constructive perception*' and argue it as being integral to creativity (2003).

'Constructive perception' involves firstly, a *perceptual reorganisation* of elements, which may include a designer regrouping visual elements, changing the reference frame and altering perspective—processes we can understand in terms of binding. Secondly, it was argued as constituting *associative fluency,* which is where new and related concepts are generated—something we could perhaps understand as facilitated by the top-down associative processes of seeing explained above.

The work in constructive perception points to the role of emergent shapes in the creative drawing process. As discussed in Chap. 2, architect Bill Mitchell and other design researchers have asserted that emergent shapes are an integral part of the drawing process during which explorative design occurs: "*Designers... frequently recognize emergent subshapes, and subsequently structure their understanding of the design and their reasoning about it in terms of emergent entities and relationships—ones that they never explicitly input.*" (Mitchell 1993). As Edmonds also said, emergence is a part of creativity (Edmonds 1995). By highlighting the different aspects of perceptual reorganisation and conceptual associations, theories of perception facilitate better understanding into these creative processes of seeing.

Computing Emergent Shapes While designers and people are able to perceive emergent structures, it is not so simple for the computer. As Bill Mitchell wrote in 1993, "*emergent sub-shapes are, from the computers viewpoint, unrecognizable*". Creative design using the computer and, in particular, supporting perceptual structures or emergent shapes, is still limited today. Computational sketching tools would potentially facilitate a designer or user to 'read off' new understandings from sketches, i.e. facilitate additional perceptions and understandings from them. They could also improve the ability of novices to use sketches in this way. One description of this idea is as follows:

> Our vision is of a tool that will, when a user draws a new figure, present visual stimuli e.g. 'animation' or 'highlighting' of sketched items (as 'figure') as well as of interspaces among the items (as 'ground'). The basic concept is that if the look of visual features of items (e.g. shapes, angles, sizes, textures and line-features) and of patterns produced by their spatial arrangement fluctuates, then the fluctuation may encourage the user to 'read off', beyond just their visual features, their potential appeal to perception in unanticipated ways (Akin et al. 1997).

A difficulty with implementing such a system is due to the mode of representation in the computer system. That is, geometric forms are not directly represented. For example, emerging forms such as the heart shape in Fig. 1.2 require a new schema for representation over and above that of the original shape (Gero 1996). Thus the CAD software's algebraic representations of geometry need to be augmented to support the extraction or manipulation of emergent shapes. Furthermore, it is only those shapes that are made up of elements depicted in the graphics that can be extracted—the perceptual, mental objects which are not represented by the system cannot be recognised.

Research to address these limitations has covered a range of computational models for shape emergence. Decomposition into intermediate representations such as vertices, maximal lines or region was proposed, prior to recombining these parts into new shapes (e.g. Soufi and Edmonds 1995). Different methods to inform the selection of elements and recombination were also explored. For example, Gestalt principles and some psychological criteria could help to correlate emergent shapes with a designer's expectations. Other approaches include the use of shape grammars to model sets of possible permutations (such as the work of Stiny 1993) or generative methods such as the use of artificial life algorithms to model shapes for emergence (Poon and Maher 1996). Neural networks have also been proposed to inform a 'curious design agent' to augment the designer's process (Saunders and Gero 2001). More recent research does, however, appear limited.

Instead, current design discussions describe a preference for exploration to be done with freehand sketching. For example, in architecture and industrial design magazines and online forums we can see comments like that of one ArchDaily reader, who writes in: "*...we always start by hand drawing sketches. Why? Because that's the early stage and we're developing alternatives with our clients to explore which one works best.*" Or another designer who speaks more personally: "*For me, sketching in the office is used when I run into the limitations of the software... I get out the trace when I need to "let a line go for walk." Sketching allows me to quickly rethink things, just to see if it is worth doing in the computer*" (Stott 2015). These indicate that the early ideation and exploration of concepts—that stage where we tend to see a lot of emergent shapes and structures and new understandings—is something explored by hand. The computer is used in design but Computer Aided Design, it seems, becomes beneficial when more refined focused or clarification of designs is undertaken (e.g. Self 2012; Stott 2015). There is, however, another area where research around the computation of emergent images is growing: internet security.

A Human Quality? Internet login for sensitive information facilitates client privacy and protection from unauthorised users. 'Bots' or software programs that run through login and password combinations can, eventually, come up with viable combinations, hacking internet sites to forcibly gain access to private data. The CAPTCHA method is a common approach to this situation. CAPTCHA stands for Completely Automated Public Turing Test to tell Computers and Humans Apart. It was developed to separate humans from the software bots. However, as image analysis algorithms and machine learning techniques have improved, the CAPTCHA method has become less secure. New research looks at images with emergent shapes, or features, as an alternative to CAPTCHAs. Given the difficulty of computer modeling of emergent shapes, such an approach can provide a way to ensure that people are accessing the system rather than bots. They are more difficult for bots to identify while still remaining fairly quick for people to interpret and decipher. Both still and moving 'emerging images' have been found viable, however moving emerging images seem particularly promising, offering both a high ease for human eye interpretation and a high degree of difficulty for bots to 'hack' (Mitra et al. 2009; Xu et al. 2012, 2014; Gao et al. 2015). As discussed previously, the ease with which we can perceive features is due to our specialised neurons for detecting motion; that is, our human and pre-attentive capacity for isolating certain features to interpret images. It informs our capacity for visual creativity and, quite possibly, sets us apart as human.

Reflections

Different domains describe the same concept of emergence. Across all there is the appearance of something new that is qualitatively different to what was there before. It is a whole that is greater than the sum of its parts—be they grains of sand in a ripple, neurons in the brain that spark an idea, the hydrogen and oxygen atoms in water, the water molecules in a snowflake crystal or the designer's sketch marks that through mental imaginings can reveal an organising shape. While we may be able to explain and understand an instance of emergence, that instance was not planned but is rather unpredictable.

For our purposes, we can see the many different approaches, from chaos and complex systems theories through to perceptual re-organisation as facilitating means to generate patterns, structures and order for audiences to interpret creatively and make meaning, or to see new forms in themselves. Models like the local majority rule (Fig. 7.2), Langton's Ant (Fig. 7.3) and the Koch curve (Fig. 7.5) can help us understand, explain and even model emergence in interactive systems. People who interact with these systems can do so to extend the range of possibilities in them, 'opening them up'. Their emergent experience will be informed by the generative potential of that system. New, emergent understandings and creative behaviours can be facilitated in the participant-observer.

Perception also plays a role. We understand from studies in design research and visual thinking that the human eye will more efficiently respond to some visual phenomena over others (e.g. Fig. 7.8), and that designers identify new features by reorganising perceptual elements as well as imposing understandings based on past experience. The perception of emergent shapes is relevant to data visualisation as well, where finding trends or meaning in the ever-growing sea of data is an increasing challenge. In addition to marketers, data miners and analysts, the everyday person also needs to engage with their own digital footprints and growing data trails. How are they to continually manage and make meaning from this information?

While the demands for making sense of the sea of information are growing, it would seem that digital tools have limited capacity. It may be that identifying new visual patterns, or emergent shapes, is an activity that is unique to being human. Recent research in internet security points to this given the identification of emergent images has been found to differentiate human client from trawling software bot. We could infer here that it is exactly our human-ness that facilitates this creative seeing. Or conversely, we could think of our capacity for creative interpretation as core to being human. At the very least it would seem that creative interpretation is a uniquely human quality. Closing the gap between seeing those patterns and effecting or modelling them in interactive art and design could not be more exciting!

References

Akin O, Suwa M, Tversky B (1997) What do architects and students perceive in their design sketches? A protocol analysis. Des Stud 18:385–403. doi:10.1016/S0142-694X(97)00008-2

Animatrix (2015) Reaction diffusion VOP node. www.orbolt.com/asset/animatrix::reactionDiffusion::1.00

Bar-Yam Y (2002) General features of complex systems. Encyclopedia of Life Support Systems EOLSS. UNESCO Publishers, Oxford, UK

Bedau MA (1997) Weak Emergence. Philosophical Perspectives: Mind, Causation and World 11:375–399

Bedau MA (2008) Is weak emergence just in the mind? Mind Mach 18:443–459. doi:10.1007/s11023-008-9122-6

Bergson H (1978) In: The New Encyclopaedia Britannica in 30 Volumes, 15th edn. Encyclopedia Britannica, Inc., pp 843–845

Bohlen T (2016) Langtons' Ant software model. www.turnerbohlen.com/langtonsant

Cariani P (1991) Emergence and artificial life. In: Langton CG, Taylor C, Farmer JD, Rasmussen S (eds) Proceedings of the workshop on artificial life II. Addison-Wesley, USA, USA, pp 775–797

Crutchfield JP (2003) What lies between order and chaos? In: Casti J, Karlqvist A (eds) Art and complexity. Elsevier Science, pp 31–45

Darley V (1994) Emergent Phenomena and Complexity. In: Proceedings of the Workshop on Artificial Life IV. USA

Davidson K, Hermanovic G (1998) Houdini. Side Effects Software, Toronto, Canada https://www.sidefx.com

Dietz S (2002) Ten dreams of technology. Leonardo, The MIT Press 35:509–522

Edmonds EA (1995) Creativity: interacting with computers (panel discussion). In: Edmonds EA, Katz I, Mack R, et al. (eds) CHI'95 conference on human factors in computing systems.

SIGCHI: ACM special interest group on computer-human interaction. ACM Press, Denver, USA, pp 185–186
Emmeche C, Køppe S, Stjernfelt F (1997) Explaining emergence towards an ontology of levels. J Gen Philos Sci 28:83–119
Fry B, Raes C (2001) Processing. Aesthetics and Computation Research group at MIT Media Lab, https://processing.org
Gao S, Mohamed M, Saxena N, Zhang C (2015) Emerging image game CAPTCHAs for resisting automated and human-solver relay attacks. Proceedings of the 31st annual computer security applications conference. ACM Press, Los Angeles, USA, pp 11–20
Gero JS (1996) Creativity, emergence and evolution in design. Knowl Based Syst 9:435–448
Hanes DM, Anderson RS, Hoagman W (2016) Why do regular, wavelike shapes form when the wind blows over the sand on the beach for a long time? And what determines the spacing (frequency) of these waves? In: Scientific American's ask the experts: the environment. Macmillan Publishers Ltd
Hornby GS, Pollack JB (2001) Evolving L-systems to generate virtual creatures. Comput Graphics 25:1041–1048. doi:10.1016/S0097-8493(01)00157-1
Kim C-H, Kim S-J, Kim S-K, Kang S-J (2015) Real-time visual effects for game programming, 2015 edn. Springer
Langton CG (1987) Artificial life. In: Langton CG, Taylor C, Farmer JD, Rasmussen S (eds) Proceedings of the workshop on artificial life I. Addison-Wesley, Los Alamos, USA, pp 1–47
Laughlin RB, Pines D (2000) The theory of everything. Proc. Nat. Acad. Sci. (PNAS) 97:28–31. doi:10.1073/pnas.97.1.28
Lee KJ, McCormick WD, Ouyang Q, Swinney HL (1993) Pattern formation by interacting chemical fronts. Science 261:192–194. doi:10.1126/science.261.5118.192
Mandelbrot B (1982) The fractal geometry of nature, 1st edn. W. H. Freeman and Company, San Francisco, USA
Mccormack J (1993) Interactive evolution of l-system grammars for computer graphics modelling. Complex Syst. From Biol. Comput. 118–130
McCormack J (1994) Turbulence: an interactive installation exploring artificial life
McCormack J (2004a) Generative modelling with timed L-Systems. In: Gero JS (ed) Design computing and cognition'04. Springer, Netherlands, pp 157–175
McCormack J (2004b) Impossible nature: the art of Jon McCormack: Jon Mccormack. Australian Centre for the Moving Image, Melbourne Australia
McCormack J, Dorin A (2001) Art, emergence, and the computational sublime. Proceedings of the second international conference on generative systems in the electronic arts. Centre for Electronic Media Art (CEMA), Victoria, Australia, pp 67–81
Mill JS (1889) On the composition of causes. In: A system of logic ratiocinative and inductive being a connected view of the principles of evidence and the methods of scientific investigation, Peoples edn. Longmans, Green & Co., London, England, pp 242–247
Mitchell WJ (1993) A computational view of design creativity. In: Gero JS, Maher ML (eds) Modeling creativity and knowledge-based creative design. Laurence Erlbaum Associates Inc., Hillsdale, USA, pp 25–42
Mitra NJ, Chu H-K, Lee T-Y, et al (2009) Emerging images. In: ACM SIGGRAPH Asia 2009 papers. ACM, New York, USA, pp 163:1–163:8
Nagel E (1961) The doctrine of emergence. The structure of science problems in the logic of scientific explanation. Routledge & Kegan Paul Ltd, London, England, pp 366–380
Dictionaries Oxford (2010) Reductionism. Oxford University Press, UK
Pearson JE (1993) Complex patterns in a simple system. Science 261:189–192. doi:10.1126/science.261.5118.189
Penny S, Schulte J (1995) Sympathetic Sentience, artwork
Poon J, Maher ML (1996) Emergent behaviour in co-evolutionary design. Artificial intelligence in design. Springer, Netherlands, pp 703–722

Prusinkiewicz P, Hammel M, Hanan J, Mech R (1996) L-Systems: from the theory to visual models of plants. In: Michalewicz M (ed) Proceedings of the 2nd CSIRO symposium on computational challenges in life sciences. CSIRO Publishing
Prusinkiewicz P, Lindenmayer A (1990) The algorithmic beauty of plants, Electronic version published Springer, New York, in 1990 and reprinted in 1996. Springer
Rinaldo KE (2000) Autopoeisis, interactive artwork
Saunders R, Gero JS (2001) Designing for interest and novelty. In: de Vries B, van Leeuwen J, Achten H (eds) Computer aided architectural design futures 2001. Springer, Netherlands, pp 725–738
Schmidt K "toxi" (2016) toxi.sim.grayscott
Seevinck J (2014), Of me With me, interactive artwork
Seevinck J (2016) Dichroic Wade, interactive artwork
Seevinck J (2008) +−now, interactive artwork
Self J (2012) CAD versus sketching, Why Ask? Core77
Solkoll (2005) Fractal trees. Images of the trees generated from a L-system. commons.wikimedia.org/wiki/File:Dragon_trees.jpg
Sommerer C, Mignonneau L (1994) A-Volve, interactive artwork
Sommerer C, Mignonneau L (eds) (1998) Art as a living system. In: Art @ science. Springer, Austria
Soufi B, Edmonds EA (1995) A framework for the description and representation of emergent shapes. In: Teh M, Tan R (eds) Proceedings of computer-aided architectural design (CAAD) futures. Singapore, pp 411–422
Stiny G (1993) Emergence and continuity in shape grammars. In: Flemming U, Van Wyk S (eds). North-Holland Publishing Co., pp 37–54
Stott R (2015) The Computer vs the hand in architectural drawing: ArchDaily readers respond. ArchDaily
Suwa M, Tversky B (2003) Constructive perception: a metacognitive skill for coordinating perception and conception. pp 1140–1145
Thomas NJT (1999) Are theories of imagery theories of imagination? An active perception approach to conscious mental content. Cogn. Sci. 23:207–245. doi:10.1207/s15516709cog2302_3
Turk G (1991) Generating textures on arbitrary surfaces using reaction-diffusion. Proceedings of the 18th annual conference on computer graphics and interactive techniques. ACM, New York, USA, pp 289–298
Ware C (2008) Visual thinking for design. Elsevier Inc., Morgan Kaufmann
Whitelaw M (2004) Emergence. In: Metacreation: art and artificial life. MIT Press, pp 206–237
Witkin A, Kass M (1991) Reaction-diffusion textures. Proceedings of the 18th annual conference on computer graphics and interactive techniques. ACM, New York, USA, pp 299–308
Xu Y, Reynaga G, Chiasson S et al (2012) Security and usability challenges of moving-object CAPTCHAs: decoding codewords in motion. In: Proceedings of the 21st USENIX conference on security symposium. USENIX Association, Berkeley, CA, USA, pp 4–4
Xu Y, Reynaga G, Chiasson S et al (2014) Security analysis and related usability of motion-based CAPTCHAs: decoding codewords in motion. IEEE Trans Dependable Secure Comput 11:480–493. doi:10.1109/TDSC.2013.52

Chapter 8
Insight for Emergent Interactions

Abstract Emergent participant experiences offer potential for creative and complex interactions. These run counter to usability expectations of HCI, though that domain is increasingly broadening its scope. Emergent experiences with art can offer more insight to interaction design, as well as the understanding of interactivity generally. Emergence is characteristically surprising, unpredictable, open-ended and with a capacity for creativity. These are complex ways of being that resonate with our experience of the natural physical world. Investigations into emergent interactions can help us move towards understanding interactivity in a similarly more complex way. The creation of emergent experiences is, however, not without challenge. The practice-based research effort taken in this text has revealed design insights and mechanisms for addressing unpredictability of the artwork and participant perceptions about lack of control. These are presented here. Insights into the creative co-creation of participant alongside artist are also provided. All of these efforts aim to better articulate the many facets of interaction for more differentiated interactive art, understanding and participation.

Emergence is a debated concept and interactive art is still young. This text has drawn on literature, practice and evaluation research to reconcile these areas and map their intersection. Emergence has been broadly defined as *occurring when a new form or concept appears that was not directly implied by the context from which it arose. This new 'whole' is more than a simple sum or grouping of its parts.* The Taxonomy of Emergence in Interactive Art (TEIA) organises different views of emergence and, as has been shown, can be used to identify new opportunities and mechanisms for facilitating emergence in creative practice as well as characterising it in people's interaction with art systems. It has also helped to identify non-emergent behaviours including generic behaviours. Identifying these typical interactive art experiences assists us in understanding the nature of interactivity more generally as well. I have also shown that emergence can be intentionally facilitated by the artist. This can be in a number of ways—from the simulation of complex processes such as artificial life through to the perception of emergence by participants of interactive systems. This latter type of perceptual emergence has

J. Seevinck, *Emergence in Interactive Art*, Springer Series on Cultural Computing,
DOI 10.1007/978-3-319-45201-2_8

been the focus of this book. The specific area of emergent participant experience, provides new ways for both understanding and 'sculpting' that art audience (participant) experience. Artists can design for emergence and it can also happen without their intention. In Chaps. 5 and 6 I discussed interactive artworks that intentionally seek to facilitate emergent participant experience, and were evidenced to do so. I have also discussed artworks that, from documentation and descriptions of them, can be characterised as facilitating emergence (Chap. 4). Whether the artists intended them to facilitate such novel and surprising behaviours or not, the artworks seem able to support these. These findings provide new ways of appreciating the artworks. The findings also increase our understandings of emergent experiences and the nature and dimensions of interactivity: when looking through a lens of emergence we can characterise the meaning making that happens during participant interaction. This ranges from Ted's '*stir, wait, feel*' behaviour, described as having a "*magical depth*" with "*infinite variation*" like looking at the stars (Seevinck 2008, Chap. 6), through to the taboo behaviours that happen when conventions or rules are transgressed, such as the mocking the police in imagery in *Body Movies* (Lozano-Hemmer 2001) or the explicit posing in *Text Rain* (Achituv and Utterback 1999) (Chap. 4).

Physical emergence, such as the simulation of emergent processes on the computer, has many opportunities for art and interaction design. While it is more established in the computing and interactive art domains, it's useful to think about the different ways in which it relates to a participant as well. Physical emergence has been used to generate complex rich environments for participant engagement—that is, a simulated rich landscape resonant of the complexity and diversity we see in the natural world. On the other hand, simulated physical emergence can also involve a participant directly in its processes of unfolding, such as the inclusion of people to initiate and direct the creative experience and evolution of artificial creatures in Christa Sommerer and Laurent Mignonneau's *A-Volve* (1994). In this work we do, in fact, see both. The participant is engaging with a complex emergent environment both from the position of external spectator and as an interacting agent themselves. These artists' approach to working with artificial life art is also very open. That is, they open up the determinism of the computer by including the participant in the art system, and in a very substantial way. This is to draw the initial forms that are then interpreted for populating the virtual world. Including the participant in the system means that they are extending the domain of the system and it is no longer finite—it has opened up to include the openness inherent in the natural system of a person. In so doing there is opportunity for more possibilities and potential forms: they are '*informationally open*' systems, as was discussed in Chap. 7. A finalsignificant point about physical emergence here is that it does notpreclude perceptual emergence from occurring. Just as we can perceive a V shape in a self-organising flock of birds, here the participants may also experience perceptual emergence during their interaction with the system modelling of physical emergence.

Interactive art is a key concern for this book. There is still much to learn and understand about interaction as a medium. The palette of interactivity is limited—at least in comparison with the millions of hues we demand of colour every day. Artists working with interactivity are exploring these questions, not the least of which is the notion of longer term or influencing interaction, as in Edmonds Shaping Form artwork (Edmonds 2007, see also Edmonds 2011). This runs counter to the seductive gaming experience—and prevalent utilitarian experience—of action-response. Furthermore, an influencing type of interaction is something that resonates with memory and our experience of the natural world: *what you said to me yesterday is still with me today* and *the resources we use today will affect the planet for our children, tomorrow*. Emergence, with its inherent affinity to the natural world, can extend our understanding of interactivity. Ted compared his experience of interacting with +−*now* with looking at the stars, and described it as having infinite variation. There is an openness to both emergence and the natural world. Open works are, like Eco asserted, inexhaustible with a field of possibilities. They may be ambiguous and they require interpretation (Sengers and Gaver 2006) as well as creativity to interact with. These are complex and promising areas for interaction design and interactive art.

Design for Unpredictability and Understanding

There is a tension between influence of the artwork and control of the artwork. Emergence, with its characteristic unpredictability, pushes the envelope of how we may design and understand participant engagement. It can point towards more complex experiences of creativity and ambiguity. Designing for these can, however, be challenging, because participants can disengage. If they are frustrated they may give up and leave. These concerns relate to unpredictability. Unpredictability is valuable given its necessity for novelty, creativity and emergence. But how can we engender these aspects while sustaining participant engagement? One answer is to facilitate participant understanding of what is going on in the system, at least in part. That is, to design for participant anticipation of the events and to generate system feedback to respond to participant actions. Mechanisms towards this are:

- Structural transparency
- Priming
- Combined directly responsive and influencing interactions
- Finally, conducting evaluation research in order to understand what participants are thinking.

Structural Transparency and Feedback

My creative work draws on a constructivist approach to art making (Gabo 1937; Gabo and Pevsner 1975; Chilvers 2009 see also discussions in Chaps. 3, 5). This has meant that I make aspects of interaction and interface—those materials that go into constructing the artwork and experience—evident, rather than trying to cover them up. While this approach may not be attractive to all designers, in this case it allowed me to provide a certain amount of awareness about the structural aspects of the work as well as leading to design mechanisms such as *structural transparency*. It is also useful to remember that providing feedback is one of the basic tenets of good interaction design (e.g. Bowman et al. 2001; Norman 2002). In fact, giving feedback is one of Ben Shneiderman's 'Eight golden rules of interface design' (2010).

Feedback works by confirming to users that theirinput is registering with the system. For example, in *+−now* (Seevinck 2008) the colourful, augmented sand surface provides immediate feedback that gestures in the sand have registered successfully. This confirmation is needed as there is a delay for the more complex, sustained interaction to develop; that is, until the layered images on the large screen build up enough for emergent shapes to become visible.

Structural transparency works by establishing a causal relationship between the participant and system. In *+-now,* the process by which the emergent shapes are created is clearly presented. That is, the transparent layers of imagery that add together over time and result in opaque, emergent shapes are easily observed to follow each gesture in the sand. This communicates understanding as well as feedback. It provides a sense of control for the complex, unpredictable interactive work. Another example is *Homographies Subsculpture 7* where artist Lozano-Hemmer includes a representation of the tracking system as a part of the work's installation (Lozano-Hemmer 2006). This provides participants with insight into how their movements are affecting the work, similarly generating understanding. *Homographies Subsculpture 7* also features intermittent '*interludes*' when the moving fluorescent tubes briefly cease being influenced by people to instead run through a series of pre-set arrangements. We can understand this ordered choreography as communicating the system's potential for order. In combination with the tracking information, it provides the participant with the means to infer a relationship between their action and the system. By facilitating an understanding of the underlying structures, a sense of control afforded to the participant.

The addition of the *Crescendo motif* to *Dichroic Wade* (Seevinck, 2016a) is anotherexample. Here, after an approach to the work has been sensed, the glass and reflections are manipulated into escalating waves of movement. This is intended for an additional direct, responsive interaction with the work. In addition to rendering immediate feedback, this also demonstrates the potential for order in the work. Making the structure evident can be considered a design tactic. Of course, it is also consistent with a constructivist approach.

Priming

Also related to the unpredictability and novelty of emergence is the issue of being able to detect an emergent feature. That is, a participant's ability to recognise something not previously seen, detecting emergence for the first time can be quite a challenge. *How do they know what to look for? How will they know it when they see it?* The priming techniques discussed here aim to address the novelty and unpredictability of an emergent structure for a participant in order to make it easier for them to perceive it. They come from information visualisation literature, where the concern is with detecting patterns in data representations. Priming involves exposing the person briefly to some patterns prior to their interacting with the visualisation (Ware 2004). This increases their receptivity to any subsequent patterns. Prior exposure to sample emergent features may also be useful for the participants in an interactive artwork. This is because it could also increase their receptivity to any incidences of emergent features.

We can see priming used in the installation work of Lozano-Hemmer. For example, in *Homographies Subsculpture 7* (Lozano-Hemmer 2006) the '*interludes*' mode can be considered a form of priming in that it communicates the system's potential for order. In this way it facilitates detection of emergent patterns or compositions in the behaviour of the robotic fluorescent tubes. The *Crescendo motif* in *Dichroic Wade* also communicates a potential for order in the artwork, priming the audience to look out for other patterns of movement from the weather and participant sensor movement data (Seevinck, 2016a, b).

Influence, Response and Feedback

Influencing interaction does not, by definition, involve direct feedback. This can make it challenging for a participant to have a sense of control with the work. Similarly the more open-ended works are also more unpredictable, compounding participant concerns with control. *Dichroic Wade* does not facilitate an action-response type of interaction. Instead it focuses on visualising data from the broader environment and layering this with data about participant presence. Given the added input of that weather data, the work is necessarily more open-ended. For example, it will move and, in a sense, be completed without the need for participation. These aspects made it more challenging for participants to identify a feedback loop of understanding with the system, something which the findings also showed (Chap. 6). Audience engagement with the work remain of interest to me, and in reflecting on the findings from the *Dichroic Wade* prototype study, I implemented additional, more distinctive and responsive behaviours such as the approach feedback and *Crescendo motif.* From an aesthetic point of view, the *Crescendo* reinforces the approach behaviour as well as integrating the two data sources. The overall effect was that as one approached or 'waded in' towards the work, the glass pieces and reflections would become more and more disturbed, creating a turbulence of light and movement.

The iterated *Dichroic Wade* work therefore is a combination of both influencing and responsive interactivity in order to generate imagery informed by weather data and participant interaction, respectively. Moreover, these are integrated here into a physical system with its own turbulence and capacity for harmonics—an open-ended complex system. I added the more overtly responsive aspect to facilitate feedback and increase opportunities for perceiving order with the work. Future evaluations of the system will provide data on this design approach as well as further insights.

In considering open interactions in art and design, we start to engage with the range of possibilities that characterises the open work. Open interactions also alter the participant's role from a user to a collaborator, increasing the opportunity for creative collaboration between artist/designer and participant. Since emergence is open, the creation of interactive systems that facilitate emergence can, firstly, result in open interactions, and secondly, create interactions that are similar to those we have in the natural world. But for many participants the openness and richness need balancing with a sense of control or, as argued here, understanding facilitated through feedback. This may only provide a short term understanding, but it can work to sustain engagement such that they may explore for interaction with the more creative, richer and complex aspects.

These insights were facilitated through evaluation research as well theoretical and practical investigations. Conducting evaluations on near-complete prototype works can help ensure that the artist's understanding of the experience generated is consistent with that which participants have. Evaluations have been an integral part of this PBR approach, directing practice and generating evidence for the insights. Here they have contributed to understanding different types of emergence, and what it might be like for people.

Evaluation for Perceptual Emergence

Given that emergence's characteristics (lack of predictability, control and multiplicity/ambiguity of interpretation) differ from the prevalent HCI approach, the emergent interaction environment may run counter to a participant's expectations. These differences to typical HCI design necessitate developing specific evaluation criteria. Sengers and Gaver (2006) argue that when evaluating open designs one cannot focus on whether a single interpretation was generated, but should instead be asking questions like 'how many interpretations were generated?' Similarly, the evaluation of emergence in interactive art or design might endeavour to find out about the diversity and quality of interpretations afforded. Here I have identified different types of emergence, guided by the TEIA and emergence mapping and coding schemes. Evaluation was used to find out whether or not perceptual emergence occurred, as well as what types of these were found, if any. It has also informed subsequent design and development cycles, such as the progression from *Glass Pond* to *+−now* to increase participant feedback and enable understanding of how it behaved, in order to improve the quality of participant experience. Similarly I iterated *Dichroic Wade* to become more explicitly responsive in addition to retaining its influencing interactive behaviours.

As stated, this effort has relied on evaluation to learn about the quality of the participant's experience. While it focused on emergent participant experiences, other interesting events were also identified in the data. These provide insight into participation with interactive art more generally.

Non-Emergent Behaviours

Looking for emergence and finding what is NOT emergent of that artwork but still an interesting behaviour of artworks in general, is very useful. Non-emergent behaviours can inform our understanding of interactive art by helping us to identify generic ways in which people engage with interactive artworks. In so doing it also extends our understanding of interaction.

Three interesting but non-emergent behaviours were identified in the evaluations. These generic activities are predictable and not new, discounting them from being considered emergent. They are:

- Assessing (trying to figure out how it works)
- Resetting the artwork to return it to a starting condition
- Anthropomorphising.

Another type of non-emergent behaviour relates to instances where participants did not engage with the artwork as a 'whole'. Here instead the construction of meaning was limited to just a part of the work. For example, in some cases participants engaged only with the sand and ignored the projected lights in *+−now*, or they ignored the grey marks in *Of me With me*. In these situations their interaction and meaning-making was informed by the affordances of sand and black marks respectively, rather than the artwork. That is, the participants' aesthetic experience was at the level of constituting materials and objects (parts) rather than the compositional whole. Fortunately this was rare. Were it prevalent then the integration of the composition of the work's elements would likely need to be reconsidered.

Reflections on Evaluation and PBR

While evaluations are certainly helpful, they can present creative challenges for the practitioner and researcher. A seemingly simple first challenge is successfully designing the evaluation for the experience under investigation. Given the diversity of interactive artwork and practice, however, there is no single approach that will work. In some cases observation needs to capture gross body movement while in others, fine finger movement. Demands can differ between what is possible technically and in the field and what the researcher and artist require—typically a non-intrusive research design. Trade-offs necessarily occur, and sometimes the data collection suffers. In my latest study of *Dichroic Wade,* constraints from the installation environment and camera technology impacted on the data collection so that the light reflections that were of interest to participants, influencing their experience of the work, were not always visible in the post-event protocol video imagery. Opportunities for that video to prompt discussion of participants were missed. This points to a larger issue for the creative practice-based researcher: the installation of interactive artworks has two sets of requirements. There are those relating to the aesthetic experience of the work, and there are those that are necessitated by the research questions and design. Hopefully these will have limited trade-offs. For me, it means that for a future study I would need to consider a location with reduced ambient lighting—not because the work needs it, but because the recording video cameras do!

The second, more complex issue concerns the integration of evaluation research and creative practice. Specifically, what voice must the artist give the research findings generated from evaluations? My thoughts are that this is a question for each artist, every time. There is no obligation for art to attract or please participants, and an evaluation must reflect the aesthetic intention of the work (which may be to repulse, disengage etc.—all of which are equally valid). The artist needs to ensure an internal coherence in their work, that the aesthetic intention behind the work is met by the artefact. Methods from evaluation and reflective practice can assist, but the practical implementation of these methods during a creative process is another matter. Evaluation findings can become an intrusive voice in creative practice. Maintaining distance or balance with outside voices (such as through the evaluation feedback) is a challenge. Here I found the conceptual structure useful. It provided space for exploring my own voice in a way that is unmediated by others. It can operate in parallel to the *situation talk-back* from evaluation studies. The added presence of the conceptual structure throughout a project helped me maintain focus and coherence in the work. It offset the risk of simply embodying other's desires and, through *reframing*, also integrates with other reflective practice and PBR methods.

In some ways the question of involving evaluation feedback in the creative process is a part of the broader issue of the open-ended work (Eco 1962). That is, that authorial, creative control becomes shared between artist and the participant who interacts to realise or *complete* the work.

Evaluation is valuable for understanding participant experiences of emergence with one's work. And viewing (any) interactive work through the lens of emergence can reveal its depth and reach—the horizons and openness of the work. Seeing a work realised by a participant in unexpectedly new ways also reveals its creative potential. When a participant exercises their creativity in a way that extends the artist's compositional efforts, this can be very exciting for the artist. And seeing new horizons for your work, when it seems to take on a life of its own, is even more rewarding still. Analysing work through the lens of emergence can determine its potential for emergence and, in so doing, its open, creative potential.

Creativity in Emergent Interactions

Creativity has featured throughout this book. Emergence is fundamental to creative thought (Edmonds 1995) and the emergence of shapes during creative design processes has been researched by architects and designer researchers across the world (e.g. Mitchell 1990; Mitchell 1993; Edmonds et al. 1994; Gero 1996). The interactive artwork +−*now* has also demonstrated how such processes of perceptual emergence can lead to other creative interpretive behaviours, from '*playing the piano*' through to animating. The interactive drawing artwork *Of me With me* engages with ideas around 'distributed creativity' as it developed out of shared creative drawing efforts, and the interaction itself retains this conversational, creative engagement (see Chap. 6 and for example, Seevinck et al. 2006; Seevinck and Edmonds 2008). We have seen potential for emergence and creativity in people's interaction with artworks from around the world as well (Chap. 4). These indicate a capacity for creative interaction in the art audience. As audiences interpret work interactively to compose, sometimes breaking taboos, they are realising new possibilities for these artworks—new to audience, artwork and artist alike.

The artworks discussed have shown potential for emergent and creative audience interactions. Other facets of these experiences have also come to light, however, including some sharing in the creative responsibility for the 'completed' art experience.

Capacity for Expression

Firstly, emergent interaction places the participant in a creative role with opportunity for expression, but also responsibility for that creative expression. Like the open-ended system, where a participant is involved in co-creating an interactive artwork with the artist or system, they are also sharing creative responsibility for the experience. The artist cedes control to the participant in the interactive artwork, and also cedes control to the emergent system in emergence-based works.

The works discussed here demonstrated a number of different types of emergent and creative audience interactions. They ranged from the collages of text and image or shadow and photo in *Text Rain* and *Body Movies* respectively, through to the game-playing, animating and collaborative drawing in the case study artworks of Chaps. 5 and 6. This variety of emergent interactions indicates that there is an audience capacity for metaphor as well as abstraction in their engagement with these interactive art works.

On the other hand, evaluation findings and artist discussion alike haveshown that expectations of action-response and unambiguousinteraction, as in the traditional HCI model and the unchanging, more closed artwork, can be detrimental to participant engagement. Feingold expressed his frustrations with audiences of his open-ended work *The Surprising Spiral* (Feingold 1991), while some of my evaluation feedback similarly indicated participant expectations to control the work (Seevinck et al. 2006). More recently, Edmonds has described his *Shaping Forms* body of work as engaging people on a longer-term and influencing way, rather than the *'seductive interactive approach made popular in computer games'*. For the artist navigating this minefield of popular expectation and aesthetic innovation/ *avante garde* expression, I would argue that ensuring the aesthetic intention of the work is realised is the priority. After all, internal cohesion of concept and form are critical aspects to a resolved composition. Of course this composition and intention can vary in any way, popular or no, as desired by the artist. Where the work is concerned with interactive experience, an understanding participant experience is most likely essential in determining this has occurred. And methods of evaluation can help gain that understanding of people's experience. While the processes of evaluation can, be challenging in terms of involving other 'voices' in the creative processes, as was discussed above, this can be managed. Furthermore, once one accepts the active role of the participant in completing an artwork, making this shift to consider other voices becomes inevitable. Including the participant as a collaborator or co-performer can also become a creative opportunity. Here I see it as facilitating the exploration of perceptual emergence.

'Completing' the Work

Secondly, the open work typically needs participant engagement for it to be completed, or closed. That is, one can argue that it may not be realised until someone interacts with it.[1] This further confounds the artist or designer seeking to challenge preconceptions of engagement or present controversial subject matter. While such efforts are legitimate and even necessary in order to explore a more differentiated understanding of interaction, it must also be acknowledged that where a participant declines interaction with the interactive artwork this can mean the interactive artwork is unfinished in a sense that is different to someone who simply refuses to view a painting they find objectionable or unpleasant. In the painting, its form has already been set and finished. The form of the interactive artwork is, however, indeterminate until a participant engages with it.

One approach to address this concern is to look towards theories of engagement. The attract, sustain, relate model (Edmonds et al. 2006) may guide system design that prioritises participant attraction to the work in a non-controversial way, while the sustained, longer term interaction could develop that more challenging aspect. Certainly seduction and beauty are not new to the artist, who has practiced these to similarly engage audiences in artworks throughout our history.

[1]An exception is where the openness of the work is due to other factors, for example natural processes such as the use of weather data input in *Light Currents* (Seevinck 2015) and *Dichroic Wade* (Seevinck 2016a). In these situations it is that input which is helping to generate the form of the work.

It is also useful to recall Bilda's findings in their Creative Engagement Model. This showed that when participant expectations were not met, this could lead to frustration; however, for some, this experience led to curiosity and even creative engagement (Bilda et al. 2008).

As we look towards audience experience of, or creative *completion* of, theopen-ended, interactive artworks, it is also useful to consider thequalities of these creative completions. The Taxonomy of Emergence in Interactive Art (TEIA) is a theoretical framework that guides such an interpretation and analysis. For example, a comparison between instances of concrete and referenced emergence in participant interaction with a given art system provides a range of possible interpretations of that work. In a sense, it draws a spectrum of interactivity for the work. An analogy is looking for new compositions versus looking for motifs. In looking at both aspects we reveal a potential range of completions as well as any references the participants are drawing on, pointing towards the open nature of the work.

Materials as Rules

The affordances of materials used in interactive art systems will influence the ways in which people understand and interact with those works (Gibson 1977). Gibson's theory of affordances can direct the ways we think about emergence in interactive art in a couple of different ways. We can think of interface affordances as guides and constraints, or rules for interactive behaviours. They can facilitate so-called 'transparent' or intuitive interaction for the participant because they set up expectations of how to interact. The use of sand in *+−now* (Seevinck 2008) is one example—it needs no instructions about how to interact with it. Sand is also an open material, facilitating a range of different behaviours.[2] Choosing interface materials that are open-ended may similarly facilitate openness in interaction and, by extension, opportunities for creativity. That is, we can choose materials based on their capacity for ambiguity and multiple interpretations—for their open nature. This increases the space of possibilities for interaction and the openness of the work. It may provide opportunities for creative insertions and emergent experiences, though design and evaluation are still needed to develop opportunities for order. Evaluation may provide insight into emergent perceptions that people can come up with, and how, for example, design intervention for additional feedback or reduced openness might be needed to tune it towards facilitating interpretations of meaning, pattern or order of some other kind.

The choice of material in *Dichroic Wade* can also be understood interms of its affordances: glass affords 'looking through' and'reflecting'. Here the dichroic glass

[2]Sand play therapy cites the use of sand for this reason of open-ended play, as is also articulated in the humorous essay on open-ended gameplay with simple wooden blocks by H.G. Wells (Wells 1911; Kalff 1991).

generates colourful reflectionsand transmissions of light (Seevinck, 2016a, b). We can also think of these affordances as building blocks for the work, and the way in which they integrate we can think of as the compositional whole. When they prompt participant movement and sense-making, these parts may inform an emergent whole. For example, participants were found to interpret new shapes and forms ranging from a bird or butterfly through to looking through layers of a *story within a story*. These instances of perceptual emergence were described in Chap. 6.

Artists and designers select materials for their affordances as these suit the audience/participant and creative intention. Selection can also be informed by site when looking at ambient environments and architectural installations, like the choice of reflective glass in *Dichroic Wade* was informed by looking at light on the water currents in the adjacent river. But selection of materials can also operate on another level. If we think about the affordances as rules for behaviour and how these rules might be transgressed, we might see opportunities for emergence … and things get interesting when rules are challenged. Emergent behaviours operate outside the rules. Game strategies like 'bluffing' in Poker are not explicitly defined by the rules, but they are an integral part of the game play (Salen and Zimmerman 2004).

Rules need not only be driven by materials, however. The broader context of an artwork may impose social constraints as well. Behaviours that transgress these, or taboo behaviours, may exhibit potential for emergence. As was found during participant interaction with Lozano-Hemmer's *Body Movies* (2001) and with Achituv and Utterback's *Text Rain* (1999) some surprising things can happen when people transgress social convention—from changing the projected image of two men side by side into two men holding hands in *Body Movies*, to forming the new word 'pussy' not in the original poem through a sexual pose, people can interact with artworks in emergent ways: they can generate new meanings not explicitly identified in the 'rules' of the artwork.

The Structure of Interaction

The audience's role has changed through the last hundred years of contemporary art and led us to interactive art. We have come from an interest in critical spectatorship, through to active audiences and participation. Within interaction, there are other trajectories as well: our movement from linear and hypertext structures of interaction to networked, generative, evolving and open-ended or emergent structures, as well as the varied qualities of direct action-response modes of interaction through to more distended, longer-term influencing modes.

It's likely that we will continue to develop our understanding of interaction in even more qualitatively different ways. For example, if we compare the structure of interaction to advances in science, we may see the multiple yet coincident interactions that quantum physics ascribes to particles. Similarly a deeper analysis of the physically real, natural interactions, such as conversations, that occur in our every day lives can provide insight and stimulus for thinking about computer-mediated interaction.

A more differentiated and subtle understanding of the structure of interaction would also approach the depth of understanding that is integral to the other arts. The texture and rhythm of a piece of music, or the use of mass, light and ritual in architecture are dimensions for those disciplines, but similarly concrete elements are elusive to the interactive arts and interaction design. Greater understanding of interaction,particularly as it approaches surprise, unpredictability and emergence, can expand the palette available to interaction artists, designers and participants. Very little work has been done in this area as yet. Extending our understanding of interaction has the potential to enrich our increasingly computer mediated existence. I hope that as we discover and define its unique and novel qualities we can move towards the day when Interactive Art, like Architecture and Music, has its own Muse.

References

Achituv R, Utterback C (1999) Text Rain, interactive artwork

Bilda Z, Edmonds E, Candy L (2008) Designing for creative engagement. Des Stud 29:525–540. doi:10.1016/j.destud.2008.07.009

Bowman DA, Kruijff E, LaViola JJJR, Poupyrev I (2001) An introduction to 3D user interface design. Presence: Teleoperators & Virtual Environ 10:96–108

Chilvers I (2009) Constructivism. Oxford University Press, Oxford, UK

Eco U (1962) The poetics of the open work. In: Bishop C (ed) Participation. Whitechapel The MIT Press, London, pp 20–40

Edmonds EA (1995) Creativity: interacting withcomputers (panel discussion). In: Edmonds EA, Katz I, Mack R, et al. (eds) CHI'95 Conference on human factors in computing systems. SIGCHI: ACM special interest group on computer-human interaction. ACM Press, Denver, USA, pp 185–186

Edmonds EA (2007) Shaping Form, interactive art installation

Edmonds EA (2011) Art, Interaction and Engagement. In: Candy L, Edmonds E (eds) INTERACTING: Art, Research and the Creative Practitioner. Libri Publishing Ltd., Faringdon, UK

Edmonds EA, Candy L, Jones R, Soufi B (1994) Support for collaborative design: agents and emergence. Commun ACM 37:41–47

Edmonds EA, Muller L, Connell M (2006) On creative engagement. Visual Communications 5:307–322

Feingold K (1991) The Surprising Spiral, interactive artwork

Gabo N (1937) The constructive idea in art. In: Circle: International survey of constructivist art, 1st edn. London, England

Gabo N, Pevsner A (1975) 1920 Naum Gabo/Antoine Pevsner: basic principles of constructivism. In: Conrads U (ed) Programs and manifestoes on 20th-century architecture, Revised ed. edition. The MIT Press, Cambridge, USA

Gero JS (1996) Creativity, emergence and evolution in design. Knowl Based Syst 9:435–448

Gibson JJ (1977) The theory of affordances. In: Shaw Robert, Bransford John (eds) Perceiving, acting, and knowing. Lawrence Erlbaum Associates, Hillsdale, NJ, USA, pp 127–143

Kalff DM (1991) Introduction to sandplay therapy. J Sandplay Ther (JST) 1:1–4

Lozano-Hemmer R (2001) Body Movies Relational Architecture No 6, interactive art installation

Lozano-Hemmer R (2006) Homographies Subsculpture 7, interactive art installation
Mitchell WJ (1990) The logic of architecture design, computation and cognition, 2nd edn. The MIT Press, Cambridge, USA
Mitchell WJ (1993) A computational view of design creativity. In: Gero JS, Maher ML (eds) Modeling creativity and knowledge-based creative design. Laurence Erlbaum Associates Inc., Hillsdale, USA, pp 25–42
Norman DA (2002) The design of everyday things. Basic Books, New York, USA
Salen K, Zimmerman E (2004) Rules of play game design fundamentals. The MIT Press, Cambridge, USA
Seevinck J (2008) +-now, interactive artwork
Seevinck J (2015) Light Currents, interactive artwork
Seevinck J (2016a) Dichroic Wade, interactive artwork
Seevinck J (2016b) Dichroic Wade. In: CHI EA'16 Proceedings of the 2016 CHI conference extended abstracts on human factors in computing systems. ACM Press New York, NY, USA, San Jose, USA, pp 3889–3892 doi:10.1145/2851581.2891094
Seevinck J, Edmonds E (2008) Emergence and the art system "plus minus now". Design Studies (Interaction Design Special Issue) 29:541–555
Seevinck J, Candy L, Edmonds E (2006) Exploration and reflection in interactive art: glass pond. ACM Press, Sydney, Australia, pp 143–150, doi:10.1145/1228175.1228202
Sengers P, Gaver B (2006) Staying open to interpretation: engaging in multiple meanings in design and evaluation. In: Designing interactive systems DIS'06. ACM Press, pp 99–108
Shneiderman B, Plaisant C, Cohen M, Jacobs S (2010) Designing the user interface: strategies for effective human-computer interaction, 5th edn. Pearson, Boston, USA
Sommerer C, Mignonneau L (1994) A-Volve, interactive artwork
Ware C (2004) Information visualization perception for design, 2nd edn. Morgan Kaufmann, Amsterdam, The Netherlands
Wells HG (1911) Floor Games. E-Book available through Project Gutenberg, http://www.gutenberg.org/ebooks/3690

Index

J. Seevinck, *Emergence in Interactive Art*, Springer Series on Cultural Computing,
DOI 10.1007/978-3-319-45201-2

MIX
Papier aus verantwortungsvollen Quellen
Paper from responsible sources
FSC® C105338

If you have any concerns about our products, you can contact us on
ProductSafety@springernature.com

In case Publisher is established outside the EU, the EU authorized representative is:
Springer Nature Customer Service Center GmbH
Europaplatz 3, 69115 Heidelberg, Germany

Printed by Libri Plureos GmbH
in Hamburg, Germany